AF568064

MEDIA EDUCATION

DPH Education Series

MEDIA EDUCATION

UTTAM KUMAR SINGH • K N SUDARSHAN

DISCOVERY PUBLISHING HOUSE
NEW DELHI-110002

Discovery Publishing House
4831/24, Ansari Road, Darya Ganj
New Delhi - 110 002 (INDIA)

Media Education

Edition : 2012
ISBN-81-7141-366-8

PRINTED IN INDIA

Published by Discovery Publishing House, New Delhi and Lasertypeset at Technographics and Printed at Dynamic Printers

Preface

The *DPH Education Handbook* has been created to provide access to information about contemporary topics in education. Practitioners and students at all levels in education have a need to know what is happening today, in addition to historical treatments within the literature.

Each chapter within the Handbook is designed to provide the user with needed "state-of-the-art" information as well as further sources of information. One of the significant features of each chapter is the inclusion of specific programmes, projects and activities so that the researcher can locate human resources as well as the literature.

The handbook will be of use to graduate and post graduate students in education and to practicing teachers, administrators, librarians and planners. The chapters and the further sources of information cited in each book should lead the reader to thousands of people and documents for either research or programme planning purposes.

An effort to achieve universal and effective education is based on a recognition of the rights of students to basic education that enables them to thrive in a complex society, as well as a realization the technological and economic growth is facilitated by increasing the numbers of students, even those with poor academic progresses, who are, in fact successful in learning. Thus, recent and current efforts improve education serve both private and social interests.

This series is addressed to administrators, planners and educators working in the field of education and training with a view to stimulating interest and attention in the areas of education and its related fields. It is also addressed to a growing number of teachers and instructors who will be practitioners in education and who will need to be acquainted with the modern aspects of educational practice and development. Many ideas, generalisations and discussions presented in this series should also prove useful to employing organisations committed to provide training facilities within their establishments—leading to effective mutual participation by institutions and organisations.

The editors wishes to thank the contributors, as well as those organizations that gave permission to publish their extracts, chapters etc.

Editors

Contents

Preface v

1. New Technology on Educational Broadcasting 1

2. Communication Satellites in Education 55

3. The Social Functions of the Press 65

4. Responsibilities of the Media 100

5. Motion Pictures in Relation to Social Control 135

6. The Motion Picture Business 172

7. Current Issues 204

8. Administration of Educational Media 237

9. Improving the Media 246

10. Freedom of Access to Broadcasting 282

11. The Future of Educational Broadcasting 328

Index 347

1 New Technology on Educational Broadcasting

Radio and cassettes

A great deal of publicity is being given to 'high technology' in education, particularly micro-computers and video-discs. There is a danger though that these developments are diverting attention away from the effects of equally powerful low-cost technology. Audio recording is not new in education, nor glamorous, but the development of cheap, easy-to-use audio-cassette equipment has already had a major impact on the use of educational broadcasting, both in schools and adult education.

For many years, schools have used tape-recorders to record school radio broadcasts. Recording is ubiquitous, and the ability to record has been much enhanced by the introduction of combined radio-cassette machines. Recording became even more significant in 1983 when the BBC switched secondary school radio broadcasts from afternoon to night-time transmission. This move, resulting from the wish of the BBC Radio 4

Controller to offer width, requires recording to be made in schools automatically at night-time using time-switches. This change has been implemented despite initial opposition from the BBC's own Educational Broadcasting Council. In 1982 less than 25 per cent of secondary schools has electronic time-switches, and night-time transmission requires local education authorities to spend over 200,000 on extra equipment. It entails centralised planning of recordings in advance, and a pilot showed that there was a high failure rate in overnight recording due to teachers not correctly operating the automatic recording equipment. The BBC radio producers, the Educational Broadcasting Council and the local education authorities all thought that the move would reduce the use of radio in secondary schools. At the time of writing, it is not known whether these predictions will come true. However, in Norway and Sweden, an alternative system works very effectively. Most local education authorities have set up an audio-visual unit in one of their local teachers' centres. Radio, and increasingly television programmes, are recorded off-air by a full-time technician in each centre. Schools are sent a catalogue of programmes from which they request the programmes that they need. The service is relatively cheap to run and there is virtually no failure rate in recording, with all programmes available to all schools. Indeed, there is no real need to broadcast radio at all, since all programmes could be mailed on tape at very low cost to the local centres.

At the Open University, the impact of audio-cassettes on radio has been dramatic, with radio transmissions in 1983 dropping to less than thirteen hours a week, and over 500,000 cassettes being mailed to students. Furthermore, more than a third of the students who listen to the radio programmes that remain do so on recordings. In 1982 91 percent of Open University students had audio-cassette players. Just under half of the radio recordings are made off-air by students themselves but the majority are heard from cassette tapes ordered by students through an audio-cassette loan scheme which has been in operation since 1977. Students wanting to hear a radio programmes on cassette may obtain up to four programmes at a time by sending a request card to the University's headquarters. In 1981 42,000 programme recordings were requested, and the loan scheme increased the average listening rate by 6 per cent to 44 per cent, at an average cost to the University of 28 pence per programme request. It is clear that even when made originally for radio transmission, programmes available on cassette are more helpful for students than when broadcast. On a five-point scale, the mean helpfulness rating for broadcast radio in 1979 and 1980 was 3.42. When the same material was used on cassette, the helpfulness rating was 3,79.

However, there is a big difference, both in production style and educational effectiveness, between programmes made originally as radio programmes, and programmes created from the beginning for use specifically in a cassette format.

Course designers can make full use of the stop-start and review facility, and the hidden nature of the next part of the tape to be played can also be exploited. Thus students can be talked through diagrams, tables or formulae in a text, can stop the tape and carry out activities, and return to the tape for correct answers or comment. Cassettes combined with text allow the simultaneous use of sound and vision, with freedom for the students to move from one medium to another in their own time, and with the ability to rewind and repeat as necessary. Thus students have full control over their use of the medium.

Cassettes can be used for a variety of educational purposes for which radio is less suitable or convenient: practice leading to mastery of a technique; commenting on diagrams, charts, tables or text; talking students through a home experiment; backing up or commenting on the television programmes; recordings of conversations, interviews, language use and discussions, which can be replayed several times for the purpose of analysis; and many other uses. Durbridge has designed an audio-cassette package which demonstrates various ways in which audio-cassettes can be used in a home-learning situation.

Academic staff at the Open University like audio-cassettes because they can easily integrate them with the texts as they design their courses. They can take a recorder home and rough out ideas as they develop the text, whereas with a radio programme, with its continuous and uninterrupted flow, it is impossible to develop such close integration between sound and print. The final cassette tape still benefits from being 'produced' to ensure good sound quality and to avoid mistakes or ambiguity in the script, but academics generally feel that they have much more control over the cassette script than with radio.

The Open University students also like audio-cassettes. In a majority of courses where audio-cassettes have been used, students rank them as the most useful course component after the correspondence texts, and in a few courses, they have been ranked even higher than the texts. The features that appeal to students are their convenience, the control they have over them and their informality. Students frequently comment that listening to an audio-cassette is like having a personal tutorial in their own room with the course author, a quality that appears to be lacking in most radio programmes no matter how skillfully they are made.

Lastly, cassettes distribution is remarkably cheap in large quantities compared with radio transmission costs, which themselves are not expensive. A C60 cassette can be copied, packaged and sent to a student as part of the course materials for less than fifty pence. Even including copying and clerical costs., it is generally cheaper for the Open University to mail cassettes to students than to pay radio transmission costs for two transmissions of each programmes, when there are less than 1,000 students on a course.

Cassette, though, become increasingly more expensive than radio as student numbers increase beyond 1,000.

The initial choice of media for the Open University was made in 1967. Since then, audio-cassettes have been the University's most successful media innovation. Audio-cassettes are more widely used and more effective than computer-assisted learning, video-cassettes, telephone teaching, or even television and radio. It is surprising then that few other institutions have exploited this cheap, convenient and effective teaching medium. The Open University's success has been due to course tams not using audio-cassettes as lectures, but instead tightly integrating them with the printed material.

Video-cassettes

The pattern regarding audio-cassettes and radio is repeating itself with video-cassettes and television to some extent, although there are important differences. As with audio recorders, a video-cassette player in a school gives more flexibility to the teachers in their use of broadcast materials. However, there are far fewer video-cassette machines in schools, although the numbers are rapidly increasing. While the proportion of primary schools with video-cassette machines in Britain doubled from 1980 to 1981, this brought the number up to only 25 per cent, and few schools had more than one, which meant that they could not play back and record at the same time. Nearly every secondary school had a video recorder in 1981, but the average number per school was only two, not really enough to give the ease of access and flexibility required in secondary schools. Hayter concluded that an increase in video recording and playback equipment would do more than anything to increase the effectiveness of schools television. It is significant that the increase in equipment over the last five years has been paralleled by an increase in the overall use of television, particularly in secondary schools. Nevertheless, there is still not enough equipment yet in schools to justify the transfer of schools television to night-time transission although, technically, it is easier to record television than radio off-air because of the in-built clock on most video-cassette machines.

The Inner London Education Authority used to distribute its own programmes, and those of the broadcasting organisations, via a cable system at all the schools in its areas. Because of the high cost of renting the lines from the Post Office it closed down its cable service in 1979, since when it has distributed its programmes on video-cassettes. By 1981 over 75 per cent of the primary schools in the ILEA area had bought video-cassette machines, largely due to a deal worked out between ILEA and a commercial rental company which gave the schools large discount prices. ILEA schools pay a nominal rental for the hire of each cassette loaned from their television service.

Nothing is more volatile at the time of writing than the expansion of home ownership of video-cassette machines. At the end of 1983, nearly 30%

of all households in Britain had video-cassette machines in their homes, and sales are roughly doubling each year. Furthermore, according to the BBC Audience Research Department figures video-cassette machines are just as likely to be found in lower income as in more wealthy households. The rate of growth of video-cassette access is greater in Britain than in any other country. By 1986 it is expected that half the homes in Britain will have a video-cassette machine.

This rapid growth is due to several reasons. Machines can be rented for as little as 10 per month, and there are many High Street shops and back-street dealers from which video-cassette programmes, including feature films, can be hired at little cost. Because many of the broadcast programmes are still of high quality, it is also worth while recording these at home, especially since the range of choice at any one time is limited to four channels in the current absence of a widespread cable TV system.

In 1981 11 per cent of Open University students had access to video-cassette recorders in their homes and another 8 per cent had easy access to recorders elsewhere. By the end of 1982, 20 per cent of Open University students had access to machines in their home and another 22 per cent convenient access elsewhere.

The advent of video-cassette technology has caused often bitter arguments within the Open University, although now its advantages are generally recognised by the academic staff. The

Open University experimented as early as 1974 with a video-cassette replay service to students in its South region. Eventually, the University set up a modest loan scheme on a national basis in 1982. The University's reluctance was due to the fact that any video distribution system becomes an additional cost to broadcasting since although the quality of times has deteriorated, the amount of transmission, and hence its cost, has remained the same. Video distribution costs-like those for audio-cassettes-therefore have to be found from the University's academic budget, at the expense of alternative academic programmes, such as new courses or more research, and not from the part earmarked for the BBC.

The loan scheme in 1982 was limited to thirty-seven courses with low student numbers and courses without repeat transmission times. The scheme was designed to cope with a limit of 20,000 programme requests in the year. In 1983 the scheme was expanded to cover eighty-four courses, all with less than 850 students. Students obtain copies of programmes by sending in a request card to the University's headquarters. A small stock of each programme recorded in advance has been made and any demands over that basic stock are met by making extra copies. The cassettes are mailed directly to the students' homes. Students inn 1982 and 1983 could either watch at home or on machines placed in local study centres or colleges. Cassettes are returned by students after use, and stored for re-use. In this way, 20,000 cassette copies can be added each year to the stock, thereby increasing the number of student requests that can be met within a relatively stable budget from year to year. The full cost of the scheme, including the rental of over 240 machines in regional study centres, was 150,000 in 1982.

An evaluation of the first year's operation showed that, in general, the scheme had been successful. Programmes with a single transmission and a cassette loan facility had higher viewing a single transmission and a cassette loan facility had higher viewing rates than comparable courses with two transmissions. The availability of programmes on video-cassette made it easier for students to integrate television with the rest of their studies and increased students' perception of the helpfulness of the programmes. There was also a high demand for cassettes from non-students, mainly from tutors for use in group sessions. However, few students used the machines located in study centres. The equipment appealed mainly to non-students since fifty-seven machines were stolen from study centres in the first year. Rental for study centre machines accounted for over half the cost of the scheme, so, in response to yet another round of government cuts, there will probably be no national provision of replay machines in study centres in 1984. Regions will be left to make their own arrangements from their own budgets. It is expected though that demand for loan copies will increase as more students get their own machines.

Indeed, many more students make their own

recording than borrow through the video-cassette loan scheme. Home recording increased viewing on post-foundation courses by 8 per cent in 1983.

The Open University faces a difficult situation over the next five to ten years, until most students have access to a video-recorder. It takes two years to plan an Open University course, then it runs for about eight years. Courses are now being planned which will be running in 1993. Some course teams are anxious to design video-programmes which will exploit the educational advantages of cassette facilities, such as the ability to stop, carry out an activity, rewind and review, or pause on a still-frame. It is the lack of student access to video-cassette machines rather than the costs of physical distribution which makes the University cautious about producing programmes which can only be used on a cassette machine. Calculating the costs of physical distribution of video-cassette is complicated, and at the time of writing hypothetical, but it appears that it will actually be cheaper to mail video-cassettes to students than to pay for two transmissions when there are less than 500 students on a course, provided cassettes are returned and re-issued each year. This allows for costs of cassette copying, clerical staff, post and packing, and a 10 per cent loss or replacement annually. Four programme equivalents would be transferred to an E-120 cassette and mailed to students with their course material. Students would return the cassettes at the end of their course. Over an eight-year course life, the distribution cost would be as little as 1 per student per programme equivalent. Consequently, the University has decided the following policy for all new courses from 1985.

(1) Programmes on courses with less than 300 students will have no transmissions but will be distributed on video-cassette to students' homes.

(2) Programmes on courses with between 300 and 1,00 students will have one television transmission and can also be borrowed on video-cassette through the loan scheme.

(3) Programmes on course with more than 1,000 students will have two transmissions but will not be available through the loan scheme.

(4) Individual course teams may deviate from this policy if they can make a special case.

The aim of the policy is to encourage course teams to design programmes from the outset using either a broadcast or a video format but not confusing the two. It is also hoped that this will encourage a number of course teams to experiment with the design of video-cassettes, to build up experience about the best way to use the format. The policy at the same time limits the number of students who will have to use a video-cassette machine to about 6,000, possibly requiring about 3,000 students still without access to machines to get one.

In the long term, it is possible that only programmes on the foundation courses and two or three large second-level courses will be broadcast at convenient times. Programmes on courses with more than 300 students are likely to be made in a video format, but broadcast once during the night for automatic off-air recording, with a loan scheme back-up. On courses with less than 300 students, the cassettes will be mailed directly to students.

Why does the University believe that there is such a difference between broadcast and video formats? The first Open University course to be designed for use on video-cassettes was EM235, 'Developing Mathematical Thinking', presented for the first time in 1982. It was aimed at teachers and the programmes were planned to be viewed in groups at local teacher centres or schools already equipped with video-replay machines. In fact, about half the students watched in groups, with the rest watching at home on their own. The programmes were deigned differently from broadcast programmes, although they were transmitted for off-air recording. Each twenty-five-minute programme consisted of a series of segments, each lasting from two to seven minutes, observing children carrying out mathematical operations. After each segment it was planned that the tape should be stopped and followed by group discussion of the segment. Suggested questions for discussion were contained both in the programme itself and in the accompanying broadcasting notes.

An evaluation of this course showed that students in groups used the programmes differently from students watching individually.

Individual students used the replay facility more, while group students found that the discussion after each segment provided sufficient recall. Individual students were less confident about their interpretation of the material than group students and tended to concentrate on details rather than on more general points. Students in the group situation were sometimes anxious about using the equipment, not always being familiar with it, or were more self-conscious about stopping, starting or replaying the segment when others were present.

This course is perhaps unusual, being designed for group work, and great care must be taken in generalising to video programmes designed for individual use. It does, however, demonstrate that there are different design features of video programmes if the potential of the medium is to be exploited, and their structure and format will differ from broadcast programmes, just as audio-cassettes that exploit their medium differ from radio programmes. This principle has by no means permeated to all producers. Many programmes, with a continuous, uninterrupted format, nor does the Open University's own drug therapy course, made for general practitioners, really exploit the cassette medium. Cassettes were used mainly because they would not be seen by the general public and consisted of a series of interviews between doctors and patients, but with no explicit instructions to stop or interrupt the tape.

While video-cassette programmes require

different production formats from broadcasts, the design features of audio-cassettes will not always be appropriate for video production. The production requirements of a video programme are much more demanding technically and in terms of manpower. This means that recording of material, and its editing, is separate from the preparation of the texts to which it relates, and makes it more difficult at the design stage to develop the very close integration between text and programme that is possible with audio-cassettes, although careful advance planning and editing of both programme and text can go some way towards this. Nor can students so easily integrated video programmes and text simultaneously, because they cannot watch video and read the text at the same time. Taking notes during a video sequence is much more difficult than during an audio sequence and tends to lead to concentration on detail rather than on principles or general points. In practice, this means that video sequences will tend to run for longer without interruption, with interrogation of the material taking place segments, with some replay to assist. Particularly where students are having to share equipment-either a machine at a study centre, with other students waiting to use it, or at home, with the television set wanted by the rest of the family-it will be more difficult for students to spend a great deal of time working repeatedly through the cassette. This is less of a problem with audio-cassettes. It is clear that in the next few years there will be scope for a great deal of experiment and innovation to identify suitable video-cassette formats for education.

The most important aspect of both audio-and video-cassettes is the control over the medium that they offer the learner compared with broadcasts. It is worth looking more carefully at this comparison since it highlights some of the unique characteristics of television, as well as certain weakness of broadcasting as an instructional medium. Table 1 lists the control characteristics of broadcast television. A comparison with table 2, which lists the control characteristic of recorded materials, bring to the fore some of the differences between broadcasts and cassettes.

In comparing these two tables, it would be an advantage to have an audio-cassette so that you could look at the framework while I comment upon it. It will be seen, though, that it is difficult for a learner to integrate or relate broadcast at a set time and the impossibly of stopping or interrupting a programme at a specific point. If ideas or thoughts are simulated during a broadcast, learners run the risk of either losing the thread of the programme of being unable to follow through their own ideas. Some producers at the Open University have argued that one of the values of a broadcast is its ability to teach learners to think 'on the run', and that this is an essential everyday skill. We have found little evidence that broadcasts do this, and some may well argue that education is more concerned with teaching students to think carefully, rather than quickly.

Table 1. Control characteristics of broadcasts

Broadcast characteristics	*Learner implications*
fixed schedules	Fixed time to view
Scarcity of time	Limited response to material
Ephemeral	Non-repeatable; non-retrievable
Continuous	Thinking 'on-the-run'
Holistic	Reflection, analysis, restructuring, relating to other materials, all difficult.
Aimed at 'average' target viewer	No room for individual differences in pace
'Rich' in meaning	Interpretable in different ways and at different levels-but only a limited range of interpretation permissible in time available for any one student.

Table 2. Control characteristics of recorded material

Recorder characteristics	*Learner implications*
Available when required	Convenient
Rewind/fast forward facility	Repetition; mastery learning; search
Stop/start facility	Integration with other media; activities integrated with cassettes; more room for individual variation
Non-continuous/segmented	Reflection, analysis, restructuring easier

With either a broadcast programme or a cassette, each individual member of the target audience is sent the same material. No matter how specialised the target audience, each individual will vary in ability to learn from the programme. Programme makers have to make assumptions about the 'appropriate' level, but there will always be a majority of the audience who will not find the pace quite right in terms of their own learning needs. With recorded material, provided that the level of the material is not too wide off the mark, it is possible for learners over a range of abilities to repeat the material until they have mastery over it. Furthermore, with a recording, learners can stop to reflect on the material, analyse it or restructure it, as it best suits them.

Salomon has pointed out that television is particularly rich in the quantity and variety of information it conveys. It uses a wide variety of symbol systems-sounds, pictures, colour, movement. Television is also highly ambiguous in the way it conveys meaning. This results from the techniques used in production-camera angles and movement, editing procedures, manipulation of structure-and from the richness of the information television conveys. Because of its ambiguity, television material lends itself to a wide variety of interpretations from each individual viewer, many different interpretations being equally valid. This means that each viewer will abstract different meanings from the same programme. Television should therefore be valuable for developing creative or 'open-ended' thinking because it forces learners to impose their own Construction of meaning from the programme material. If such a hypothesis is correct, it makes it all the more important that learners have the opportunity to explore television material more fully than is possible with a single, unbroken transmission.

Broadcasts thus appear to be much weaker instructionally than cassettes in terms of integration with other material, ease of recall, mastery learning, deep thinking and possibly creative thinking. By their very nature, broadcasts tend towards stimulating more superficial levels of response compared with cassettes or books.

I have left the most controversial, and potentially most challenging, implications of cassettes until last. Cassettes could free educators from the dominance that broadcasters have exerted over the design and distribution of educational audio-visual materials. Until recently, distributing audio-visual material widely through formats other than broadcasting has been unrealistic because of the high costs of distribution on alternative formats, such as film or open-reel vide tape, and because of the lack of playback equipment in schools or homes. On the other hand, the distribution of broadcasts has been largely seen as a 'free' service from the user's point of view. The increasing accessibility of video-cassettes, are changing that situation. With broadcasting, the broadcasting organisations set the priorities, select content, determine style and decide production and technical standards for what they broadcast. In practice, they only transmit material that they themselves have originated.

Video-cassettes can change all that. It is now realistic for other agencies-universities, colleges, local authorities, voluntary organisations, even schools-to commission, reduce and distribute effective video material for the specialized audiences that broadcasters have been unable to serve adequately in the past. Costs will depend very much on what kind of programme is required and on whether full or marginal costs are charged. There is, however, a good deal of spare production capacity, particularly in the public education sector, so marginal costing is often realistic. Highly effective, professionally-make half-hour educational vide-cassettes can be produced for between £8,000 and £20,000, depending on the nature of the material. Cheap programmes which nevertheless are very effective in certain contexts if carefully designed can cost as litter as £2,000 to produce. This should be compared with a full production cost of around £35,000 or an average of £8,000 for a programme budget for a BBC/Open University television programme.

You get what you pay for, of course. BBC/ Open University programmes often include overseas filming, expensive computer graphics or animation, glossy drama productions, or complex and originally designed physical models. However, form may educational purpose, much expensive facilities are just not necessary. It depends on what the teacher wants to do.

The implications of lower production costs and relatively low-cost non-broadcast distribution are far-reaching. Because wide distribution costs are related to the number of assets to be distributed, video programmes for very small minority audiences become a real economic possibility, provided that there is a framework through which they can be marketed. Secondly, educators can make programmes in the style, pace and format which they believe to the important. There are obvious dangers that the full potential of television will not be developed by people who are not professional broadcasters. On the other hand, there are many able and trained production staff outside broadcasting organisations willing to work to a clear educational brief. Also, those who regularly deal with specialist groups are likely to be better judges of their needs than professional broadcasters. There will still probably be a shortage of educators with the talent to exploit the advantages of television on cassette, but the technology does open up the market to those who want to try.

Over the next few years, I foresee rapid expansion of an educational video production and distribution industry in parallel to broadcasting. This in itself is unlikely to lead to the end of educational broadcasting. Broadcasters still have two strong advantages: their programmes are available to schools and the general public at no extra direct cost; and they have a wealth of resources, experience and a powerful reputation behind them. Non-broadcast video is likely to serve rather different needs from those of broadcasters. Nevertheless, there will be areas of overlap, and where the broadcasters do not meet the needs of their target groups, they are likely to lose audiences to enterprising video producers. A number of agencies are now gearing themselves up for production and distribution of non-broadcast educational video. ILEA in particular has a large stock of cassette programmes available for hire by other local authorities, as does the recently established Educational Video Index.

It is unlikely that the commercial television companies will move into producing their own non-broadcast educational video material, but the BBC might, through BBC Enterprises. More likely is that educational broadcasting will be moved to night-time transmission for off-air recording, or be abolished completely, to free the air-waves for extended morning television in order to compete with cable and satellite competition. If the broadcasting organisations do start extensively producing non-broadcast material for education, it will raise some interesting legal and financial issues. Will they reflect the true cost of making the programmes, or will they merely charge copying, marketing and distribution costs? The true cost is likely to be too high for schools. On the other hand, if the price of cassettes does not reflect the true cost, would broadcasting organisations be open tot he charge of using licence-holders' money or profits from advertising to undercut independent, non-broadcast production companies?

Whatever happens, it will be interesting over the next few years to see whether there will be such an expansion of non-broadcast educational video as predicted, and if so, how the broadcasting organisations will respond to the challenge.

Video-discs and interactive video

There are different manufacturers' formats for video-discs and a variety of models within each format but, nevertheless, the principle of video-disc technology is relatively simple to grasp. The more advanced systems using laser technology allow up to 54,000 single still-frames, with full colour, to be stored on side of a disc. Each frame can be individually identified and accessed almost instantaneously. The rate at which these frames can be played can be varied across a wide range of speeds, from stepping through single frames, through slow motion, up to normal or even fast speeds. Two high-quality independent sound tracks capable of synchronisation with the pictures when played at normal motion speed are also available.

These features allow a combination of moving and still pictures to be played linked to stereo or two independent sound-tracks. The systems allow for slow-motion, frame-by-frame presentation, fast motion, fast or slow forward or reverse search, or still-frame presentation, with no picture jitter at all on still-frame, each feature under the direct control of the viewer. More significantly, full computer control over the video-disc player is possible, either using an 'in-board' computer or an 'out-board' microcomputer linked to the video-disc player through an 'interface', i.e. a processor or computer programme that allows the microcomputer electronic assess to the video-disc player's controls. With the right interface, it is possible to link up low-cost domestic video-disc players with low-cost micro-computers, and to combine graphics or keyboard symbols from the computer with sound and pictures from the vide-disc, on the same television set, with pictures from both sources either overlaid, or presented in sequence.

Because the laser-based systems use light to read the disc, there is no mechanical contact. Therefore disc life and quality are not likely to be affected by constant use. Picture and sound quality, even on the cheaper players, is better than on video-cassette machines, although as yet commercial vide-disc machines cannot record, only play back. The low-cost and simpler domestic models retail at around £400, with the more advanced commercial machines costing £1,200.

Video-discs certainly provide more sophisticated and better quality video and audio facilities than video-cassettes, but it would be a mistake to think of video-disc systems as merely a more advanced form of video-cassettes in terms of educational functions. We shall see that video-disc technology is a distinct teaching medium in its own right, with a unique potential for education, and its own unique requirements for design and production.

Because access, control of speed and search facilities are more refined on video-disc machines, they allow learners even grater control over video materials. Furthermore, by linking video-discs to microcomputers, learners can interact with the video-disc and the computer. This means that the computer can provide feedback to learners on what they have learned from the disc and can guide learners through appropriate 'routes', so that the learning experience is more individualized and suited to each learner's needs.

Video-cassettes can also be linked to computers in this way, but less efficiently than video-discs. Video-cassettes do not have individual frames like video-discs, so on all but the highest-cost machines, it is difficult to get completely still pictures. While it is possible to lay electronic pulses as markers along a videocassette tape, thus enabling each point on the tape to be identified and accessed, this cannot be done so accurately and cleanly as with a video-disc. It also takes time for video-cassettes to wind backwards and forwards to the point to be accessed, whereas video-disc access is virtually instantaneous. Nevertheless, a microcomputer linked to a video-cassette machine can do many of the things that a video-disc can do, if less elegantly.

At the time of writing, very few educational video-discs have been made, so the educational potential of interactive video is still to be explored. The reason for the interest is that interactive video combines two well-established learning media, video and computer-assisted learning, in the hope that it will bring together the advantages and overcome the deficiencies of both.

So far, three rather different ways of using video-discs in education seem to be emerging. The first is to use video-discs to provide a superior form of control and access. Thus a 'normal' television programme can be made available on disc format, with perhaps a second sound-track added. The learner can then use the still-frame, slow motion on fast search facilities as required. A refinement would be the provision of an index at the start of the disc so that the learner can go immediately to the section of most interest. Such discs can be useful for showing model procedures, such as the correct positions or movements for gymnasts or golfers and the correct procedure for striping down a car engine, or for showing animals operating in their natural habitat. The BBC has produced a video-disc of this kind on

British garden birds, with linked bird song on one track, and a commentary by David Attenborough on the other. No computer control is needed for this kind of programme but it is possible for those who purchase such a disc to add their own computer control relatively easily. In this way, tests, feedback and suitable routing through the disc dependent on test responses, can all be added through a linked computer.

Alternatively, vide-disc and computer control can be designed together as the video-disc is being planned. The resulting package can be extremely complex, both to design and to work through as a student. Student responses via the computer need not be limited to selecting from an array of multiple-choice answers, but can involve feeding in data, or more complex problem solving. Very sophisticated programmes are possible in this form. For instance, a video disc made at the University of Nerbraska provided training on instrument reading for flying light aircraft. After a short period of instruction, the learner is given a set of instrument readings, then has to make decisions about operation of the plane's controls in order to bring the plane in to land. Dependent on the action chosen, the disc shows the position of the plane relative to the earth. This is done by the computer processing the student's answer and selecting the appropriate part of the disc for such an action. Learners can in this way be provided with very realistic simulation exercises with the consequences of their decisions becoming painfully clear! The computer programme that accompanies such a disc can either be physically separate, on cassette or on a computer disc, or it could be contained on the video-disc itself and 'dumped' from there into the computer when played. Computer programmes stored on vide-discs, though, can be used only on the type of computer for which the programme was designed. The first commercial interactive educational video-disc, on teaching physics, was made at the University of Nebraska and marketed in 1982 by John Wiley.

There is a third way of using video-discs which is just beginning to be explored in an educational context. Video-discs can provide an efficient and substantial data-base, with information stored in a variety of ways: as computer data, still-colour pictures, moving pictures, or text. Video-discs could therefore be used as a resource base, which the learner searches or used for a particular purpose. For instance, in training historians, or archaeologists, a whole set of materials could be archived on disc-pictures of archaeological sites and are facts, historical documents, short, dramatised extracts from historical events, archive film and so on. Students could be asked to work through this material, drawing conclusions and testing hypotheses, with students to some extent imposing their own structure on the organisation of the data. A teacher could use the video-disc material to show a sequence of pictures as desired to students. The first such 'archival' video-disc commercially marketed featured the satellite photographs of Jupiter and Saturn.

These are merely glimpses of the potential for education of video-discs. But what are their implications for educational broadcasting? Although the cost of making the master for discs from the final edited tape is not expensive given the cost of production, video-disc production seems to require broadcast which, unlike video-cassette production are likely to be found mainly in production centres concerned with broadcasting. Secondly, to exploit the advantages of video-disc, programme production costs are likely to be towards the more expensive end of the scale. Broadcasting organisations thus are well placed to exploit video-disc technology, at least technically.

The design requirements of interactive video-discs and their implications for broadcasting organisations, through, are critical. Where programmes are to be designed from the outset to be used in an integrated way with computer control, difficulties are likely to arise. The structure of the video-disc, the choice of responses required from learners, the extent to which learners will be free to choose their own paths, through the material, what paths are permissible or desirable, the number of difficulty levels to be built into the disc, the balance between computer and video graphics, and the design of the computer programme, all have major educational implications and go far beyond the normal brief of an educational television producer. It would be a fundamental mistake to the normal television production is merely a mild extension of the normal television production process, with the computer programming contracted out as an afterthought almost. This kind of disc requires a team approach, involving teacher, television producer, computer programmer and instructional designer/evaluator, working as equals from conception to final credits. This inevitably slows up the production process, limits the producer's freedom and increases the cost of production. It will be interesting to see whether broadcasters will be willing to enter into this more complex from of video-disc design and, if so, under what conditions; or whether they will prefer to stick to the safer form of video-disc design, where the disc can stand alone without being tied to predetermined computer control.

How realistic is it to expect video-discs or interactive video to become widespread in education? Video-discs have only just come on the market and their commercial viability as a consumer product has yet to be proved. There are at the time of writing few commercial discs available for sale in Britain and it is not yet possible to record off-air on the disc. Video-cassettes are in the process of becoming well-established, at least in Britain, as a consumer product in direct competition with discs. It may be many years before home wonder ship of video-discs is a more realistic possibility. The Open University has already produced a video-disc production is irrelevant when set against the phenomenally high cost or disastrous consequences of mistakes made in real circumstances.

The use of video-discs in schools is less certain. The cost of a video-disc machine is not out of the question, but given the slow growth of video-cassette machines with far greater amounts of suitable programme material, I do not see schools rushing to get disc technology. Even more of a problem will be the cost of discs if they have to cover their full production costs. It is difficult to imagine a well-designed interactive video-disc costing less than £25,000 to produce. To retail at £10 a disc, at least 3,000 discs would need to be sold to recoup costs, and this is a high target for the school market given that there are less than, 6.000 secondary schools in Britain. It is likely therefore that video-discs will have a more specialised and restricted use than video-discs will have a more specialise and restricted use than video-cassettes, at leas over the next ten years, but where they are used and well designed they could prove to be extremely valuable.

While the combination of video and computer-assisted learning may bring together the advantages of both, it is as well to remember what Bernard Shaw once said to a lady suggesting an experiment in genetic engineering: 'But what if it has my looks and your brains?' After all, there is only one medium more expensive in education than television-and that is computer-assisted learning. Without careful design and choice of appropriate situations for its use, an interactive video-disc could easily turn out to be a horribly ugly and expensive baby.

Cable and satellite

Cable and satellite developments are also likely to have some impact on educational broadcasting, although less immediately than video-cassettes or even video-discs Should anyone be reading this book in 1988, or beyond, they will no doubt obtain some perverse satisfaction in seeing how wrong my predictions have turned out to be, but, for reasons which I shall explain, I suspect that there will be no significant expansion of cable for educational purposes much before 1990, although no doubt there will be a number of significant experiments. Similarly, the first UK direct broadcast satellite will not be launched until 1986, and while there will be four DBS television channels available from around that time, none will offer educational services.

Cable and satellite could have major implications for education, but given the slowness with which they are likely to develop in the United Kingdom I shall limit myself to a very brief outline of their potential and limitations and the likely consequences for educational broadcasting.

There are four basic characteristics of cable television that are significant for education: the ability to provide a large number of channels-from thirty to a hundred, dependent on the technology thereby theoretically increasing choice of service; the possibility of two-way communications through the cable system; the possibility of local programming; and the ability to 'filter' or 'select' viewers electronically. Satellite television can provide national coverage but, due to international regulations, Britain is limited to only five channels.

A study of the implications of cable developments for the Open University suggested the following *potential* advantages of cable for education: better transmission times, more time available for educational television: channels dedicated solely to educational use; access to more potential students; more specifically targeted programming; increased interaction and student participations; more choice of educational programming; easier access to television for teachers; more scope for experiment; multiple sound-tracks or radio channels.

These are all possible, but whether they are likely depends very much on political and financial decisions yet to be finalised. At the time of writing, though, it seems most unlikely that these benefits will be realised in Britain, and, in fact, cable developments are more likely to have negative educational effects. For instance, even the most optimistic forecasts predict that less than 50 per cent of the United Kingdom population will be on the cable by the end of the century. Given the current unbridled commercial basis on which cable is to expand, the first and most profitable areas to be cabled up will be the outer suburban areas and commercial centres of large cities. Rural communities and the poorer inner city areas are less likely to be cabled up quickly, yet this is where the educational need and lack of provision is the greatest.

Currently it seems that there will be no statutory obligation for British cable operators to carry educational or community programmes, unlike practically every other major developed country with cable systems. Nor are there plans yet to ensure the establishment of a nationally linked cable network. Current proposals are based on the establishment of independent local systems. This does not guarantee local programming, though. At least one commentator, John Howkins, of the International Institute of Communications, predicts that London-based communications companies will make up 'packages' of programming which will then be sold to local stations. The lack of a national network is a severe limitation for the Open University, but if there is spare capacity for local programming this would provide opportunities for other educational institutions to negotiate deals with stations in their own area.

The key question, though, is who will pay for the educational services on cable, and how? Some stations, just to earn 'brownie points', may allow local colleges to use spare studio capacity and an otherwise unused channel to provide low-cost programming free of charge. More likely, companies such as Rediffusion Ltd will put together an educational package of programmes, using whatever existing material it can obtain at nil or low cost from current educational providers, such as those universities, colleges and local education authorities that have their own production facilities. Some courses may be mounted on a 'pay-per-view' basis, or made available only to students who entorl. Enrolled students could be given an electronic code or key which would enable them to access the relevant programmes.

It is difficult, though, to see coherent educational offerings of any quality being offered in these ways. Educational broadcasts and Open University programmes are strongly protected by copyright, and its is unlikely that such material will be released free of charge for use by cable operators. The real issue is who is going to pay for the costs of creating original educational material for use on cable. It is unlikely that students will be able to pay the sort of charges that would be necessary to recoup 'true' production costs. At the time of writing there is no lobby for education among the political debates on cable, and the educational and voluntary agencies seem to be too diverse and unco-ordinated to sort out any agreed policy.

One of the major attractions of cable for education frequently claimed by politicians is its potential for two-way communication, allowing the viewer to interact, respond or participate in the viewing event. This is the sort of claim that needs to be taken with a good pinch of salt. There are major financial and technical obstinacies that limit the likelihood of cable being a truly two-way communication system for some time. There are two types of cable that can be laid. Co-axial cable is the basis of virtually all current systems but, for practical purposes, co-axial systems tend to be limited to a maximum of thirty to forty channels in one direction. Co-axial cable is not really suitable as a two-way communication system. Fibre-optic cable has much greater capacity and is a realistic proposition for two-way communication. However, It is still a largely untried technology in a fully operational sense and it will probably be more expensive than co-axial cable to lay.

Secondly, two-way communication will depend crucially on the configuration or design of the cable system. Co-axial cable uses a 'trunk and branch' system, i.e. a central 'trunk' cable running down a street with 'branch' off to each house. The street cable itself is probably a branch of a more central trunk running through the town. Even with fibre-optic cable laid in a trunk and branch configuration, 'backward' communication from the home could only follow the same route as the downward signal, i.e. back to the 'head-end', the local station. It would not be possible to communicate across branches. I.e. with neighbours in the street, or the local college on the other side of town, unless this communication was relayed from the head-end. If all communications have to go thorough the head-end, this obviously limits the amount of communications that can be handled, even with a hundred channels.

The alternative, only possible with fibre-optic cable, is a configuration similar to that of the public service telephone system. This has been named a 'star' system since each house would be linked directly to a central switchboard, which in turn would also be linked up with other switchboards. This would allow any one point to communicate directly with any of the others, as with the current telephone system but using much wider band-widths, including even television transmission 'outwards' as well as inwards. Fibre-optic cable would be essential for such a system. Also, a national grid or satellite-linked system would also be necessary for cross-connections between different cable also be necessary for cross-connections between different cable systems. Unfortunately, because of the amount of switching gear required, a 'star' system would be much more expensive to introduce.

For these reasons, interaction is most likely to be limited to user typing, i.e. keying-in instructions along the lines of PRESTEL responses, enabling home banking and possibly some computer-assisted learning responses, through a local viewdata system. In other words, it would give little more than is currently available through PRESTEL. Until a national fibre-optic 'star' system is established, it will still probably be more practical to use the public telephone network for voice interaction or even telewriting.

These technical considerations indicate quite clearly the kind of framework required for education from any national policy for cable development: statutory obligation on cable operators to carry at least one educational and community channel; a policy which will encourage cable operators to provide services in areas of greatest educational need-i.e. inner city and rural areas-as well as in commercially attractive areas; cable systems based on fibre-optics technology; 'star' cable configurations; and a national grid or a satellite-linked system for cable allowing inter-communication between all cable users.

Unfortunately, at the time of writing, most of these developments are unlikely for some time given the 'free market' policy of the present Conservative government. The use of cable for educational purposes, therefore, is likely to develop very slowly and to be very piecemeal, as indeed will cable be generally. The original reason for setting up cable systems in North America was to provide decent signals for the many areas not covered by adequate off-air transmission, but in Britain most homes can receive high quality, off-air broadcast transmissions. Secondly, there is no guarantee that an increase in channels will lead to an increase in the range of quality of programmes available. Anyone who has switched from channels to channel on cable system in America cannot fail to have noticed the similarity of programming on each cannel. It is significant that the BBC plans to use one of the new statellite channels merely for repeating old BBC programmes. Leaps in technology are not necessarily accompanied by leaps in imagination. The growth of video-cassette machine ownership, the ease of hiring video-cassettes for a small fee from the local corner shop and the opportunity to record high-quality broadcast programmes, are all real threats to the competitiveness of cable television. Most of all, laying the cables, connecting up homes, providing extra programming and linking cable systems together, will be extremely expensive and financially risky. There is likely to be a great deal of caution exercised, therefore, before there is a major expansion of cable services.

For all these reasons, I am very sceptical of cable being of any significant value for education in the 1980s and early 1990s, despite its potential. The main danger of cable developments is that, despite their slow growth, they will put yet more pressure on channel controllers in the broadcasting organisations to remove educational programmes from transmission. Only the national broadcasting organisations are in a position during the 1980s and 90s to provide a national educational television services. Cable would be a very poor alternative.

Teletext and viewdata

Teletext systems such as CEEFAX and ORACLE which broadcast 'frames' or 'pages' of information that can be called up at any time by the viewer, have at the moment only two real educational advantages; they are useful for up-dating informations, such as news headlines and weather forecasts; and the services is free. Their educational limitations though are considerable The number of pages that can be accessed is limited, in 1983 to around eight hundred, and since each teletext page holds far less information than a printed page, the total amount of information that can be accessed is very small indeed. Because of the inherent nature of the technology, teletext information tends to be geared to maximum audiences with common interests, and to deal primarily with information that can be easily condensed and up-dated. Thee is no possibility of two-way communication, and a viewer can have irritating time delays while waiting for pages called up. Teletext services have been used, however, for transmitting computer programmes to schools, which are received on a standard aerial and 'dumped' into a BBC microcomputer, again offering a free, if limited, distribution services.

Viewdata systems based on the telephone, such as PRESTEL in Britain, ANTIOPE in France and TELIDON in Canada, have a much wider range of features which may prove more useful in education, but not to the extent of having much impact on broadcasting. Viewdata systems also have major educational limitations. In theory, the number of pages that can be accessed is limited only by the size of the computers that store the pages. However, like teletext systems, the technology limits the amount of information that can be displayed per page. Also, because of the cost of creating and accessing viewdata pages, information again tends to be presented in a condensed and simplified form. Viewdata systems, also like teletext, have no sound. The lack of synchronised sound and pictures is a major disadvantage, as too is the lack of movement, compared with broadcasting. Lastly, the way viewdata systems structure information is still unsatisfactory, searching through the branching structure for the information one needs is a tedious business-especially if it was never there in the first place. This technology structures knowledge in a way that is unhelpful for learning. Attempts to base systems on keywords may improve access and structuring, but it is hard to see how the system can ever have the flexibility and richness of an educational television programmes.

There have been some experiments, particularly in Canada, to create teaching materials for use on viewdata systems. TV Ontario located Telidon terminals in 120 primary schools throughout the province, and asked teachers to create their own programmes by sending in specifications to TV Ontario where skilled Telidon advisers created the frames and stored them on the mainframe computer. Teachers could then call up on the mainframe computer. Teachers could then all upon the telephone not only their own programmes but also all the other programmes so created. However, despite the superior picture quality compared with Prestel the quality of the programmes that I saw was poor, being limited to testing recognition skills. There was of course no sound, and very primitive animation. Pupils appeared restless and easily distracted without the sound facility.

It may be too early yet to judge but it seems there are inherent problem with using systems such as teletext or viewdata extensively in education for teaching purposes, although they may have their use as a data-base or for general informational purposes. If they do have their values, they are more likely to complement than compete with educational broadcasts.

It is the microcomputer which is likely to have the greatest long-term impact on educational broadcasting, as on many other aspects of out lives. Microcomputers will enable individual teachers to create their own audio-visual teaching materials quickly, easily and economically, and will enable the individual learner to interact in a wide variety of was with such audio-visual materials, which can be tailor-made to the individual's needs. This material is likely to be highly motivating both for the teacher and the learner. To do this, teachers will not need to be highly skilled in using computers, and the learner need not have any programming expertise to study in this way. Furthermore, this is not a Utopian dream; such a situation could be widespread in British education by the early 1990s. The ability to create one's own audio-visual materials on microcomputers will not eliminate altogether the need for educational broadcasting but it will require educational broadcasting to be used more precisely.

Currently, this potential has not been realised, because of technical limitations. Designing computer-assisted learning programmes is at the moment extremely time-consuming, requires a good deal of computer power, and needs a sensitive combination of high-level computing and teaching skills. Effective CAL programmes tend to be expensive to produce in terms of the actual use made of them. The learner is generally limited to responses via the keyboard, and the range of responses in this mode is also limiting. Another very real limitation of CAL is the lack of adequate sound, particularly the teacher's voice. This means that CAL programmes have a heavy reliance on textual and simple graphical presentation, although animation is also available at a price. Creating good quality, effective graphics and animation requires a lot of programming time and can be difficult to achieve on the lower-priced microcomputers. The major limitations, however, at present is the need for teachers to become skilled programmes. Many have neither the time nor the inclination to do this, and in terms of what CAL can currently offer on microcomputers, they are probably correct in assuming that the results are not worth the effort. Those who have proved skilful in this areas have tended to produce packages which are used by other teachers-resulting in a degree of centralisation of teaching which in practice limits the use of such materials.

But all that is changing. By the late 1980s 'peripherals' to standard microcomputers, and special packages of programming which can be loaded into a microcomputer so that it can be operated easily in certain way, will allow teachers to create their own sophisticated audio-visual materials very simply and without needing computer programming skills. Similar developments will also allow audio-visual material to be sent down a telephone line and for learners at home to communicate back with a teacher and other learners, both with voice and visually.

It is possible to predict fairly accurately what a low-cost micro-computer-based audio-visual teaching system will look like, partly as a result of experience gained from using a prototype system called CYCLOPS at the Open University and in schools. CYCLOPS digitally converts simple colour-video graphics-handwriting, text, diagrams and very simple animation-into sound codes. These graphics can be very easily generated using a combination of a standard computer keyboard and an electronic writing-pad which also displays graphics on the TV screen. Still images from a video-camera can be similarly coded. Because the video signals are converted into a sound code, they can be stored on audio-cassette or transmitted down standard telephone lines, then decoded back into a video signal. Using either standard stereo audio-cassettes or two telephone lines, full sound can be synchronised with the visuals.

The crucial point is that audio-visual materials can be created very simply and quickly this way without any need for computer programming skills. The system has been successfully used in the Open University for three years for running distance audio-visual telephone tutorials. Students and tutors may be scattered across as many as seven different locations at any one time. Each person though is able to communicate with everyone else taking part., both visually and orally, using a standard teleconference bridge, The same equipment has been used in schools. Three teachers with no previous experience of using computers created their own CYCLOPS materials for use by individual children in their classes using the audio-cassette facility. It proved possible in this way to develop very quickly highly motivating and interactive audio-visual materials. CYCLOPS is basically a 'peripheral' system for a standard microcomputer since its 'core' can be made available as a cartridge or a ROM to be added to a standard microcomputer.

While it may not be the CYCLOPS system that eventually gets used, by the late 1980s microcomputer-based audio-visual teaching systems will be common in schools. A probable configuration will consist of a standard television receiver, a stereo-cassette player and microphone, a light-pen or an electronic writing-pad, and a standard microcomputer. This will incorporate a CYCLOPS-type facility, either built into the microcomputer itself, or as an add-on accessory, and a connection to the public telephone system. Most of this equipment is already available in schools in Britain at the time of writing. For instance, in 1983, 98 per cent of british secondary schools were equipped with a microcomputer. The additional components-the light-pen and the CYCLOPS-type cartridge-will cost approximately 50 each, and in the future, facilities similar to CYCLOPS are likely to be built into a microcomputer as a standard feature. Microcomputers will also increase in power and reduce in price over the next few years.

With such a facility, teachers can create their own teaching materials. They can draw on the screen and add text via the keyboard. They can also use standard graphics facilities in the cartridge or the microcomputer itself, to create shapes such as triangles, squares and circles, and to 'fill-in' these shapes with different colours. They can also create certain forms of animation. The facility enables a teacher to build up pictures or frames which are then transferred to a standard audio-cassette. Each picture or frame can be coded and stored, enabling editing to be carried out simply and easily by the microcomputer. When all the pictures have been assembled, edited and correctly ordered, the teacher can add the sound-track using the microphone and the audio-cassette player. As well as the teacher's or the pupils' voices, music or special effects can be added. The computer controls the length of time each frame is displayed to enable sound-track and picture to be synchronised. The programmes can be exchanged with other schools, ordered from a central bank or used for distance teaching. Teachers can learn how to use the system either by following a simple manual or by loading on a cassette containing a training programmes. It is likely to take teachers two or three hours to learn how to use the system, after which time they will have no difficulty in creating their own materials.

Learners will load the audio-cassette and work through the programme very much in the same way they would work through an audio-cassette or video-cassette. In addition, though, they can use the light-pen or keyboards or microphone to give answers to questions on the tape, and their responses can be recorded together with the original programmes, for later inspection by the teacher if so desired. CAL features can also be added, with feedback given on keyboards.responses, and the tape can be directed to appropriate sections according to the learner's responses.

The technology to so this is already here and will be introduced to schools and colleges in the mid 1980s. We will have to wait and see whether teachers will want to create their own materials in this way or whether they will prefer to use materials prepared more professionally by others, probably marketed by publishers. Such developments, however, have obvious implications for broadcasters since microcomputer programmes of this kind will have a number of advantages over video materials. They will be much cheaper and easier to produce and distribute than video-cassettes. They will be much more interactive and specific to the needs of individual teachers and learners, especially if created by teachers themselves. But there will also be disadvantages. It is likely that a majority of teachers will prefer high-quality, off-the-shelf material that is readily and easily available. The 'cottage-industry', teacher-generated computer materials cannot currently match the quality of professionally produced broadcasts, or even non-broadcast video-cassettes. Even with the advanced CYCLOPS-type facilities, computer-generated materials will still lack many of the features of video, no matter how professional the computer design. There will still be need for film or tape of overseas situations, for portraying human interactions, for presenting the world in a fully representational manner, for the more personal aspects of seeing a human face, for seeing things as they happen. Microcomputer-based programmes will not eliminate the need for video. They will, however, provide teachers with a convenient and cheaper alternative. Video programmes will therefore have to compete against other highly effective media for the limited time of teacher and learners. If video is to compete successfully, broadcasters and video producers will need to identify and exploit to the full the unique advantages of their medium.

The main developments likely to impact directly on educational broadcasting are cassettes and microcomputers. Both will develop independently of and in parallel with broadcasting, and are likely to reduce to some extent the use of educational broadcasts, particularly in schools. Cable and satellite may have a further negative effect, increasing pressure on broadcasting organisations either to transfer educational programmes to inconvenient or impossible times or, for financial reasons, to drop educational programmes altogether. Cable is unlikely though to offer an effective alternative for education. The main overall effect on broadcasters will be the need to identify and exploit the unique educational advantages of broadcasting, since a range of highly effective audio-visual alternatives are now becoming available to teachers and learners.

Selection of media materials

Meeting the instructional needs of the learner requires excellent instructional materials, excellent teachers, cooperative parents and rich, challenging experiences both in and out of school, says Edgar Dale, writing in Audio-visual Instruction, 'Toward Excellence in Institution,' September 1973.

We are considering improved instructional experience in all fields of learning today, both in the classroom and out. Changes in the needs and interests of students, in modern life, and the curriculum demand many resources for learning.

Selection of those materials is the responsibility of many of us today in our nation's schools and universities and colleges. Leslie Cottardi, writing on "A Survey of Instructional Budgets" in Audiovisual Instruction, December 1971, points out that money for institutional materials in our schools is only an average of five percent of the nationally recommended amount.

Most school districts, however are increasing expenditures. Teachers, administrators and librarians are all involved in selection of instructional materials.

In a survey done by Myles P. Breen and Donald A. Ary, of some 174 school districts selected from the 14,000 listed in Education Almanac, the individual teacher was cited as the most important element in film selection by 54.5 percent of the respondents; teacher committees were cited by 28.7 percent of the respondents. Administrators also have an important voice in film selection; 45.5 percent of the respondents in the Breen and Ary study indicated that building principals are involved in selection. And 40.5 percent of the respondents named the librarian as the person who makes or shares in the selection decision. Such selection involvements often carry over into the selection of all media, with the possible exception of books, in the library media center.

Considerable financial support for audiovisual equipment and materials has come from the federal aid to education programs. The National Defense Education Act of 1958 provided funds that enabled local school units to purchase audiovisual equipment and materials for the purpose of strengthening instruction programs in selected curriculum areas. The Elementary and Secondary Education Act of 1965 was the largest single commitment by the federal government to strengthen and improve the educational quality of schools. Title II recognized that teaching and learning depend upon effective school library materials, high quality up-to-date textbooks and a variety of other educational resources. Such federal support increased in dollar support in the 1970 fiscal school year, but the percentage of the total expenditure decreased one percent in comparison to the two previous fiscal school years.

The teacher of today realizes that motivation to learn is the key to excellence in instruction. The roles of teacher and student are changing as we aim towards individualization of instruction. Every classroom can have the best instructional materials now produced. Excellence in learning involves use of many educational media as the student learns to read critically, listen critically and observe critically.

As the librarian, teacher or administrator selects media materials for the learning resources center, the library media center or the classroom, he must evaluate effectiveness of resources in meeting objectives, production standards, acceptability for acquisition, and whether the resources meet a specific need. Evaluation must precede selection. The supply-support function includes evaluation, selection, acquisition, distribution/retrieval, description and storage functions.

Basic indexes and catalogs are used by every librarian selecting material and recommending selection aids to the teacher or administrator. This list of selection sources is intended to bring up-to-date selection in certain areas, to point out some sources which discuss selection criteria, and to list important selection sources for the teacher, administrator and librarian.

Media research

The Winter 1974 issue of *School Media Quarterly* introduced, in its Current Research column, a listing of "School Media Dissertations in Progress." The idea for this came from the Journal of *Education for Librarianship,* which lists "Doctoral Dissertations Topics Accepted in Library and Information Science." The editors of *School Media Quarterly* hope to develop a listing of school media, dissertations which will tap non-library/information science programs and isolate the school media dissertations found in the JEL list. This current-awareness listing of dissertations on the school library media program is a step toward creating more interest in media research.

Much more research in educational media and technology is needed to define and implement solutions to the needs in education today. In research, *media* is defined broadly as including all print and non-print aids to instruction. Research is needed, in both education and librarianship, on educational media and technology, its uses, preparation, selection, distribution, research, preservice and inservice education, design and evaluation.

A broad definition of educational research appears in Carter V. Good's *Dictionary of Education* "study and investigation in the field of education or bearing upon educational problems." A more specific one is: "an inquiry-oriented activity employing an objective, empirical and controlled methodology, the findings of which must be replicable when subjected to scrutiny by other investigators, must instill a high level of confidence and must be generalizable beyond the local setting in which they are obtained".

The systems approach is a methodology which shows promise in research in new classes of education endeavors. Systems technology has strengthened educational research, and research can make a contribution in educational systems, engineering: the two, in a sense, are complementary. The systems, approach as research methodology denotes a collection of procedures directed toward realistic effects. Systems, methodology may enable the researcher to focus on larger phenomena and hence produce findings of broad significance. The value of a research study or a systems design, however, depends always upon the researcher's ability to abstract effectively from the "rich complexity of reality". In general, one might say that research emphasizes the general principle, while systems methodology is generally applied to specific situations.

2 Communication Satellites in Education

Planning studies and experiments are underway to explore the use of communications satellites in education, both in the United States and in other countries and regions. These studies and experiments seek to take advantage of the ability of satellites to deliver educational radio, television, digital data, and other signals over wide areas, to reach remote areas, and to tie together people and institutions to share resources, experiences, and ideas.

Applications Technology Satellites I and III, developed by NASA, have been and are being used in the U.S. for educational communications experiments of limited scope. More extensive educational television distribution, and institutional broadcasting experiments involving inexpensive, community-reception-type receivers, are planned during 1974-1976 in the U.S. and India, using the ATS-6 satellite. A number of educational experiments or demonstrations during 1975-1977, using a joint U.S.-Canada

Communication Technology Satellite, have been proposed by U.S. and Canadian educational institutions and other agencies. Major planning efforts for operational satellite systems which serve education are underway within large countries like India, Brazil, Indonesia, and Iran. UNESCO has supported studies of regional satellite systems for Africa, Latin America, and the Arab countries.

Communications satellites are one of many technologies of current or potential interest to educational technologists and planners. The extent to which satellites will be used depends upon the extent to which educational and communications technology proves responsive to educational needs, the extent to which "cost-effectiveness" can be demonstrated, and the extent to which technology in general finds future use in education. In particular, satellites have the potential for providing relatively low cost educational services-computer-aided instruction, radio, one-way and talk-back television, library and computer resource sharing, etc.-to large numbers of people and institutions, provided that economies of scale can be achieved. Such services may prove to be responsive to calls for greater access, individualization, and productivity in U.S. education, as well the need to extend education and literacy to greater numbers of individuals in developing countries. However, to achieve this potential suitable organizational arrangements and structures must be devised which respond to the particular educational setting of the country or regions.

Communications satellites

Use of satellites for communications was first outlined by the radio engineer and science fiction writer Arthur C. Clarke in 1945. Just 18 years later, after a series of experiments with low and medium altitude satellites which required large and complex earth-stations, the stationary satellite Syncom-II was successfully placed in geo-synchronous orbit. In such an orbit the satellite is some 23,000 miles over the equator, and stays in one fixed position relative to points on earth. Three of these satellites in the proper position could beam signals which cover almost the entire surface of the earth.

The demonstration of the feasibility of using a stationary satellite in geo-synchronous orbit for communications paved the way for commercial communications satellites. Since the orbiting of the Early Bird satellite, launched for the International Telecommunications Satellite Consortium in 1965, communications satellite technology has come a long way and has acquired a high degrees of sophistication. Intelsat has launched four generations of satellites; investment costs per circuit year of satellite capacity dropped from $15,000 for Early Bird to $500 for Intelsat IV; earth-stations have increasingly become less complex and less expensive; and satellites have moved from international to domestic communications. Canada has a full-fledged domestic communications satellite system of its own, and a small number of commercial domestic communications satellite systems have begun operating or are being planned for the U.S.A.

It is important to recognize that satellites in use for international telecommunications today, and the present generation of domestic satellites coming into being, have relatively low power transmitters which provide "fixed-satellite services," to connect relatively large and expensive earth stations. However, the satellite technology has reached a point where relatively inexpensive, roof-top type receivers for receiving radio and television programs or broadcasts over a wide area from relatively high-power satellites will be feasible shortly. In recognition of this possibility, the 1971 World Administrative Radio Conference, held in Geneva, defined and allocated radio frequencies for a "broadcasting satellite service" in which signals transmitted or retransmitted by satellites are intended for direct reception by the general public. Two distinct categories exist in this service; systems that allow individual reception by simple receiving units in homes, and systems that are designed for community reception, either by a group of the general public at one location or through a distribution system covering a limited area. However, it should be pointed out that WARC regulations for broadcasting satellite service do not permit direct reception by unaugmented conventional TV receivers of the type in use today.

Educational uses of satellites

The applications currently contemplated for communications satellites in education are indeed diverse, reflecting the differences in educational systems and needs of the nations or regions where uses of communications satellites have been proposed. In the U.S., formal systems of education have been serving large portions of the school-age population, and higher education is becoming more widespread with the inception of the community college. According to Koerner, three current educational demands center on greater access to education by those not served, greater individualization of education, and greater economy. There is also current emphasis on nontraditional forms of study. These movements may provide clues as to opportunities for satellite utilization in the U.S. In a developing nation like India, higher priority may be given to building a system of basic education and an infrastructure, almost from scratch, to communication skills and attitudes necessary for the economic and social development of the nation, with particular emphasis on rural areas.

In the U.S., with its relatively well developed telecommunications infrastructure, including considerable investment in educational telecommunications facilities, the rationale for utilizing satellites for educational communications differs from that in countries which may not have well developed telecommunications plants. The key to satellite utilization, as opposed to other communications technologies, lies in provision of significantly new services that existing terrestrial facilities are unable to accommodate or provide, and provision of services similar to those provided by existing technologies but at significantly reduced cost. Educational satellite planners are emphasizing educational networking for sharing of library, computer, and human resources, educational services which are not adequately provided by the existing formal system; direct delivery of high-quality educational material and resources to small and remote institutions; and educational television and ratio networking.

In developing nations like India, the emphasis is on taking advantages of the wide-area coverage and broadcast capabilities of the satellite to provide a quantum jump in the, ass-communication capabilities of those nations, and to expand and improve their basic education system quickly. Brazil's extensive satellite planning effort emphasizes educational radio and television programming, to be used in formal education in the remote, less developed areas of the Northeast.

Table 1 summarizes primary roles in Education which satellite may provide. If and when educational services are implemented, they are likely to be developed in conjunction with local distribution facilities such as cable-television systems, Instructional Television Fixed Services systems, regional terrestrial networks, and broadcast facilities. The use of satellites for direct delivery of services to rooftops of schools and learning centers is of interest in areas where tropical and/or demographic conditions make local distribution and interconnection stems less attractive economically-areas such as Alaska, the Rocky Mountains, and parts of Appalachia. Satellites look promising for delivery of educational services to wide but sparsely populated areas, and for interconnection of cable systems, but the cable-television headend interconnection is not necessarily promising unless educational interests can make greater inroads into local cable systems. Cable systems tied together by satellite could conceivably provide a second interconnection for public television programs.

Table 1. Primary roles for satellites towards the delivery of certain educational communications media and services

Service	*Primary roles for satellites*
Instructional television	Direct delivery to schools and learning centers, to broadcast stations, ITFS and cable headends for further redistribution.
Computer-assisted instruction	Delivery of CAI to small, remote institutions, particularly those 70-80 miles or more away from a major metropolitan area.
Computing resources multi-access interactive computing	Delivery of interactive computing to remote institutions for the purposes of problem solving and implementation of regional EIS.
Remote batch processing	Delivery of raw computing power to small, remote institutions for instructional computing and administrative data processing.

Computer interconnection	Interconnection of the computer facilities of institutions of higher education and regional computer networks for resources sharing.
Information resources sharing interlibrary communication	Interconnection of major libraries for bibliographic search and interlibrary loans, etc.
Automated remote information retrieval	Interconnection of institutional and/or CATV headends with major information storage centers.
Teleconferencing	Interconnection of educational institutions for information exchange without physical movement of the participants, and for gaining access to specialists.

Educational satellite experiments

In 1969, after two years of studying the application of communications satellites for mass communications, education, and telecommunications, India became the first country to commit herself to a large-scale experiment in satellite delivery of institutional television to rural areas. This experiment, scheduled for 1975-1976, will be conducted in cooperation with NASA by the Indian Space Organization, using NASA's Applications Technology Satellite. In this experiment, the ATS-6 satellite will be used to broadcast directly to 2500 rural community receivers. Some 2000 additional receivers will be served by rebroadcast through low-power VHF transmitters interconnected by ATS-6. The primary instructional objectives of the experiment involve family planning, improved agricultural practices, and national integration. Certain portions of the programming will also be devoted to general school education and teacher training.

The history of experiments with satellites for educational communications in the U.S. dates back to January 4, 1970, when the Corporation for Public Broadcasting initiated an experiment in transcontinental interconnection employing NASA's Applications Technology Satellites 1 and 3. Since then a number of educational communications demonstrations and experiments using ATS-1 and 3 satellites have been completed or are continuing. With the sole exception of the CPB transcontinental interconnection experiments conducted using C-band transponders, experiments continuing or completed to date have employed Very High Frequency transponders on-board ATS-1 and 3-using frequencies that are nor assigned for operational services, and that are incapable of accommodating wide band or high data-rate communications such as television relay/ distribution.

The Health-Education Telecommunications experiment, jointly sponsored by NASA, the department of Health, Education and Welfare, and the Corporation for Public Broadcasting, involves educational experiments in Alaska, Appalachia, and the Rocky Mountains. This experiment, which began in late spring of 1974, employs the ATS-6 satellite to distribute health and educational material to public broadcasting stations, cable television headends, translators and community centers in S-band using low-cost/receive terminals. It also was designed to use VHF transponders on-board the ATS-1 and 3 spacecrafts to accommodate limited narrowband interaction from selected remote installations.

In addition to demonstrating the feasibility of distributing ETV signals to low-cost terminals, the HET experiments were planned to explore the three dimensions of educational delivery arrangements-the hardware, soft-ware, and human-support elements. These were to be weighted in different ways to assess the impact of different combinations on the learning, participation, and opinion

3 The Social Functions of the Press

Theoretical basis of press freedom

As the libertarian philosophy of freedom developed in England and America, the press became accountable for performing at least six social functions. In brief, its six assigned jobs are these: (a) enlightening the public, (b) servicing the political system, (c) safe-guarding personal liberties, (d) making a profit, (e) servicing the economic system, and (f) providing entertainment. It is easy to see that some of these functions arose naturally from our ideas of freedom of speech. A brief review of our traditional theory of press freedom will show also that certain characteristics of the press system make it difficult for the press to perform some of these functions adequately.

The traditional Anglo-American theory of freedom of the press rests on a belief that man has certain inalienable natural rights, one of which is the right to free expression. It assumes that man is disposed to seek truth and will be guided by it. Using his reason, man can find truth if he has free access to ideas and information. For the theory also puts strong faith in what has been called the "self-righting process," the unfettered clash of ideas and information in the free and open market, which ultimately results in the emergence of truth. As men find truth in the free play of ideas, social change results from conversion instead of from revolution. The theory makes virtually all ideas welcome. If they are true, men will embrace them; if they are false, men will reject them. More probably, however, men will find some truth amidst falsehood, some falsehood amidst truth, because truth and falsehood rarely appear in simple shades of black and white.

Prepublication censorship, under the theory, is abhorrent. In the long run, suppression is effectual, for sooner or later a suppressed idea will make itself known. Meanwhile, however, suppression may land a fictitious validity to invalid ideas. Furthermore, the theory recognizes that no person or group of persons is wise enough to distinguish between valid and invalid ideas before they have been put to the test of the market. Even traffickers in lies and distortions must be free to have their say. There is no need to fear them; other men will find it profitable to expose them so that in the long run lies and distortion will be shown up for what they are.

As fighters against tyranny traditionally regarded the government as the chief foe of liberty, the Anglo-American concept of press freedom came to be predominantly one of negative liberty. Primarily, it emphasizes freedom from government intervention. But the theory does not regard press freedom as absolute. The theory sanctions certain minimal restraints. For example, it sanctions postpublication libel laws and laws regulating obscenity. More recently the "clear and present danger" doctrine, first expressed by Justice Holmes in 1919, has been generally sanctioned. This doctrine holds that free speech may be abridged when the words in question are used "in such circumstances and are of such a nature as to create a clear and present danger that they will bring about the substantive evils that Congress has a right to prevent." Wartime limitations on press freedom, too, have been justified. The protection of the Constitution has been held to be less in wartime than in peacetime because "the character of every act depends upon the circumstances in which it is done."

So, somewhat simplified, runs the traditional Anglo-American theory of freedom of the press. It is a theory evolved by scores of philosophers, statesmen, jurists, and practitioners. If only a few names are usually associated with it-those of John Milton, Thomas Jefferson, and John Stuart Mill, for example-it is because those men best caught the spirit of their times or overshadowed other men who expressed the same ideas. As this theory of press freedom developed, the press came to be held responsible for performing certain social functions.

Social responsibilities of the press

Enlightening the public

Man can explore at firsthand but a tiny fraction of the world of which he is a part. To know and understand the world, man must depend largely on the printed word. Not only can the press furnish man with the information he needs to formulate his own ideas but it can also stimulate him by offering him the ideas of others. For centuries, the press has been regarded as an important carrier of information and ideas. Running through John Milton's Areopagitica of 1644 is the theme that a free press is indispensable in the quest for truth. As Milton put it, "Where there is much desire to learn, there of necessity will be much arguing, much writing, many opinions; for opinion in good men is but knowledge in the making." Although Thomas Jefferson wrote no unified work on the press, his scattered writings time and again touch upon the importance of a free press to public enlightenment. In a letter to M. Coray in 1823, he remarked: "The press is the best instrument for enlightening the mind of man, and improving him as a rational, normal, and social being."

By implication, John Stuart Mill, too, recognized the role of the press in enlightening the public; for much of his essay, On Liberty, dwelt on the necessity of free discussion for the individual's self-development and the mental well-being of mankind. Nor were these moulders of traditional theory the only ones to assign the press a public enlightenment function. More recent writers, including some who would modify existing theory-as, for example, the Hutchins Commission on Freedom of the Press-have made much of the importance of the press in informing and educating the citizenry.

Servicing the political system

Closely allied with the public enlightenment function of the press is the second function of servicing the political system. The very nature of democratic government imposes a heavy responsibility on the press, which is granted a privileged position under the Constitution. As Carl Becker once remarked, "Democratic government rests on the assumption that the people are capable of governing themselves better than any one or a few can do it for them." If the citizens are to rule themselves wisely, they must be aware of the issues and problems at stake and must have access to views and information on which to base sound decisions. Therefore, the press must serve as an engine of democracy, as a transmission belt between the people and their elected representatives. The very success of government may depend in large measure on the extent to which the press services the political system and the extent to which the people make wise use of the press.

Safeguarding personal liberties

Not far removed from the two foregoing functions of the press is the third-safeguarding personal liberties. Individual liberty is the core of democracy, which is founded on the assumption that the individual citizen \knows what is best for himself. John Stuart Mill expressed the happy idea that only the free individual can develop his capabilities to the fullest; as the individual develops, Mill believed, society as a whole benefits. Although infringements on an individual's freedom may come from many sources, the government has long been a potential enemy of liberty. As the theory of press freedom evolved, the press came to be assigned the task of watchdog, to sound the alarm whenever personal liberties are infringed.

Jefferson reiterated the importance of the press in safeguarding democracy by exposing infringements on personal liberties. "If a nation expects to be ignorant and free, in a state of civilization, it expects what never was and never will be," he wrote in 1816. "The functionaries of every government have propensities to command at will the liberty and property of their constituents... Where the press is free, and every man able to read, all is safe." And earlier, in 1792, he wrote to George Washington: "No government ought to be without censors; and where the press is free, no one ever will be. If vircuous, it need not fear the fair operation of attack and defense." Not only must the press preserve its own freedom of expression but it must also be alert to all infringements on freedom, wherever they occur.

Making a profit

The traditional concept of press freedom lends cogent justification to a fourth function of the press-making a profit through proper use of its freedom. The theory holds that only a free press, operating under a system of private enterprise, can fulfil the tasks of enlightening the public, servicing the political system, and safeguarding personal liberties. The syllogism behind that assumption runs somewhat as follows: Only a free press can serve the cause of truth. A press beholden to the government or to any special interest group cannot be free, because it will inevitably be subjected to environmental and financial pressures. Therefore, to be free to present news and views without fear or favor, the press must be a self-sufficient business enterprise. Carried a step further, this line of reasoning has been used to justify large communications enterprises. The argument is that a large, prosperous medium is better able to withstand pressures than a small, marginal one.

The entry of the government into the communications field, according to traditional theory, is per se bad. For one thing, governmental media would no doubt be more interested in perpetuating the party in power than in truth. For another thing, a subsidized governmental press would threaten the economic sufficiency of a private enterprise press. With no need to show a profit, such a press would have an unfair economic advantage over the regular commercial press.

In a sense, this correlation of press independence with profit-making has a strong kindship to Adam Smith's idea in classical economics that as each individual works for his own gain, he serves the welfare of the community. The necessity of showing a profit, the theory runs, assures us of a press closely attuned to the needs and wants of the community. George Sokolsky, columnist for the King Features Syndicate, expressed this view in the Don R. Mellett Lecture at Syracuse University in May, 1947.

The battle for circulation, Sokolsky said, is the battle for truth. Although a few publishers may find it profitable to pander to the lowest taste and to deal in falsehood, a far greater number of publishers will find it even more profitable to deal in truth and good taste. As readers vote with their coins and subscriptions, the publications they do not want wither and die from lack of financial support. The publications they do want will grow financially strong and flourish. By serving his own personal interest in making a profit, then, the publisher almost automatically gives the community the sort of newspaper it wants and needs. The system is the essence of democracy; according to some spokesmen for the theory; for, by expressing its pleasure or displeasure with coins as ballots, the public gets the sort of newspapers, magazines, and books it wants.

Critics of the press have taken sharp issue with this aspect of press theory. By a sort of Gresham's Law of Journalism, they say, bad publications tend to drive out the good. They summon a number of examples in evidence. Boston, for example, has long been known for the low quality of its newspapers; and the best paper in the city, the Christian Science Monitor, is not even a home-town paper but a national one. They call the roll of the fallen giants of New York-the World, for example, and the Sun-and they point out that the huge circulation of the News is more than quadruple that of the Times.

A press system devoted to the irresponsible pursuit of profit, critics say, results not in publications serving the wants and needs of the community but in publications ill-equipped to meet the demands of complex contemporary society. It results in publications aimed at the lowest level of public taste. It results in publications for which the sensational is more important than the significant. Moreover, the critics say, the public, unacquainted with the possibilities of the media and conditioned to like what it gets, often cannot tell what it would really like and what it does need.

Servicing the economic system

Related to the profit-making function is a fifth task of the press, one which emerged with the development of modern advertising, that of servicing the economic system. Long before advertising assumed the importance it has today, the press fulfilled this task to some extent. In Colonial America, newspapers filled their columns with information about commerce and shipping, material important to an economy in which foreign trade and shipping bulked large. And newspapers devoted to commerce continued to flourish, even after the penny press of the 1830's made its pitch for the masses with human-interest copy.

But it was with the rise of a complex system of mass production and mass distribution that the contribution of the press to the national economy became of major importance. Today a task of the press is to bring together, through advertising, the buyers and sellers of goods and services. In performing that seemingly simple task, the press, according to some scholars, has helped to promote a dynamic, expanding economy. Such is Borden's general conclusion in The Economic Effects of Advertising. Sandage has credited advertising with contributing to a high level of consumption, with helping to allocate resources, with stimulating product variety, and with helping to bring about prices favorable to the consumer. Although critics have charged advertising with fostering wastefulness, monopoly, and other evils, the press as an advertising medium certainly has contributed to a high material standard of living.

By editorial fare as well as by advertising, the press oils the wheels of commerce. For instance, approximately two thousands trade, technical, and business publications in the United States are important to manufacturers, wholesalers, retailers, and others engaged in commerce. They keep their specialized readers abreast of new developments in the fields they cover, and they carry news on which many of the decisions of business are based.

Providing entertainment

Almost from the time that Caxton introduced printing to England, the press has devoted a part of its output to entertainment. However moralizing may have been their tone, the broadside ballads which flourished in Britain for more than three centuries, were intended less for edification than for amusement. Other offerings-pamphlets and books-were also intended to amuse the reader. Early newspapers in England and America were primarily informational, but they, too, ran human-interest copy from time to time. As the press tapped mass audiences, there seems to have been an increase in the proportion of material frankly designed to afford amusement, entertainment, or escape. Today, serving up entertainment seems to be one of the main functions of the press.

Evaluating the services of the press

Those, then, are the six functions ascribed to the press. Historically, some of them are of longer standing than others. Public enlightenment is one of the oldest functions; servicing the economic system is a relatively recent addition. As has been shown, some of the functions are inherent in the theory of political freedom. The responsibilities of the press for enlightening the public, for servicing the political system, and for safeguarding personal liberties are intimately identified with the Anglo-American concept of freedom of the press. At least one of the functions, however, is not inherent in the theory. The role of the press in servicing the economic system was recognized only after the development of modern advertising.

In practice, of course, some of the functions may conflict. Entertainment, for example, may clash with public enlightenment. A magazine publisher may wish to explore seriously the nature of the struggle between East and West; most readers may want slick fiction and features that do not strain their intellect. The book publisher may wish to publish a philosophical work; the book-buying public may prefer to spend its dollars on historical novels with bosomy heroines. So, at bottom, the function most likely to collide with others is making a profit. The magazine publisher runs fiction because it is more profitable than articles analyzing the struggle between East and West. The book publisher brings out historical novels because bosomy heroines are more profitable than philosophical discussions.

One must remember that a given medium need not carry out all six functions by itself. Newspapers, as a medium, need not perform all six tasks. It is enough if newspapers, in conjunction with the other media, do the job. Nor does every publication have to carry out all of the functions all the time. A given publication may do only two or three of the tasks and still be making a genuine public contribution. The six functions are those of the press as a whole, working in concert.

What should be the proper balance among the six functions in the press as a whole? The answer involves subject judgments which will depend on the importance one attaches to each of the six tasks and what he expects from a press system in a democratic society. Nonetheless, certain characteristics of the United States press system make it difficult for the press to strike what some persons regard as a proper balance among the six functions. The press has performed some of these functions admirably. It has done a good job of profit-making, and by doing so it has remained free from its traditionally feared foe, government. It has done a good job of servicing the economic system. Despite the faults one can find with advertising, there can be no doubt that the press has contributed to a high material standard of living by bringing together the buyers and sellers of goods and services. It has done a good job of providing entertainment, however much the critics may quarrel with the cultural level of that entertainment. If anything, the press has performed the entertainment function so well that it has neglected some of its other tasks.

There are other functions which, some critics believe, the press has not performed as adequately. In its task of enlightening the public, they say, the press has fallen far short of the requirements of contemporary society. Aiming at the lowest common denominator of its mass audience, the press gives superficial treatment to significant issues and events, too often, its emphasis is on the what rather than on the why.

Contributing to this evil, they add, is the insistence of the press on a curious sort of objectively-a spurious objectivity which results in half-truths, incompleteness, incomprehensibility. In adhering to objective reporting, newspapers try to present both sides of a story; but in doing so, say the critics, they do not bother to evaluate for the reader the trustworthiness of conflicting sources, not do they supply the perspective essential to a complete understanding of the situation. Instead of assuming that two half-truths make a truth, the critics say, the press should put facts into a context that gives them meaning.

Moreover, the critics continue, the press does not give adequate attention to minority views; and even when it does give space to minorities, it invariably emphasizes the humorous, the ludicrous, the insignificant aspects of the minority viewpoint. Nor is that all. Because of design or because of design of because of the way the system works, the press often biases and distorts informative material.

The foregoing summary by no means completes the inventory of charges against the press as public enlightener, but it does indicate the general nature of contemporary criticism. In its job of servicing the political system, too, some critics think, the press has fallen down. Its shortcomings in this regard are essentially the same as those in its attempts to enlighten the public.

The press also has been remiss in safeguarding personal liberties, some critics say. To be sure, the press has championed its own freedom and has been quick to protect itself against potential threats to it. It has been less ready, however, to expose and denounce infringements on the liberty of others. Indeed, by some of its excesses, some critics think, the press has violated the rights of some citizens. It has invaded their privacy without just cause; it has destroyed their reputations by publishing malicious gossip and by headlining irresponsible charges made by politicians using Congressional immunity for their own self-aggrandizement.

The critics' charges have some validity. However, one should remember that their generalizations do not apply with equal force to all media or to all units in a given medium. Perhaps the criticisms hold most strongly for newspapers and the mass circulation magazines, least strongly for small circulation magazines and books. And within each medium, there are publications which carry out their functions superbly. The newspaper field is brightened by such conscientious and responsible organs as the New York Times and the St.Louis Post Dispatch, to name but two. In their own ways, such magazines as Harper's, the New Yorker, and others have performed with exemplary integrity. Nearly every book publisher can name a number of books he has published without expectation of profit in order to give a deserving author a hearing.

Problems involved in publishing

What hinders the press in carrying out its functions? There are many things. There are limitations imposed by the communication process itself-by the way in which we send and receive spoken and written messages. There are limitations imposed by the nature of the media. In this chapter, however, we will consider but two major problems-concentration of ownership of the media, and the commercial basis of the press system.

Concentration of ownership of the press

The concentration of ownership of the press-which has resulted from, among other things, technological advances and the demands by readers for improved service-has alarmed many observes. In the daily newspapers field, the number of papers has gone steadily downward as circulations have steadily mounted. As the number of dailies has diminished, more and more cities have been left without competing newspapers. Nixon has thoroughly documented this situation.

The number of English-language dailies of general circulation reached its peak-2,600-in 1909, according to Nixon. Since then, the number has gone steadily downward as a result of suspensions, mergers, and changes from daily to less frequent publication. Between the two world wars-between 1918 and 1944-the total number of all dailies declined 19.4 per cent. Yet, in the same period, the total circulation of daily newspapers increased 60.4 per cent. The following figures indicate the trend toward fewer general circulation English-language newspapers with increased circulations:

Number of Daily Newspapers and Their Circulation, 1930 to 1951

Year	Total Dailies	Total Circulation
1930	1,942	39,589,172
1935	1,950	38,155,540

1940	1,878	41,131,611
1945	1,749	48,384,188
1950	1,772	53,829,072
1951	1,773	54,017,938

A glance at these figures shows that fewer papers are accounting for larger circulations. And as the number of dailies has declined, so has the number of cities with competing papers. Cities without competing papers rose in number from 1,114 in 1930 to 1,277 in 1945. Of all United States cities with dailies in 1945, 91.6 per cent did not have competing papers. Wrote Nixon in 1945: "Daily news-paper competition, certainly in the full economic meaning of the word, has been eliminated from all but 117 American cities. Ten entire states have no local competition whatsoever."

The growth of newspaper chains, especially in view of the declining number of newspapers, has also caused observers some concern. The national chains had their greatest growth after the first world war. Today they have been largely supplanted by state and regional chains. Nevertheless, the number of dailies affiliated with chains has been on the increase, as the following figures testify.

Control of Daily Newspapers by Newspaper Chains, 1929 to 1949

Year	Number of Chains	Number of Chain Dailies	Percent of Total number of Dailies	Average number Dailies per Chain
1929	52	267	13.7	5.0

1935	63	328	16.8	5.1
1939	77	364	18.8	4.7
1945	76	370	21.2	4.8
1949	70	386	21.6	5.5

Cross-channel ownership has intensified the seriousness of concentration, some observes believe. And, indeed, a trend of the last twenty-odd years has been for chains linking radio stations and newspapers under the same ownership to replace chains consisting entirely of newspapers.

The magazine industry, too, is characterized by a few giants with mammoth circulations. Despite their dominance, however, the industry is still highly competitive. Although the voices of the mass-circulation leaders are loud and ubiquitous, they cannot entirely shout down the many small circulation magazines which, in the aggregate, offer a wide range of editorial fare. And despite the financial hazards endemic to magazine publishing, the fields is still open to the small publisher who does not try to compete with the giants but seeks to publish for a relatively small circle of like-minded readers.

No published study has ever dealt with the amount of concentration in the magazine industry, which has oddly escaped the attention of scholars. Even much of the available data about the industry must be regarded warily for a number of reasons. For one thing, different persons use the term magazine in different ways. For another, there is no central clearinghouse for data, although there are agencies which collect certain types of information. The United States Census dos collect some types of data, but they lack comparability and are often unreliable.

Yet one can get some idea of the amount of concentration in several ways. One way is to look at the relative size of magazine publishing establishments. The 2,166 periodical establishments in the United States in 1947 employed 68,823 persons, according to census reports. But just three establishments of the 2,166 employed about 17 per cent of the total-11,701 workers. And just ten of the 2,166 establishments employed nearly one-third of the total number of workers.

A second way of getting an idea of the amount of concentration is to look at circulation figures. To do so, though, one must necessarily use figures from various sources, figures often not strictly comparable. The 4,610 periodicals in the United States in 1947 had an aggregate per issue circulation of 384,628,482, according to census figures. Other sources show that 33 magazines, each with a circulation of a million or more, accounted for more than one-fifth of that aggregate circulation. At least 27 of those 33 magazines were published by companies having two or more publications.

Since magazines depend heavily on the post office for distribution, the use of the mails also gives some clues to the dominance of magazine leaders. Reporting on the use of postal services in 1949, a Senate committee said that 18 of the largest magazines and two of the largest newspapers accounted for 43.6 per cent of the weight and 43.2 per cent of the revenue in second class, the postal class which gives preferential rates to publishers of bona fide periodicals. Ten companies published these 20 publications; just three corporations controlled the nine largest.

Rare is the publisher who is content to publish just one magazine. Although it is scarcely feasible to determine the number of publishers who issue more than one magazine, the author, using two standard listings of magazines, counted 68 multiple-title publishers of general-interest magazines and comic books, another 12 multiple-title publishers of farm magazines. The number of magazines issued by a single publisher ranged from two in several cases to 53 for Fawcetr, 38 for Popular, and similarly hefty numbers for several others. Since the listings were incomplete-they did not cover business and trade journals, for example-those figures are conservative.

Still another way to get an idea of the extent of concentration is to learn how advertising funds are allocated. In 1950, the 2,257 national advertisers spent some $416,898,000 on advertising in general and farm magazines. Well over half of that national total was accounted for by the gross advertising revenues of just three publishers-Crowell-Collier, Curtis, and Time, Inc-whose combined gross in 1950 was $231,380,947. And just two publications of Time, Inc-Time and Life-grossed $104,159,377, roughly one-fourth of the national total.

Yet these figures should not distract attention from the fact that there are many small circulation magazines with variegated editorial policies. There are perhaps 6,500 magazines in the United States, even though the census shows considerably fewer than that. And although individual publishers and their magazines come and go, there seems to be no downward trend in either the number of publishers or the number of magazines. One reason for the relative stability of magazines numbers may be that publishers need not invest heavily in plant and equipment; they can have their printing done for them on contract. Nor are they limited by geography as are newspaper publishers and radio station operators; they can draw their audiences from the nation as a whole.

Today the odds in starting a new magazine seem to favor the established publishers, but many newcomers in recent years have become highly successful. In fact, a good share of the current circulation leaders has sprung up since the 1920's and 1930's-among them Reader's Digest, Better Homes and Gardens, Time, Life, Look, Coronet, Woman's Day, and Seventeen.

Although a handful of large publishers turns out a disproportionate share of books, the book industry is also composed of many relatively small, highly-competitive firms, a situation desirable for the free flow of ideas. In some ways the book industry is akin to the magazine industry in that the publisher is limited neither by geography nor by large investments in plant and equipment. The lack of integration in the book industry favors the existence of a sizeable number of small, competitive firms, according to Robert W. Frase, economic consultant to the American Book Publishers' Council. Frase gave this picture of the industry:

> The United States book trade is in many ways an industry of the 19th century type, composed of relatively small, personally-managed, highly competitive firms, and with very little vertical integration. This situation is highly desirable so far as the end product is concerned-it maintains freedom of the press to a maximum degree. It insures publication of works which might not find a publisher if there were only a few giant integrated firms; and it is free of much of the pressure of serving a mass market with something which will offend or antagonize no one. On the other hand, this same lack of size and integration imposes economic handicaps, especially since the competition in the communications-of-ideas industry is generally more integrated and has, moreover, a major additional source of revenue in advertising.

While it is true that the giants do not monopolize the book industry, it also seems true that a small number of houses is responsible for the bulk of the books published in the United States. Much of the information about the book industry, like that about the magazine industry, is sketchy and unreliable; but, however one reads the available figures, they do point to the important of the large publisher. For instance, census reports for 1945 show that less than 3 per cent of the 1,080 publishers in the United States brought out more than 60 per cent of the total books sold, while 67 per cent of the publishers accounted for less than 1 per cent of the total. But the census figures inadvertently tend to exaggerate; they include many firms which cannot realistically be considered as publishers. Therefore, they are not as dependable as the data of William Miller, who estimates that the number of book publishing firms, year in and year out, averages about 250; of these, he says, some 42 account for the great bulk of the original book business.

Many of the large trade-book publishers are affiliated with reprint houses. The "big three" hard-cover reprint houses are Garden City Publishing Company, Grosset & Dunlap, and World Publishing Co. World is the only one of the three not associated with a large trade-book firm, according to Miller. Garden City is a subsidiary of Doubleday, the largest hard-cover reprint house in the world; it issues Blue Ribbon Books, Star Books, Sun Dial Books, Permabooks, and other lines. Grosset & Dunlap was bought out in 1945 by the Book-of-the-Month Club and a group of publishing firms including Harper & Brothers, Little Brown & Company, Charles Scribner's Sons, and Random House. Some of the paper-back reprint firms are not associated with regular trade-book publishers, but the largest ones are. Simon and Schuster, for instance, has an interest in Pocket Books; Grosset & Dunlap and Curtis

Publishing Company own shares in Bantam Books.

One of the largest trade-book publishers is also one of the largest operators of book clubs. Doubleday's clubs include the Literary Guild, Junior Literary Guild, the Dollar Book Club, and the Book League of America.

Undeniably, then, the big publishers are important. They can most readily afford to bid for potential best-sellers and are most likely to attract the best-known authors. They are most likely to share in the economies of large press runs. And they are in the best position to advertise and promote their lists.

It is not only concentration within the book, magazine, and newspaper industries that has worried observes of the press system. Accompanying such concentration has been cross-channel ownership. Many newspaper publishers operate radio and TV stations, some publish magazines, and some do both. Some magazines publishers operate TV stations, own studios for producing documentary movies, and issue original or reprint books in paper-back editions. Some book publishers also issue magazines, and at least one operates a major book club and runs a string of retail bookstores.

Moreover, there are instances of strong vertical integration. Some newspapers own paper mills. And a few magazine publishers exhibit varying degrees of integration. Curtis Publishing Company, for example, owns forests and paper mills, has its own engraving and printing plants, operates a subsidiary which conducts market surveys and statistical studies, owns agencies for soliciting subscriptions and for distributing magazines of its own and of other publishers.

Complicating this whole situation is the fact that the press is controlled by a single socioeconomic class-loosely, the "business class." Earl L. Vance wrote in the Virginia Quarterly Review:

While there is nothing singular about newspapers being private business, there is cause for concern about business having a monopoly on a nation's sources of information. The reason is not that business is sinister. Monopoly of the press by any group-by labor or government no less than by business-is the one thing that freedom cannot endure.

The problem of concentration has inspired a number of proposed remedies. Some writers base their remedies on the implicit conviction that bigness is necessarily badness. Ernst in his The First Freedom would improve press performance by what he calls "old fashioned, approved techniques-right down the middle of our traditional legislative paths." His recommendations, in essence, include the breaking up of communications empires and the fostering of small communications enterprises.

There is some support for Ernst's point of view in the argument of Maclver in The Web of Government that too much power in the hands of any group, that every monopoly or approach to monopoly, is inimical to democracy. While recognizing the merits of large communications enterprises if they are checked by public safeguards, Maclver warms: "Of all such monopolies, the most immediately fatal to democracy is the monopoly of the media of opinion, or any approximation to it."

Other writers have assailed the thesis that bigness is necessarily badness. Economist Robert A. Brady contends that Ernst's recipe of competition is outmoded; that, for all practical purposes, it has been abandoned by business, government, economists, and others; that as therapy for the ills threatening democracy it is essentially worthless.

Brady fully recognizes the evils of concentration under which the few can determine policy for the many. He says in effect that economic power perhaps cannot be separated from political power; that to gain political power, business must, among other things, manipulate the media. But he denies that large-scale activities are irresponsible with democracy; there are ways of making them compatible. In the interests of democracy, he thinks, policy control of the media must be shifted back to the people affected by the decisions of the policy-makers. He believes that there can be such democratic participation in policy-making, but with experts to implement the policy decisions.

Nixon also doubts that it is possible to return

to the yesteryear of many small, diversified communications units. He remarks that the one-newspaper town is not an evil in itself; what matters is the sense of social responsibility possessed by the publisher. One poor newspaper is no worse than several poor ones, he adds; and one good newspaper is better than several poor ones. Believing that journalism is entering a new period in its history, that of "scientific direction," he suggests that the fruits of communications research may make the press more and more responsive to the wants and needs of the community.

Still other writers discount the dangers of concentration. A common argument is that the nature of press competition has changed. Fortune magazine for April, 1947, reviewing the report of the Hutchins Commission on Freedom of the Press, questioned the often-made assumption that a smaller proportion of the people can express their ideas in the press today than in former times. Fortune contended that too much fuss has been made about the diminishing number of newspapers and of the increase in one-newspaper cities. Said Fortune:

The trend cannot be interpreted except in the light of the development of transport, which brings out-of-town dailies to ever widening areas. It cannot be interpreted except in terms of the rise of weekly news magazines, general magazines, radio newscasting, radio forums, national hook-ups, and the nationally syndicated column. Competition has not disappeared; its form has changed. And no basic research has been done to determine exactly what its present form is or what its present effects are.

The commercial basic of the press system

Posing perhaps even more perplexing problems than concentration is the commercial basis of the press. The problems it raisers become especially serious in view of the high degree of ownership concentration. The situation can be simplified somewhat as follows: To remain free, the publisher must be self-supporting; to be self supporting, the publisher needs a large number of readers. If his publication does not carry advertising, he needs many readers to keep down the per unit cost. If his publication does carry advertising, he needs a large number of readers not only to keep down per unit cost but also to justify profitable advertising rates. In either event, therefore, there is pressure upon the publisher to appeal to an ever expanding reader group. As the reader group widens, the publisher's chosen public tends to determine what he can and cannot publish.

In order to attract and remain readers, the publisher will tend to give the majority what he thinks it wants and agrees with. He will tend to avoid publishing material which the majority does not agree with or has no accepted. In general, the publisher seems to accept the long-term social and cultural goals of the majority, which has seldom been credited with the origination and introduction of new ideas. At times the publisher may, of course, present or espouse short-term goals differing from those of the majority of his readers.

Klapper has suggested that the commercial sponsorship of the mass media and the resultant necessity of pleasing as many persons as possible work to resultant necessity of pleasing as many persons as possible work to perpetuate the status quo. "Pleasing the majority necessarily involves hewing to majority views," he writes. "He who espouses minority opinion automatically alienates the majority; he who would immediately enlist the crowd must voice the attitude already sanctioned by most of its members." By entertainment content, by advertising, he says, the press reaffirms these sanctioned mores.

Advertisers wish their messages to appear in media which do not offend the majority and which do not attack the system under which business operates. Publishers, to get large audiences, are chary of offending many readers. As a result of these two conditions, entertainment in the mass media strengthens existing attitudes. Popular magazine stories, researchers have found, while overtly accepting racial and religious equality, in fact perpetuate minority stereotypes, approve caste lines and, in Klapper's words, "picture a world where the highest income is reserved for white, American-born gentiles who practice the protestant ethic."

Popular magazine biographies over the past half-century, one research worker found, have dealer with heroes who since birth embodied popularly sanctioned values. Advertising plays on existing drives and values to sell products, and in doing so it reinforce them. By its nature, it has a monopoly position; "two cigarette manufactures may compete with each other," says Klapper, "but neither will ever directly criticize the other's product, and never will either allow some other advertiser to inveigh against smoking."

Even casual observation shows that as the press seeks its large audiences, it resorts to the expedient of mass production techniques. The formula becomes important and is reflected in a general sameness of content and in a sameness of techniques for presenting content. Economy imposes limitations on the gathering of material. Newspapers-and to a considerably lesser degree magazines-get their material largely at stations of record.

Lippmann has observed that, since papers cannot possibly witness all of the happenings in the world, they station reporters at such points of record as courts, city halls, and so on. As papers can record only what occurs in unmistakable form, news becomes not a mirror of social conditions but of an aspect that has obtruded itself. Almost inevitably, in its quest for the large audience, the press in its content aims at the lowest common denominator. Content is thinned; drama, sensation, the unusual are exploited. Cultural minorities become "disenfranchised"; for it is often unprofitable for the publisher to cultivate certain reader groups because of their small numbers, their low purchasing power, or other reasons.

Improving the social services of the press

In the face of all this, what can be done? How can we make sure that the press will do a good job of enlightening the public, of servicing the political system, of safeguarding personal liberties? How can we make sure of a press adequate for the needs of contemporary society? Since dozens of books have already dealt with those questions, these few concluding paragraphs obviously can do no more than suggest some general points in tackling a problem for which there is no simple panacea.

First, a realistic solution to the problem must take into account the commercial basis of the press. Our system of press support is conditioned by the social and economic system within which the press operates. There is small chance of abolishing commercial support, even if it were desirable to do so. Granting that, we can see that publication without advertising do not offer a satisfactory solution. Despite its shortcomings, advertising does confer a number of material benefits on society; and even if it did not, it has become so thoroughly ingrained in our press system that it could scarcely be seriously diminished. Moreover, although advertising accounts for some of the undesirable aspects of our press system, it is not solely to blame.

Nor does breaking up concentration in the communications systems now seem a realistic corrective. The commercial basis of the press, not the mere size of the units, has caused many of the undesirable practices of the press and much of the undesirable content. It is hard to see how small publications, may more than large ones, can escape the economic compulsions of the system. In view of the pressure for large audience inherent in the commercial system, it is also hard to see how small publications could be kept from growing once more into large ones. Behind proposals to break up large communications units appear to be two suppositions of dubious validity. One is that multiplicity of publications necessarily means multiplicity of viewpoints. The other is that the small publisher is more responsible than the large one.

Secondly, and satisfactory proposal for the improvement of press performance must be based on the combined efforts of press, public, and government. On the one hand, we cannot expect the press alone to remedy its shortcomings; on the other hand, there are dangers in granting too much power over the media of communication to even a democratic government. Looking to the press alone to do away with its faults carries a rather strong implication that publishers are willfully negligent instead of handicapped to a large degree by the nature of the system. True, more publishers should put responsibility for carrying out their public service functions above profit. But in a very real sense, the press can be no better than the public it serves because it is dependent upon the public for support-directly in the case of books and some magazines, indirectly in the case of other magazines and virtually all newspapers.

Looking to the government alone is not desirable. Although the government perhaps may safely take a more active part in communications than it has in the recent past, there are good reasons for being wary of granting even a democratic government excessive power over the communications system. Even if one trusts a democratic government with the operation of the press system, there is a strong possibility that the media content would still be prepared for mass audiences; and as a result of this mass appeal, the content in the end might very well be no better than that of the commercial media and perhaps worse.

The public can, if it wills, assist considerably in improving press performance. If the public raises its own level of taste, then demands a higher standard in the media, the press may well oblige. The public can voice its discontent with low-denominator content, can protest bias and distortion when they truly occur and when it observes them, can lend its support to the worthwhile publications and withdraw its support from the irresponsible ones. The public can willingly bear a larger share of the cost of some communications services, especially those furnished by publications servicing intellectual and cultural minorities.

Thirdly, our traditional theory of press

freedom might well be re-examined, not with a view to abandoning it but with a view to adapting it to current conditions and requirements. Changing conditions have altered the nature of the right of freedom of the press. Originally, freedom of the press was a personal right. It would be exercised by anyone with the comparatively small sum needed to establish a newspaper or magazine, to issue a pamphlet or book. Today, however, the high cost of starting new communications ventures and the high degree of concentration in the communications field have left the large majority of persons unable to exercise their right of free expression. Their right is held in trust for them, for all practical purposes, by the persons in an economic position to operate the media. Thus, the press should give space to a wide range of representative views, not just the views of the majority, not just the views of the media operators themselves.

In the face of concentration of ownership and the commercial nature of the press, in the face of" disenfranchisemen" of cultural minorities and a narrowing of the areas of free discussion in the media, we might inquire if our traditional concept of negative freedom, the concept of "freedom from," is adequate for the needs of society. Traditional theory of press freedom was founded largely on the philosophical assumptions of the Enlightenment. These assumptions have been strongly challenged by the revolution in contemporary thought. Quite possibly, as Jensen has suggested, this revolution in thought might furnish the ideological basis for a new concept of human liberty and freedom of the press.

Such a new concept might involve a judicious blending of "freedom from" and "freedom for". Under the concept, we might explore the possibility of cautiously allowing government and of encouraging the large private foundations to join private enterprise as working partners in the communications system. We might find it desirable to encourage government to become a facilitating agency to help remove obstacles to the free flow of information and ideas. We might even find it desirable to encourage government, along with private foundations, to participate in the communications system, especially in serving minorities which the commercial press now finds it inexpedient or unprofitable to serve.

4 Responsibilities of the Media

Journalists in the United States have never agreed upon the media's responsibilities. The media's responsibilities are often discussed, and several groups have adopted codes of ethics, but no single code has been generally accepted. Moreover, not everyone agrees that the media's responsibilities can or even should be defined. Many journalists fear that attempts to define their responsibilities will be followed by attempts to enforce those responsibilities. They want to preserve their freedom and make decisions for themselves, without being forced to conform to the guidenlines set by anyone else.

Discussions about the media's responsibilities, however are valuable. The discussions force journalists to think about their principles, values, and obligations, and to consider how they should act in a variety of situations. Journalists are not isolated individuals: they are engaged in an old and honorable craft. Those who understand the social importance of their job and its traditions and principles are better prepared to cope with the problems that are likely to arise in the course of their work.

Gabe pressman, a television newsman, believes that, even though they have no written guidelines, the nation's best reporters have always followed a strict code. Pressman says of the unwritten code: "It's a dedication to uncovering the truth, to communicating information to people-information they're interested in getting, information with which they can most closely identify within their own lives. Its a dedication to getting information to them rapidly and accurately, to reporting the news without prejudice." Similarly, columnist walter Lipmann believed that journalists have a duty to do what every citizen should do but lacks the time and interest to do for himself. "That is, to gather information, pick out what is important, digest it thoroughly, and without passion or prejudice, relate it to the problems of the day."

Concern about the media's responsibilities is part of the general concern about the responsibilities of big business. New laws have been enacted to enforce standards considered important to the welfare and interest of consumers. Traditionalists argue that businesses exist to produce goods at a profit for their shareholders, and that they serve society best by doing so. A growing number of Americans, however, insist that businesses also have a responsibility to serve the public. Consumer advocates assert that manufacturers have a responsibility to protect the public's health. For example, children's clothing must be fireprooted, and drug companies must test the safety of their new medicines. Journalism and the media are faced with similar demands. Their consumers want-not safety-but accuracy. Truthfulness must test the safety of their new medicines. Journalism and the media are faced with similar demands. Their consumers want-not safety-but accuracy, truthfulness. And significance. These traits are, however, much more difficult to regulate and much more dangerous to enforce. In the name of truth and accuracy, the exposure of wrongdoing may be suppressed. Some societies do precisely that.

Four theories of the press

In 1956, Four Theories of the Press was published. It discusses the media's responsibilities and attempts to explain why the media vary so significantly from one society to another. The authors, The authors, Fred S. Siebert, Theodore Peterson, and Wilbur Schramm. emphasized the close relationship that exists between the media and certain basic beliefs that each society holds. These beliefs are about the nature of humanity, the nature of society and the state, the relation of citizens to the state, and the nature of knowledge and truth. Siebert, Peterson, and Schramm found four different theories or sets of beliefs that societies hold about the media: (1) the Authoritarian Theory, (2) the Libertarian Theory, (3) the Communist Theory, and (4) the Social Responsibility Theory.

The authoritarian theory

Authoritarian states dominated Western Europe from about 1500 to 1700, and their political systems had a significant impact upon the press. Citizens in authoritarian societies were expected to serve that state. Philosophers believed that societies had to preserve peace and order; that security and progress - the advance of civilization were more important than individual liberties.

There was a sharp distinction between a nation's leaders and its masses. Authoritarians believed that the leaders were more intelligent than other men and that only they possessed the wisdom and experience necessary to lead the state. Leaders often insisted that they had been selected by God and ruled by divine power. Some of the theory's advocates added that leaders were necessary to control the selfish passions of the masses; they warned that states would degenerate if the masses obtained power.

The leaders of authoritarian states considered printing a threat to their power and issued licenses to regulate its use. The licenses limited the number of persons who could operate printing presses and were issued only to persons who supported the goals of the state. Later, printers were required to submit copies of everything they wanted to reproduce to government censors, and the censors had to approve the material before it could be published. Party because censorship systems were too cumbersome, states gradually stopped licensing and censoring the press and began to punish printers only after they published anything that offended the state. Writers and publishers who criticized the government, its leaders, or policies could be charged with treason and sentenced to prison. Authoritarian theorists supported the system, since they believed that the public was incapable of understanding political problems and that governments were justified in forbidding the publication of anything that might disturb or arouse the masses.

Authoritarian states are still common in much of the world. Nazi Germany had an authoritarian press, and so do several countries in South America. Developing countries in Asia, Africa, and the Middle East often employ the same type of system. They tolerate no dissent or criticism. The press is privately owned but expected to serve the state.

The libertarian theory

Political theorists began to question the Authoritarian Theory during the sixteenth and seventeenth centuries. Established institutions in Western Europe were under attack. The Protestant Reformation challenged the authority of the Catholic church, and political revolutions challenged the power of authoritarian governments. At the same time, new discoveries were expanding human knowledge in the fields of geography and science. These changes contributed to an intellectual revolution that emphasized the role of individuals and their right to make decisions for themselves. Thinkers now began to argue that humans are rational moral beings, and that they have the right to determine their own destiny. Earlier, people were considered servants of the state. Now, political theorists argued that society was composed of autonomous individuals who created the government to protect their rights. If the state failed, they believed that citizens had the right to change or abolish it.

The Libertarian Theory also stressed the need for an "open marketplace of ideas" where conflicting opinions might be allowed to clash. John Miltion believed that truth would emerge victorious from such a clash because men were intelligent and able to distinguish right from wrong. The idea of a free marketplace of ideas rested upon the assumption that every citizen who wished to would have an equal opportunity to speak, and that his ideas would receive a fair hearing. Theorists assumed that individuals would voice their opinions and that others would listen to them.

Freedom was conceived as a natural and absolute right. Under the Libertarian Theory, individuals could do as they pleased. No one, especially not the state, had a right to interfere with their lives. Political thinkers realized that some individuals might lie, but they believed that lies would eventually be exposed. The most unpopular ideas were protected because (1) they might help lead to the truth and (2) their protection was consistent with the belief in individual freedom.

The Libertarian Theory also changed theorists' attitudes toward the media. For the first time, the media were expected to serve as watchdogs over the government. Political thinkers no longer trusted the government and felt that it would have to be watched so that it could not abuse its power. To serve as an effective watchdog, the media had to be completely free and the government had to be prevented from interfering with what they printed. The government lost the right to suppress any statements, even statements that it considered false, because men feared that the government would use it s power to suppress statements critical of its own performance.

By the end of the eighteenth century, the Libertarian theory had spread through most of Western Europe and then to America, where it influenced the men who wrote the U.S. Constitution. Thomas Jofferson voiced a part of the Libertarian Theory when he declared that governments should maintain a framework within which individuals could develop their own capabilities. Jefferson admitted that individual citizens might err, but he believed that the majority would make sound decisions. jefferson added that the press was an essential source of information for citizens who needed to be educated and informed.

The U.S. Constitution mentions the press only once-to declare that Congress cannot abridge its freedom. The Constitution does not define the term "press" or place any restrictions upon it. The authors of the Constitution feared that the press might be harassed and regulated by the government, not that the government might be inconvenienced by the press. The press was given no legal responsibilities; it cannot be censored or forced to publish anything contrary to its own beliefs. Thus, the Libertarian Theory is more than an abstract philosophy. It had a direct influence upon the Constitution, and it continues to protect journalists at work in the United States today.

The communist theory

The philosophy developed by the Soviet Union is an offshoot of the older Authoritarian Theory, but it has some significant variations. Most dictatorships have allowed the media to remain in private hands. In communist states, the media in Communist states are ideological tools used to indoctrinate the masses and help the state reach its goals. Escapism - that is, entertainment-is a sin; the media are not allowed to distract readers from serious issues.

Although at first it may seem somewhat paradoxical, the Soviet Union encourages the media to publish critical letters and articles. Major newspapers such as Izvestia receive up to 1,500 letters a day from ordinary citizens who express their personal grievances, criticize minor bureaucrats, and expose instances of corruption and inefficiency. In addition to serving as an outlet for the public's frustrations, the letters give the country's leaders an idea of the popular mood and alert them to serious problems, particularly at the local level. The criticisms expressed by the public, however, are sharply limited. The public is not allowed to question the basic system or fundamental beliefs about the governments and its policies; it cannot criticize Communist ideology, the Party, or the Party's leaders. More serious criticism reported by the media comes from the top - from Party leaders - and is conveyed down to the masses. Because the media's editors are carefully selected and watched, there is little need for censorship.

Americans argue that the media in Communist nations are controlled by their governments. Communists respond that the media in the United States are dominated by the rich and slanted to maintain the status quo. Communists claim that the American masses have no freedom of expression and no protection against capitalists who own the media and use them to promote their class interests. Americans respond by pointing to the great variety of publications and the enormous diversity of opinion that can be found here, from the most rigidly authoritarian to the most vehemently anarchistic. The masses, in the American view. Are more likely to find expression of their class and individual interests within this diversity than they could ever final within the strict uniformity of opinion imposed by communist governments.

The theory of social responsibility

During the twentieth century, thinkers in democratic societies began to express dissatisfaction with the libertarian. Theory. Many of the theory's most fundamental beliefs appeared to be mistaken. Also, the media and certain beliefs were changing. And the changes made it more difficult to endorse wholly the Libertarian Theory.

The Libertarian Theory is based upon the belief that people are intelligent, rational, and capable of making decisions for themselves. But psychologists no longer are certain that men and women can tell the difference between truth and clever propaganda. Theorists still believe that people are capable of thinking for themselves, but they now suspect that individuals are reluctant to do so. Humans seem to be more interested in satisfying their immediate needs than in searching for truth. They appear to be lethargic and easily misled by demagogues.

Political scientists also are losing their faith in the free marketplace of ideas. They suggest that the Libertarian Theory fails because there is not a real clash of ideas. Most editors either agree with one another or avoid debates. Even when conflicting ideas are available, the public fails to critically examine the information it receives. Moreover, because most cities now have only one newspaper, citizens no longer can be certain that divergent ideas will be published. The press, just as in the old authoritarian days, has fallen into the hands of a powerful few.

Twentieth-century thinkers believe that the media should remain free, but they now add that the media have certain responsibilities. The major premise of their new theory, the Theory of Social Responsibility, "is that freedom carries concomitant obligations; and the press, which enjoys a privileged position under our government, is obliged to be responsible to society for carrying out certain essential functions of mass communication is contemporary society." So freedom no longer is considered a natural right. It has become a conditional right. The new theory's proponents argue that society grants the press certain rights, and that the press loses its claim to those rights if it abuses or fails to use them responsibly.

The Theory of Social Responsibility also stresses "The public's right to know" rather than publishers' right to speak. The libertarian Theory had asserted that publishers' right to speak. The Libertarian Theory had asserted that publishers could say and do whatever they pleased. The Theory of Social Responsibility insists that the public has a right to be informed, and that the media have a responsibility to provide the information needed to be good citizens. The information must be accurate, fair, complete, and untainted by the media's own biases. The Theory of Social Responsibility insists that the press has a right to make honest mistakes, since errors are an inevitable part of the learning process, but not to deliberately lie.

Toward a definition of a responsible press

The commission of Freedom of the press

In 1942, Henry Luce suggested that there was a need to study the freedom of the press in the United States. Luce, who published Time magazine, talked to Robert M. Hutchins, chancellor of the University of Chicago, and Hutchins selected a dozen men to serve on a commission with him. All of the commission's members were scholars; 9 of the 12 were associated with a college or university. It was the first time that a highly competent, independent group with a plentiful supply of money studied the media in the United States. Luce donated $ 200,000, and another source provided an additional $ 15,000 for the study. The commission met for three years, from 1944 through 1946. Its report, titled A free and Responsible press, was published in 1947.

The commission studied all the media in the United States, including books, magazines, moves, radio, and newspapers. Television had not yet become a mass medium, and the commission found few problems in the other industries, so its report dealt primarily with newspapers. The commission concluded that the press has five responsibilities. Although intended primarily for newspapers, the responsibilities is listed might be modified into a general theory applicable to all the media. The commission declared that newspapers must provide:

1. "A truthful, comprehensive, and intelligent account of the day's events in a context which gives them meaning."

2. "A forum for the exchange of comment and criticism."

3. "The projection of a representative picture of the constituent groups in the society."

4. "The presentation and clarification of the goals and values of the society."
5. "full access to the day's intelligence."

The first requirement listed by the commissions simply that the media must be accurate; the should not lie. The commission added that the media must separate fact from opinion and report the facts in a way that can be understood. It concluded that the media do not have to publish everyone's ideas, but that they have a responsibility to publish significant ideas contrary to their own. The commission also declared that newspapers should present the truth about every group in society-not just stereotypes, whether favorable or unfavorable. The commission felt that newspapers' past performance was clearly inadequate, and it warned that if the papers continued to abuse their freedom, new laws might become necessary to protect the public. The commission's complete report, which filled a 139-page book, is considered the first clear summation of the Theory of Social Responsibility.

Journalists were generally critical of the commission's report. The complained that not a single member of the commission worked for or truly understood the news media, and that the five responsibilities listed by the commission were vague, intellectual ideals that would be impossible for anyone to attain. How, for example, could journalists determine the ":goals and values of society?" Journalists also complained that it is impossible for them to report all the news: there is simply too much of it. So they must be selective and must discriminate. The commission's recommendations failed to acknowledge the fact that newspapers entertain as well as inform, and that they are private businesses which must satisfy their audiences and earn a profit in order to survive. However, journalists were even more disturbed by the threat of new government controls.

Despite their criticisms of the commission's report, journalists have begun to accept many of the Theory of social Responsibility's most basic premises. Journalists generally agree that they have a responsibility to serve the public. The frequently acknowledge "the public's right to know," and they believe in the importance of their role as watchdogs over government, which has remained a part of the Theory of Social Responsibility. During a speech at Milwaukee, University in Milwaukee, Wisconsin, William R. Burleigh, managing editor of the Evansville (Indiana) Press, acknowledged many of the media's other responsibilities, and it seems likely that a majority of the nation's journalists would agree with his comments. Bureleigh complained about the emphasis frequently placed upon the first part of the First Amendment which guarantees the media's freedom; "Too few (journalists), it seems to me, concern themselves with the other half of the equation, in which any freedom must be weighed, the question of responsibility." He added, "The Bill of Rights recognizes the right of the people to a free press.

Note well that doesn't say right of publishers or of reporters. Neither is a special caste. The right belongs to the people. And to the degree that this confers and privilege on the press, it at the same time places obligations on us, obligations to compile and publish useful, sound, thoughtful information for the citizenry."

Other attempts to define the media's responsibilities

Attempts to determine the media's responsibilities are continuing. As one alternative, scholars have tried to identify the world's very best newspapers and to determine their characteristics. It has been suggested that the papers might be used as a "Yardstick press." Since other papers might use them as a model and try to duplicate their performance.

John Merrill, author of the Elite press, complains that most of the world's newspapers are "entertainment/play-oriented" and that they cater to the superficial whims of their mass audience. Merrill adds:

The popular press - the "hodgepodge press"-calls the people of the world to play. It does not call them to thin, to assess, to become concerned, involved, or emphatic, Its journalism is splashy, superficial, thoughtless, and tenuous. It is complacent journalism that appeals to self and to status quo, to mere verbal frolicking about the surface of vital issues. It is "supermarket" journalism-a little of everything for everybody. It shows no thoughtful selection, assessment of editorial matter, meaning, or interpretation. It is vulgar in the truest sense of the word- speaking to the masses of semiliterates who feel they need to read something called a "newspaper" but who have no desire to understand the vital issues of the day, and even less desire to concern themselves with these issues.

Despite the generally dismal picture, Merrill believes that a small group of newspapers in the world is serious and idealistic. Merrill, who calls these newspapers the "Elite press," adds that they possess several distinctive characteristics.

Merrill believes that the world's best newspapers are reliable and responsible. They are sincerely concerned with the public's right to know and stress significant ideas about politics, international affairs, business, art, science, and education. They are concerned about the future and the probable effect of current events in days to come. Elite papers also devote a large portion of their space to interpretive stories; they explain why facts in the news are significant and how they relate to ideas in other fields. The stories give readers a continuing education and most of the facts they need to make wise decisions.

According to merrill, the world's elite newspapers also are dignified, serious, and stable. Even their appearance is conservative. They publish smaller headiness and fewer pictures than other newspapers. Some contain no comics, crossword puzzles, or other popular features, Elite newspapers are more concerned about the content of their editorial pages. They try to lead rather than follow public opinion and have a reputation for being courageous and for speaking out on issues, regardless of the issues' popularity.

Elite newspapers also have a reputation for presenting all the significant alternatives to complex problems, including ideas contrary to their own. They are unbiased, accurate, and known for their consistently good writing. Unlike other papers, they are not preoccupied with trivial local events. Elite newspapers are seriously concerned about national and international affairs.

In a similar effort, Time magazine complied a list of the nation's 10 best newspapers in 1964 and again in 1974. Five of the newspapers that Time selected in 1964 did not appear on its 1974 list. They were replaced by other newspapers that Time's editors and correspondents felt had improved more sharply. Time listed the papers, in alphabetical order, and the papers selected in both years included.

1964	1974
Baltimore Sun	Boston Globe
Cleveland Press	Chicago Tribune
Los Angeles Times	Los Angeles Times
Louisville Courier-Journal	Louisville Courier-Journal
Milwaukee Journal	Miami Herald
Minneapolis Tribune	Milwaukee Journal
New York Daily News	Newsday (a Long Island daily)
New York Times	New York Times
St. Louis Post-Dispatch	Wall Street Journal
Washington Post	Washington Post

Time said it selected the latest group of papers because, "They make a conscientious effort to cover national and international news as well as to monitor their own communities. They can be brash and entertaining as a well as informative. They are willing to risk money, time, and manpower on extended investigation...they offer a range of disparate opinion." Time praised the Chicago Tribune for its investigative reporting, including stories about voter frauds in Cook county and an eight-part series about police brutality. Time cited the Milwaukee Journal's "fair-minded coverage," Newsday's "solid local coverage" and the size of the New York times' editorial staff (about 650 persons). Time also noted that the washington post, under the direction of executive editor Bean Bradlee, had tripled its news budget and recruited many of the nation's most talented journalists.

Another study provides an even better list of the characteristics that journalists themselves consider important. Journalists who wanted to evaluate the performance of all 109 daily newspapers in the New England states declared that each paper should set its own standards. However, the journalists established six additional standards or sets of responsibilities that might be used to judge the papers performance. The standards are consider ably more specific than the guidelines suggested by the commission on Freedom of the press, yet they involve many of the same basic characteristics.

Howard K. Smith of ABC Television has added that journalists should also try to be more interesting. Smith complains that newspapers in the United States are the dullest that he has read anywhere outside of dictatorial countries like Russia "Where the prose is all wood." Smith acknowledges journalists' need for scholarship, experience, and dedication but says. "The first requisite is that you know how to tell a story in an interesting way." Smith complains that readers often fail to go beyond the second paragraph of news stories and, "What that means, is that most of the news written for newspapers, possibly 80 or 90 percent of it, is wasted effort. It is just too dull to hold the reader's attention."

A final recommendation, which was offered by the Commission on Freedom of the Press, is more controversial. The commission suggested that journalists have a responsibility to criticize one another. The commission explained, 'professional standards are not likely to be achieved as long as the mistakes and errors, the frauds and crimes, committed by units of the press are passed over in silence by other members of the profession."

The new England Daily Newspaper Survey used these six criteria to evaluate the performance of daily newspapers in the region.

1. A newspaper should cover government at every level. It should devote special attention to the government agencies in its area-not only by covering meetings but by critically examining the activities of the agencies.

Recognizing its role as a check on government, a newspaper should present the views of the critics of government and those affected by its activities, as well as the statements of government spokesmen.

2. A newspaper should go beyond government news and bulletin-board journalism to reveal the quality of people's lives and the human fabric of its community. This can be achieved through several techniques-imaginative photography, personality profiles, in-depth features, and stories that provide a local dimension to important national and international issues.

3. A newspaper should attempt to publish, as best it can, a complete and balanced presentation of local, state, national, and international news, Obviously a metropolitan paper cannot be judged by the same standard as a small-town paper that prints only eight pages a day and is bought for its local news. But papers of all sizes must emphasize the news of continuing important eat all levels-international as well as local.

4. In an age when the medium is said to be the message, a newspaper must attempt to present its news as effectively and as attractively as possible. Page layouts, photographs, charts, type selection, graphics-all must help guide the reader to the news that is most important and encourage him to read what he otherwise might overlook.

5. A newspaper should stand for something. Its editorials should take a position on the important local issues-not just Watergate and the world. It should clearly, logically explain its point of view. Editorials need not argue forcefully each and every day, but regularly the reader should sense that the editorial writer truly cares about what he is saying. A paper also should encourage diversity of opinion, including letters to the editor that criticize the paper.

6. A newspaper's management-as well as its news staff-should operate the paper with integrity: the news columns should be free of bias; employee policies that avoid conflicts of interest should be enforced; pay and working conditions should encourage the professionalism of the staff.

Members of the commission warned that, "If the press is to be accountable-and it must be if it is to remain free-its members must discipline one another by the only means they have available, namely public criticism." Other critics have observed that it is hypocritical for the media to contend that they are immune to criticism themselves when they insist that they have the right to criticize everyone and everything else.

Despite twentieth-century theories about the media's responsibilities, courts in the United States continue to abide by the Libertarian Theory. Newspapers may voluntarily accept some moral responsibilities, but-because of the protection provided by the First Amendment-they cannot be forced to become more responsible. The U.S. Supreme Court still emphasizes the need for a vigorous debate and a free marketplace of ideas, and both reflect the liberation Theory, In 1945, Justice Hugo Black explained that, "The First Amendment rests on the Assumption that the widest possible dissemination of information from diverse and antagonistic sources is essential to the welfare of the public, that a free press is a condition of a free society." In new York Times Go. V. Sullivan, a libel suit the Supreme Court heard in 1964, Justice William Brennan added: "We consider this case against the background of a profound national commitment to the principle that debate on public issues should be uninhibited, robust, and wide-open." In 1966, Warren Burger, Now chief justice of the U.S. Supreme Court, bluntly ruled that newspapers do not have any legal responsibilities. Burger declared that, "A newspaper can be operated at the whim or caprice of the owners...."

Criticisms of "social responsibility"

Many journalists prefer a theory which emphasizes the media's freedom rather than their responsibilities or the need for any additional restraints. These journalists say that the United states already has the very best possible media system, a pluralistic one. Essentially, the believe that the free marketplace of ideas has succeeded and can continue to flourish - and that it is better than any possible alternative. News media in the United States are not owned or controlled by any one individual or group. They already provide a variety of ideas, and they disseminate far more information than any one person is capable of absorbing. Some media may abuse their freedom, but journalists believe that occasional abuses are more tolerable than governmental controls.

Author John Merrill, one of the most outspoken critics of the Theory of Social Responsibility, adds that journalists must retain the freedom to make their own decisions. Merrill points out that attempts to list the media's responsibilities are arrogant and dictatorial, and that the media will become more controlled if they accept the responsibilities. On the surface, merrill continues, the emphasis placed upon the media's responsibilities seems commendable. He believes, however, that the Theory of Social Responsibility must be challenged because it implies that journalists cannot determine what is socially responsible as well as some outside or impartial group.

Merrill warns that the media's responsibilities will not be defined by individual person, freely regulating their own journalistic actions, but by "some elite group-some arrogant collectivity whose members feel they can inject their senses of responsibility into each of us." merrill believes that a journalist's only responsibility is the responsibility to remain free. Journalists think they are free, says Merrill, but they are giving up their freedom and conforming to institutional and professional norms, social ethics, and fuzzy altruism. He adds that:

> American journalism is becoming so institutionalized and professionalized and so immured with the nascent concept of "social responsibility" that is voluntarily giving up the sacred tenet of libertarianism-"editorial self determination"—and is in grave danger of becoming one vast, gray, bland, monotonuous, conformist spokesman for some collectivity of society."

Merrill concludes that if journalists themselves are allowed to determine what is socially responsible, there is no need for any further debate, for that is exactly what we already have in a libertarian, laissez-fare, independent media system "That the social responsibility people are trying to discredit and change."

The Theory of Social Responsibility also has been called "idealistic nonsense." Its more cynical critics have proposed another theory, which they consider more realistic. They call the theory "Make-A-Buck." The critics explain that the media are motivated primarily by the desire to earn a profit, not by a desire to protect or educate the public. They believe that the media simply give the public whatever is most profitable. Media critic Ben Bagdikian was reflecting the Make-A-Buck theory when he commented that, "The newspaper business is a great, clanking industry that buys paper at 7 cents a pound and sells it at 36. Television owners purchase a license from the government for $ 33-33 a year and sell the results for as much as $10 million. They are corporations dedicated to profit."

Misconceptions about media responsibilities

Some demands made of the media are unrealistic and reflect an unfortunate misunderstanding about the media's responsibilities. For example: some individuals believe that the media have a responsibility to provide publicity for every group that wants it. Others believe that the media should suppress unpopular ideas, that they should report only pleasant news, and that they should offer solutions to the many problems they do report.

The media's primary obligation is to their audience, not to groups seeking more favorable publicity. The media, even those on college campuses, are besieged by individuals and groups that want more recognition, and many become indignant that the media refuse to help. Each group insists that its stories are important and that the media have an obligation to publish them. Despite their pleas, editors reject stories that would interest only a limited number of persons and that would praise rather than inform.

Editors also reject the notion that they have a responsibility to suppress unpopular ideas. Few issues are so misunderstood. Journalists want to report the truth, but stories about unpleasant happenings often distress readers When an indignant woman visited his office, the editor of the old New York Sun, apparently tried of his readers' criticisms, cried out in exasperation, "lady, the Sun cannot be blamed for reporting what God has permitted to happen." More recently, John Chancellor of NBC News noted. "Too much of the public doesn't understand that just because we report a story dos not mean we are in sympathy with what we are reporting." Katharine Graham, publisher of The Washington Posts has pointedly remarked: "To say the press ought to suppress some news, if we deem it too bad or too unsettling, is to make the press into the censor or the nursemaid of a weak and immature society. We cannot serve ourselves and our heritage by running away from our troubles.... National security does not rest on national ignorance. This is hardly the faith of a free people."

Editors also reject the nation that they have a responsibility to be popular. A strong newspaper will inevitably alienate many of its readers by reporting unacceptable ideas and by taking stands on controversial issues. When they make a decision, editors must consult their conscience-not the box office. Nor can the media solve all the problems they report. Journalist John Colburn has explained that, "While it is our responsibility to report events and their meaning, it is not the function of the press to solve all the problems of the world. That is your responsibility as citizens. Our task is to perceive, to identify, and to try to clarify issues and enable our readers to make their own evaluation in order to help solve the problems."

Radio and television: A special case

Unlike newspapers, radio and television stations are regulated by the government. The federal government is able to regulate the stations because of broadcasting's unique characteristics. Courts have ruled that the airwaves used by broadcasters belong to the public. Also, there is a limited number of frequencies, and the government must allocate them so that the signals broadcast by different stations don not interfere with one another. While serving as a circuit court judge, Warren Burger explained the philosophy that governs the broadcast media. Burger declared:

> A broadcaster has much in common with a newspaper publisher, but he is not in the same category in terms of public obligations imposed by law. A broadcaster seeks and is granted the free and exclusive use of a limited and valuable part of the public domain; when he accepts that franchise, it is burdened by enforceable obligations.

The Radio Act of 1927 and the federal Communications Act of 1934 both declared that broadcast stations could be granted a license only if "the public interest, convenience, or necessity would be served by the granting there of." Neither law attempted to define "the public interest, convenience, or necessity" nor to specify what broadcasters would have to do to satisfy the requirements. Congress left that task to the FCC, which issues licenses, sets standards, and checks to see that broadcasters are fulfilling their responsibilities.

The FCC cannot censor broadcasters; however, it can consider the general types of programs that are broadcast. The FCC often has to choose between two or more applicants for the same license. Because all the applicants usually meet the minimum requirements set by law, the FCC has generally ruled on the basis of their program proposals. It tries to determine which applicant's programs will serve the public interest most effectively.

The minimum requirements are simple. To receive a license, applicants must be citizens of the United States. They must be of good character, and they must possess adequate financial and technical qualifications. The FCC has added that broadcasters also have a responsibility to (1) offer well-rounded and varied programs, (2) satisfy the needs of their community, (3) discuss issues of public significance, and (4) satisfy the needs of their community, (3) discuss issues of public significance, and (4) threat every person and issue fairly. Also, the FCC has warned broadcasters to avoid material that might injure or mislead the public: to limit the amount of time they devote to advertisements; and to avoid false, misleading, and deceptive advertisements.

The Federal Radio Commission (FRC), established in 1927, held that radio stations have a responsibility to provide a well-rounded variety of programs "which meet the special needs and interests of substantial groups in the listening public." The FRC, suggested that stations should broadcast programs about agriculture, religion, education, and public affairs, for example, in 1960, its successor, the FCC, expanded the list to 14 types of programs that if considered necessary to adequately serve the public. As just a few examples, the FCC urged radio and television stations to broadcast programs that offered residents of their communities an opportunity to express their opinions and that developed and used more local talent. The FCC also wanted more newscast, editorials, children's programs, and political broadcasts. However, the FCC has allowed a few stations to devote most of their time to more specialized types of programs since competing radio and television stations in the same communities are expected to offer the other programs.

The FCC also emphasizes broadcasters' responsibility to serve their local communities. When citizens apply for a broadcasting license, they are required to describe their audiences' "needs and interests" and to show how they intend to satisfy those needs. Applications which failed to satisfy the requirements have been rejected. For example: the FCC refused to issue a license for the construction of an F.M. radio station in Elizabeth, New Jersey, because none of the persons seeking the license lived in Elizabeth and because the had not considered the city's characteristics and needs. The applicants planned to broadcast the same programs in Elizabeth that they broadcast on other stations in Illionis and California. In rejecting the application, the FCC explained; "Communities may offer, and so may their needs; an applicant has the responsibility of ascertaining his community's needs and of programming to meet those needs."

Two other policies, the Equal Time Requirement and the Fairness Doctrine, add to the responsibilities expected of broadcasters. Section 315 of the Communications Act of 1934 requires broadcasters who permit one candidate for public office to appear on the air to offer equal amounts of time to other candidates for the same office. However, Congress has exempted bona fide newscasts, news interviews, and news documentaries from the equal Time requirement. So stations that mention one. Candidate during a newscast are not required to devote an equal amount issues, however, all of his opponents must be offered similar 15-minute blocs of time.

The public is most likely to hear about the Equal Time requirement during presidential elections. If the television networks give time to presidential candidates nominated by the Republican and Democratic parties, they are required to give equal amounts of time to qualified candidates from every other party- regardless of how small and insignificant their parties might be. As a consequence, many broadcasters are hesitant to put any candidates on the air. In 1960. Congress temporarily suspended the Equal Time Requirement for presidential and vice presidential candidates, and its action enabled the networks to broadcast the debates between John F. Kennedy and Richard M. Nixon. If the Equal Time Requirement had not been suspended, the networks would have been required to provide equal amounts of free time for 14 minor candidates. In 1976, the networks were able to broadcast the debates between Jimmy Carter and Gerald Ford because the debates were sponsored by the League of Women Voters; they were not put on by the networks themselves. Consequently, the debates were considered legitimate news events, and the networks did not have to give any time to minor-party candidates.

The Fairness Doctrine is far more sweeping in its requirements. It declares that radio and television stations have a responsibility to discuss significant issues and to present every side of controversial issues. The FCC explained the Fairness Doctrine's philosophy and requirements in a statement issued on January 1, 1949. It declared that the broadcast media must "be maintained as a medium of free speech for the general public as whole rather than as an outlet for the purely personal or private interests of the licensee." The FCC continued. "This requires that licensees devote a reasonable percentage of their broadcasting time to the discussion of public issues of interest in the community served by their stations and that such programs be designed so that the public has a reasonable opportunity to hear different opposing positions on the public issues of interest and importance in the community."

Broadcasters cannot simply provide time when it is requested. They are expected to actively go out and seek the proponents of minority viewpoints, then put them on the air so their stations can provide balanced broadcasts of opposing viewpoints. The Fairness Doctrine also requires stations that attack an individual to show the victim a copy of the attack and given him a reasonable opportunity to respond to the criticism. Unlike the Equal Time Requirement, which applies only to political candidates, the Fairness Doctrine does not require broadcasters to give each person exactly the same amount of time - only a "reasonable" amount.

In at least one case, the fairness Doctrine has been applied to advertisements as well as to news programs. A complaint filed against WCBS-TV in New York charged that the station broadcast numerous commercials for cigarette manufacturers but refused to provide any time for persons who wanted to warn the public about the dangers of smoking. When the case was appealed to the FCC, it decided: "We believe that a station which presents such advertisements has the duty of morning its audience of the other side of this controversial issue of public importance -that, however enjoyable, such smoking may be a hazard to the somker's health." Radio and television stations that contained to broadcast commercials for the cigarette industry were required to provide free time for warnings about the health problems caused by cigarette smoking. However, when the FCC later banned all cigarette commercials, most broadcasters stopped providing time for the warnings.

As might be expected, broadcasters are generally critical of the government's regulatory powers and complain that the requirements imposed by the FCC infringe upon their freedom of speech. Reuven Frank of NBC has observed that, if the provisions of the Fairness Doctrine were applied to a newspaper, they "would be thrown out of any American court as a violation of the Constitution, as a direct contravention of the Bill of Rights." Frank believes that persons who say government regulation is necessary fail to consider what the first Amendment was intended to achieve. "Its purpose was to keep all government out of the news."

While he was chief executive officer of RCA, Robert W. Sarnoff complained that government regulations rest upon the assumption that, "in the field of journalism, the government can better judge what is in the public interest than the press or public itself-an assumption directly contrary to the Constitutional guarantee that 'Congress shall make no law... abridging the freedom of the press. "Sarnoff said the Equal Time Requirement should be repealed because it forces television networks to give time to candidates from frivolous parties in whom the public has little or no interest. He has been equally critical of the Fairness Doctrine on the grounds that it gives an arm of the government the power to second-guess the judgment of broadcasters who report events and issues that, at times, involve the government itself."

Thus, broadcasters contend that the government's regulations have failed. They explain that the Equal time Requirement was intended to give every candidate for a political office an equal opportunity to express his opinions. In reality, the requirement may compel broadcasters to deny time to distinguished men and women because they would also be required to give time to the most trivial and irresponsible candidates. Similarly, the Fairness Doctrine was intended to encourage balanced discussions about controversial issues. broadcasters contend, however, that it encourages them to avoid the issues. Broadcasters who discuss controversial issues may be asked to justify their programs, to prove that they complied with the Fairness Doctrine or to provide time for an assortment of citizens who want to express conflicting viewpoints.

Discussions about the media's responsibilities often overlook two factors of fundamental importance: financial incentives and the related responsibilities of the American public. A study in Canada found that the media there do not try hard enough to improve "because there is no economic incentive to do so-quite the reverse, in fact." Media in the United States would also be more likely to improve if there was some economic incentive to do so - if it could be conclusively demonstrated that the improvements would be more profitable. As a consequence, hope for more responsible media rests not only with journalists, but also with a more informed and discriminating audience- an audience that patronizes the best that the media have to offer.

Most persons, journalists included, generally agree upon the characteristics that are desirable in news media, but they disagree - often sharply - over the questions of who should define the media's responsibilities and whether those responsibilities should be enforced. Journalists reserve the right to determine the standards. With respect to government regulations, there is no clear eviderice to indicate that they would succeed. In the broadcasting industry, for example, critics contend that the government's efforts have backfired and stifled the very characteristics they were intended to encourage.

Despite the problems, discussions about the media's responsibilities are valuable, for they help avoid complacency and suggest standards for the craft. Through a heightened awareness of their responsibilities, journalists can only improven performance and craftsmanship. Both discussion and criticism can provide control in the absence of written laws.

5 Motion Pictures in Relation to Social Controls

Film as a mass medium

What influenced the content of the last motion picture you saw? Who was really responsible for the images and sounds seen and heard by the audience? Why was a picture made on this theme instead of on one of hundreds of other topics about which a film might have been produced? How does it happen that you, as a movie-goer, sometimes complain about shallow and tawdry film treatments of reality, distortions of truth, and double features, yet seemingly cannot do much about it? How can you, on the other hand, support the efforts of those producers who have made, and are making, really good films?

About four hundred feature motion pictures come out of Hollywood each year. It cannot be reasonably expected that all these pictures should or could be masterpieces. One does not expect every novel which is published to be on the best-seller list. Yet, for the fifty years during which story-films have been produced, religious, political, and educational leaders have regarded them suspiciously, with a critical eye. And the movie-makers have reciprocated with mutual distrust and suspicion. Why does the motion picture cause such concern? Are we expecting too much of those who make motion pictures, in contrast to those who operate other mass media?

The answers to the problems of the theatrical film can be intelligently arrived at only through an understanding of the motionpicture industry itself and how it came to be what it is.

Although films resemble other mass media in some ways, they are sharply different in others. The motion picture is made for a general, nonspecific, mass audience. Every Hollywood film is made for everybody. Thus, there are no films produced especially for children. We have no specialized films for women, corresponding to the woman's page in a newspaper, or to the soap opera in radio which is designed for 20,000,000 daytime listeners, most of whom are housewives. If we exclude a few short subjects on wildlife, hunting, or sports, we have nothing in theatrical production which corresponds to a man's magazine. What we do have are pictures which try to interest everyone, and offend no one. And the thing which interests everyone, the producer concludes, is action-action about love, crime, and sex, woven into a fantasy which spells escape from reality.

The motion picture is unlike radio, television, and the press in another respect. The general, nonspecific audience of the motion picture pays for the whole product. Advertising supports radio, TV, magazines, and the newspaper, but the ultimate cost of a movie must be paid off at the ticket office. If the press had to operate on the same basis, your daily paper would cost about fifteen cents a copy.

A third distinction about movies is that its audience is composed chiefly of young people. The 1950 Film Daily Yearbook estimates that 10 per cent of the persons attending the motion-picture theater are between 5 and 11 years of age; 20 per cent are from 31 to 45, and only 15 per cent are over 45. These young people respond to the personalities and events they see on the screen in many overt ways. What they see may influence their attitudes or give them specific, memorable items of information. One analysis of fan mail received by an actor in one of the major studios showed that 96 per cent of the writers were under 21, and that 53 per cent were under 13 years of age. A study of the composition of movie audiences, made by lazarsfeld, showed that "age is the most important personal factor by which the movie audience is characterized," and that "the decline of frequent movie attendance with increasing age is very sharp. No other mass medium shows a comparable trend." It is, moreover, an audience habituated to moviegoing. It is an audience which comes afresh to the cinema every generation.

A fourth specialized characteristic of the motion picture as a mass medium is that the audience must go to the theater. A movie is not delivered on your doorstep, is not brought free of charge to your living room like a radio program. And if first-run films are ever seen on television, it will be because some way is worked out to make a mass audience pay for the performance through some system such as phonevision where the office of the Bell Telephone company becomes a remote-control box office. The motion-picture audience, television films apart for the moment, is a mass audience in the sense that large groups of people are assembled in one place at the same time, on a voluntary basis, with at least a general knowledge of what they are about to see.

Finally, the production methods in the making of a radio program, a television broadcast, or an issue of daily newspaper are historically different from those involved in the production of a motion picture. It is to these beginnings of the industry, then, and to these methods that we must turn to assess the present condition and problems of the motion picture as a mass medium.

Patents and properties

Basically, the motion-picture camera and projector are nothing more than tachistoscopic devices for recording and projecting a series of still pictures in a succession and progression which, by virtue of a peculiarity of the human eye known as persistence of vision, makes these static images appear to move. Such devices were worked out by Thomas A. Edison as early as 1889. Edison also worked out a system to make "talking pictures," using his phonograph in conjunction with his motion-picture camera-projector. Thomas Armat, Francis Jenkins, and others in the united states and abroad developed the mechanics of projection further, and George Eastman developed the necessary flexible film base to replace glass and paper emulsion supports which were unsuitable for the motion-picture process. Color and three-dimensions pictures were experimented with at an early date, and the sound, color, "3-d" film was anticipated almost from the beginning. William Friese. Green, an English photographer, patented a stereoscopic projector in 1893 for use with color films.

Yet, many of the early technologists who toyed with moving pictures failed to appreciate their future attraction for the public. Edison felt that a projected picture would exhaust its potential audience too fast. And seldes points out that "the brothers Lumiere.... advised Georges Melies that the moving picture 'might be exploited for a while as a scientific curiosity, but it has no commercial future."

Nevertheless, Melies went on to make his Trip to the Moon and other pioneering films, and in 1903 Edwin S. Porter made The Great Train Robbery; thus, the story-film came into being.

In 1907 Porter used an unknown actor by the name of David W.Griffith in one of his films produced in New York. Griffith eventually became a director and the man who liberated film from its mechanical fetters. He exploited the close-up, the fade-out, the flash-back , and many of the techniques which are now commonly used but which before that day were not recognized by directors, who, in the tradition of the theater, planted their cameras in what would correspond to the orchestra seats, shooting the entire action from this fixed position. Griffith's most famous film, Birth of a Nation, not only established film techniques but also opened up many of the industry-wide problems which will be discussed in the following pages.

Since the illusions thrown on the screen were fundamentally the products of technical skill and equipment, the development of the technology of film-making involved a struggle among the young film companies to gain control of key patents. In 1908, ten leading companies formed the Motion Picture Patents Company and, with the co-operation of the Eastman Kodak Company which agreed not to sell raw film to nonmembers, waged war on the Edison companies which held many of the basic patents for cameras and projectors. This so-called "patents-war" went on until 1917 when the United States Supreme Court finally decided against the legality of licensed film on patented projectors.

The final struggle for the control of sound started in the early thirties. The Radio Corporation of America and Electrical Research Products, Incorporated, a subsidiary of Western Electric, through a series of alliances and agreements, finally came to dominate the field.

These two corporations held a virtual monopoly in the field of sound-recording.

Meantime, other struggles were going on between the studios. The films-markers suddenly found themselves bidding against one another for another kind of property-the "stars." The "star" system came into being as movie audiences began to identify themselves with the charming, beautiful, brave, and exciting screen portrayals they saw acted out by people surrounded by the mystery and glamour of Hollywood. And Hollywood became an Olympus where the gods of the silver-screen lived in the mist created by the fan magazine, the gossip columnist, the Hollywood "reporter," and other by-products of the industry.

The studios competed in buying the best brains and talent of the American and European theaters, initiating a period in the development of the industry which was characterized by an influx of foreign stars and directors and by fabulous salaries to attract them. Brady points out in this connection that "the device of astronomical salaries for stars was originally evolved as a means of consolidating monopoly positions."

Production, distribution, and exhibition soon became consolidated. Systems of chain theaters were bought or organized by the major producing companies, and, together with the control of production equipment and talent, the monopolistic trend of the industry became obvious. There was, too, a monopolization of film ideas.

In the early days of film-making, the ideas for

a picture were made up in the head of the director. He improvised as he went along, always with the accent on action. As the trend toward longer films developed, the need for good story material developed, too. The director needed cohesive story ideas, ideas which could sustain interest for an hour and a half of film. With the advent of sound, the need for ideas became even greater, since the presence of dialogue as well as action required writing talent of the type generally associated with the novelist, the magazine-writer, or the playwright. The natural source of film ideas was, and is, the popular literature of the day and certain well-known classic writings.

Today, the industry still seeks to "corner" the best story material. Thousands of books, plays and original stories are read by the story departments of the major studios. Each studio selects forty or fifty promising pieces of "property", buying the screen rights partly on the chance that a good film story might be made of it, partly to protect themselves by keeping the material from falling into the hands of readers in story departments of other studios. Needless to say, not all good ideas get onto the screen by this process. Some are held indefinitely. Others are rejected because they do not fit in with the studio's story requirements. Dore Schary, vice-president in charge of production for Metro-Goldwyn-Mayer, describes the story requirements of his studio as follows:

> First of all, a story must be "for us". It must fit our program, permit practical casting, and generally be ready to go. But

> it must also have wide appeal to all kinds of people, it must to adaptable to visual telling, contain fresh pictorial elements to satisfy the audience eye, must be built around strong and intriguing characters, permit telling on the screen in not much more than ninety minutes, be nontopical enough not to "date" before we get our investment back. And it must sparkle with enough of that intangible called showmanship to make millions of people hurry through their dinners on a rainy right and park too far from an overcrowded threatre because they just can't wait another day. This is an ideal, I'll admit, but we always try for the brass ring.

Stories which fail to meet these requirements, at least on the surface, are, therefore, likely to be bad risks, poor investments. Those which measure up, those which appeal to "all kinds of people," which have action and eye-appeal, which match the talents of one of the studio's acting personalities, which can be put into ninety minutes of screen time, and which won't get out of date too spoon, may be bought by the studio, in spite of the fact that the idea content may be juvenile, totally unrealistic, or similar to hundreds of other pictures made on the same theme.

By the time of World War I, the word "property" in Hollywood referred not only to production equipment, chains of theaters, and a staff of highly paid stars but also to story material-the actual content of motion pictures.

The picture business

Once it became clear that motion pictures were a commodity that people would "buy", American businessmen took an interest in this peep-show business. As with all businesses, a key objective has been to go on making money in order to make more pictures. The immediate importance of the economic aspects of film production is seen at once when we consider that it takes six months to a year to complete a picture; that its budget may run from $250,000 to more than a million dollars; and that it is expected to return close to 100 per cent of its investment within about a year after its release.

Note that the cost of a single motion picture may be more than the cost of building an average-size radio or television station and that its return depends on a ninety-minute presentation which must, in a period of three days, prove itself to the audiences of a locality in any one theater: In few other businesses is such a quick return demanded or even expected.

But before the picture can be made at all, the necessary capital must be raised. Who pays for the risk? Like other businesses, the motion-picture industry relies on the banks for funds. However, banks which finance motion pictures consider this medium and all enterprises involving show business as unstable, uncertain ventures. Collateral is required. This may include the assurance of a good story, a director who has proven himself, starring players who are currently popular, commitments for studio space, and contracts which insure suitable distribution of the finished product.

As a result of the big money and extensive collateral involved in the making of a motion picture for theatrical release, a comparatively small group of people are privileged to make films for a great number of consumers. Control is centered in the hands of a few who have been able to exist in a fabulous industry whose whole history and weed-like growth can be told in terms of the life-story of some of the men, still living, who have pioneered the industry and made it what it is.

The industry was first represented by the "Big Three"-Edison, Biograph, and Vitagraph. By 1939 the field was largely dominated by the "Big Five"-Metro-Goldwyn-Mayer, Paramount, Warner Brothers, Radio Corporation of America, and Twentieth Century-Fox-and the three so-called "satellite" companies-Columbia, United Artists, and Universal-International. These eight companies produced about 70 per cent of all feature films made in the United States in 1945. They also controlled between 70 and 80 per cent of the metropolitan first-run theaters-the big, "people's palaces" where a film has its best chance of recognition and appreciation and where it can realize its greatest financial returns. First-run theaters, controlled by these studio, came to represent 25 per cent of the total seating capacity of United States movie houses.

As suggested earlier, many exhibitors in the pioneering days of the motion picture went into the production of films to insure a constant flow of "merchandise" to their retail "shelf". Carl Laemmle, for example, organized his Independent Motion Picture Company after prospering as an exhibitor. The ownership of chains of theaters made secure the exhibition outlets for the finished products. In order to further insure their investment, producing companies required exhibitors to contract for large blocks of films, regardless or content or quality. This was known as "block booking." In some cases, the exhibitor was further required to contract for films he had never seen and for some which might not even be in production at the time. This was known as "blind selling."

These practices were only part of the list of charges made against the industry on the basis of the Sherman Anti-Trust Act. And in 1938 the Department of Justice filed a petition against the "Big Eight," charging them with restraint of trade in the production, distribution, and exhibition of motion pictures in the United States and with violation of the Sherman Act.

Not until 1940 was agreement reached with the "Big Five". Although the suit was continued with columbia, Universal, and United Artists, the five major studios-Paramount, R.K.O., Warners, Loews, and Twentieth Century-Fox-agreed that after August 31, 1941, they would sell films in blocks of five pictures each and that blind selling would be eliminated by provisions for previewing each film in the exchange area where it would be released.

In 1949, a final decree from the United States Statutory Court in New York brought about the divorcement of production and exhibition functions which had been sought by the Government since 1983. Warner Brothers, Loews, and Twentieth Century-Fox were ordered to submit plans for the ultimate separation of their distribution and production business from the their exhibition system, this to take place within one year from the date of the decree. These provisions, together with certain other concessions made by the big five of the industry, constitute the "consent Decree" which temporarily, at least, ended the suit against the companies.

The motion-picture business, like other American businesses, has gone through its period of rapid expansion, of competitive individual enterprise, has developed its leadership from a few rugged individualists who got into the infant industry, moved it from New York and Chicago to California, and built its studios, its "stars," its theaters. Like the history of the railroads, we have seen the monopolistic tendency of the motion-picture business grow. We have seen the inevitable counter-movement against such monopoly. But today, since it still takes big money to make motion pictures, competition for the American theatrical screen is relatively small. A few foreign films and independently produced documentaries have infiltrated. But what is seen on the screen is mainly the reflection of the world as seen through the eyes of a handful of professional film-makers and financiers, who represent "the industry."

The content of films

In so young an industry it is inevitable that the novelty of movie-making must take some time to wear off. The current renewal of interest in "3-D" reflects the preoccupation with cinematic effects over film content, a preoccupation expressed by Orson Welles who, when visiting a major studio for the first time is said to have exclaimed: "This is the biggest electric train any boy ever had".

Although we have been comparing the film industry with other forms of American business, the making if a motion picture can never be as simple as the production of an automobile or a pair of shoes. The psychological effect of an industry which is trading on human emotions created by flickering shadows and sound can never be simple. For this reason, from the very start and continuing with increasing force, the industry is being made to feel its social responsibility more and more, with a result that today some people consider the making of motion pictures to be not so much an industry as a public utility.

The libertarian philosophy and the philosophy of social responsibility come to a sharp focus in the motion-picture problem. The exhibitor and the producer continue to use, although with lessening effect, the argument that they are simply purveyors of entertainment, that give the public what it wants. And what the public wants, they say, is fantasy, a chance to laugh, cry, and escape from reality into the dream world of the picture palace, to live vicariously and dangerously and romantically, and to do the things which in real life they don't dare to do, or which they will never have the chance to do. "Our intent," says the movie-maker "is simply to entertain. This and nothing more."

Now, people do need "escape." They do need "re-creation". The motion-picture producer, being a shrewd businessman and a practical psychologist, can turn out pictures enough to satisfy this need. And he knows that he doesn't have to produce an Academy-award winner to do it. "Horse operas" will do it. So will most "B" pictures-and even those shadowy, shabby productions designed for the "sex circuit."

But the reverse side of the coin is that experiences do not happen in a vacuum. The content of the films affects the motion-picture audience. This does not mean that the effect are simple, linear, or immediate. Certainly it is clear that immediate effects may be slight and that there is no reason to believe that movies are the prime cause of juvenile delinquency or divorce or any social ill. Their role may be to maintain present attitudes or outlooks or, indeed, to re-enforce them. But motion pictures, like other mass media, are not innocuous. They maintain, re-enforce, or shift learning.

In another section of this book Schramm discusses the communication process and the effect of individual backgrounds on what is "seen a" and what is not seen in communications systems, film included. The most innocuous film, shown in the right climate of opinion and at a decisive moment, may take on a glow of meaning not even dreamed of by the film-maker who is communicating with a large, unseen audience. For example, some pictures shown widely in the northern part of the United States cannot be shown in the southern part. Some pictures shown in New York State cannot pass the Division of Film Censorship in Ohio. Whatever Hollywood does, however clearly labeled "For Entertainment Only," deep-seated and fundamental; ways of "seeing" films vary with the audience, with the locality, and with the climate of the times.

Furthermore, as Fearing points out, "it is probably impossible to construct a coherent sequence of audio-visual images involving human action and interaction without at the same time presenting an attitude or ideological position toward that action." Morality is always eventually expressed in terms of behavior or action. Every action which is not meaningless involves intent and, hence, a value judgment. And actions and behaviorisms of people are the essence of the film story.

What are some of the values expressed in the

American-made film? Wolfenstein and Leites, in an analysis of the content of sixtyseven Hollywood films released between September 1, 1945, and September 1, 1946, conclude:

> The major plot configuration in American films contrasts with both the British and the French. Winning is terrifically important and always possible, though it may be a tough fight. The conflict is not an internal one; it is not out own impulses which endanger us nor our own scruples that stand in our way. The hazards are all external, but they are not rooted in the nature of life itself. They are the hazards of a particular situation with which we find ourselves confronted. The hero is typically in a strange town where there are apt to be dangerous men and women of ambiguous character and where the forces of law and order are not to be relied on. If he sizes up the situation correctly, if he does not go off half-cocked, but is still able to beat that other fellow to the punch once he is sure who the enemy is, if he relies on no one but himself, if he demands sufficient evidence of virtue from the girl, he will emerge triumphant. He will defeat the dangerous men, get the right girl, and show the authorities what's what.

An earlier analysis of five hundred feature films revealed ten classes of themes: crime, sex, love, comedy, mystery, war, children, history, travel, and social propaganda. The three, major themes of pictures made during the 1930's were love, crime, and sex, or a total of 72 per cent of all themes.

These, of course, are basic motives in drama. They are inescapable. They are life. But the critical point is the kind of handling given the theme. It may be a juvenile, unrealistic treatment. Or it may be a mature, honest presentation which helps us see ourselves and our way of living a little more clearly. Hollywood had made such mature pictures. Pasteur., Treasure of the Sierra Madre, Death of a Salesman, The Men, Grapes of Wrath, and others can be quickly mentioned as examples of mature films.

In making such films, Seldes points out:

> There is no need to abandon the tempo of the American film-only to vary it in harmony with the character of any given picture. There is no need to abandon the star system-only to use stars intelligently, so that they are integrated into stories, not outside them. There is no need to abandon plot-only to develop plot logically out of character instead of distorting character to fit stereotyped plots.

In sum, the motion picture need only go on to its natural fulfillment in the direction it originally took, when it tried to tell stories to people. It has degenerated into telling myths for children. A story is always single, individual, and enhance our understanding of the many-sided mystery of the human spirit; and myth repeated without profound belief tends to become a formula, totally without reference to the actuality of our own lives, manufactured without creativeness, and deadening our capacity to see life clearly.

Social responsibility

The production of mature films implies a mature industry to manufacture the product. It also assumes a mature audience, which is to say, a mature society. It presupposes a society in which a coherent value system has been developed, a society with common goals, common morality, and common understandings. It assumes social responsibility.

Since, however, we live in a society that can hardly be described as socially mature, and since we are from decided on what kind of life we, as a nation and as a world, want to pursue, it is easy to see how the motion picture as a reflection and re-creation of that life has become involved in the conflicts we see about us every day. The honest depiction of these conflicts and the clarification of the issue involved would, indeed, be a mark of maturity for the movies. Some films have attempted this. A Man To Remember, Home of the Brave, The Ox-bow Incident, The Southerner, and other have set forth important issues and conflicts of our time. But each person views the issue and the films through his own lenses and agrees or disagrees accordingly. Conflicting judgments are made, and the question of right and wrong is involved.

Morality is always eventually expressed in terms of behavior or action. Every action involved intent and, hence, the question of good or evil. This is as true of a novel as it is of a film. But the motion picture is a special problem in this respect. Martin Quigley, long associated with the motion-picture industry, points our:

> The transcendental potency of the entertainment motion picture, in its country of origin and every where it goes, is due to the unique graphicness of the medium, plus the vast audiences which its extraordinary appeal has gained. It is thus enabled to exert an unequaled influence on the thought, and consequently the behavior, of people the whole world over. Hence, there arises an awful accountability-an accountability which insistently demands that this powerful medium be so directed as to aid and not hinder mankind's struggle toward the fulfillment of its destiny.

The industry bears a social responsibility to the estimated fiftyfour million Americans who go to the movies every, week and to the foreign audience from whom the industry gets 40 per cent of its revenue. It bears, above all, an accountability to the youth of the nation and the world who attend film showings, even though these are intended for amusement or entertainment only.

Every study of importance has shown that

motion pictures do produce effects; sometimes stalactitic, as noted by Schramm. These effects have been measured in terms of everything from restlessness in sleep to overt examples of behavior inspired by a film. Changes in attitudes have been noted by Ramseyer, and direct learning of information by film had been demonstrated by the Holaday, Stoddard, and, more recently, by studies conducted by the armed services.

The influence of the "entertainment" film thus transcends the purpose of the film-maker. It makes him a party to the social responsibility-shared with parents, teachers, churchmen, and other members of our society-of determining what kind of children we shall have and, eventually, what kind of world we shall live in.

Now, everybody has his own ideas on this matter of where we should be going and what values should be stressed. And the motion-picture industry has inadvertently, but through a natural flow of events, got itself into the war of values simply because it is a part of the society and the world in which that war is going on. People may still go to the movies to laugh, cry, escape reality. But this does not mean that such films of not have more significance. What are the people laughing at? Or at Whom? And what kinds of actions or ideas make them cry? What form does their escape from reality take? Someone once said with regard to fiction that the quality of the world from which we escape isn't as important as the kind of world to which we escape.

Traditionally, nations, through their governments, have expressed and codified the law of the land. In a totalitarian state, the codification extends to the regulation of all forms of communication. The Nazi film, says Kracauer, reflected German Culture and nationalist psychology, and in the hands of the minister of propaganda, motion pictures made in the reich presented the Nazis exactly as they wanted to be seen, reinforcing the doctrine of the National Socialist State. Lenin saw the motion picture as a tool of propaganda for the Communist-party doctrine.

But in democracy the question of controls is a delicate one. Government is traditionally obliged not to interfere with the motion-picture business as private enterprise, while at the same time it must provide protection against the allegedly licentious, immoral, sacrilegious, obscene, and indecent.

The only alternative to government control is, of course, self-regulation. Accordingly, when the motion-picture industry faced the threat of increasing censorship, especially by state and local governments, as a result of a series of scandals and unfavorable publicity involving important screen personalities, the producers decided to assume the responsibility themselves in order to forestall action which might curtail their freedom.

Censorship

The threat of government censorship, coupled with the protests of organized citizens groups throughout the country has always hung over Hollywood. Between 1915 and 1920, several attempts were made to introduce bills in Congress to tighten federal regulation of the industry, and, in 1921, "nearly one hundred measures relative to the movies were introduced in the legislatures of fortyseven states".

Chicago passed restrictive motion-picture legislation in 1907, Pennsylvania in 1911, and Ohio and Kansas in 1913. In 1815, the United States Supreme Court sustained the right of censorship by the states as a reasonable exercise of police power. At that time, Justice McKenna set the motion picture apart from the newspaper by his declaration that "the exhibition of moving pictures is a business pure and simple, originated and conducted for profit, like other spectacles, not to be regarded, nor intended to be regarded, by the Ohio constitution, we think, as part of the press of the country or as organs of public opinion." This opinion has been contested from that day to this.

Today, the states of Pennsylvania, Ohio, Kansas, Maryland, Massachusetts, New York, and Virginia maintain censorship. Twenty major cities, in addition to Chicago, censor films shown locally. In certain cities, such as Washington, Bridgeport, Hartford, New Heaven, and Greeley, police, departments have censorship powers. In Chicago, Des Moines, and Kansas City, boards of censorship do to the job. Certain cities and certain states such as Georgia and Jdaho, prohibit Sunday showings, but the pattern varies because of local options in some areas and because of a failure of the courts to uphold "Blue Laws" in other cases such as those in Virginia.

The National Board of Review was founded in 1909, a few months after the may or of New York City revoked the licenses of every motion-picture theater in New York City as a result of a series of sensational pictures shown in the local theaters. This board, composed of a group of citizens whose task was to preview and evaluate films prior to release, received its financial support from the industry and was devoted to the promotion of good films and to the idea that legal censorship was to be avoided. The board came under considerable critical fire from those who felt that it was an apologist for the industry and was failing to meet its real responsibility.

The industry, again sensing its vulnerability, appointed Will H.Hayes, Postmaster General under Harding, to head up a new organization to be known as the Motion Picture Producers and distributors of America. Hayes served from 1922 to 1945 and was succeeded by Eric Johnston in a post which required, in the interest of the industry itself, the establishment of new standards of production to keep the industry "morally clean," "artistically elevating," and as free from outside controls as possible. In 1945, under the leadership of Johnston, the name of the organization was changed to the Motion Picture Association of America, which now includes three branches. The most important branch, the Production Code Administration, passes judgment upon all scripts, which, since 1931, the members of the Association have been required to submit for approval before going into production.

The Legion of Decency, organized in 1934 by Catholic bishops of the country at their annual meeting, instituted the only successful threat of economic boycott of the motion picture. No litigation was involved here. It was simply a matter of having Catholics all over the country sign a pledge that they would not support films considered by the Legion to be undesirable. Box office receipts fell. In Philadelphia, the drop was as sharp as 40 per cent. The campaign was effective. The industry took serious steps toward further reforms, one of which imposed a $25,000 fine as penalty for producing, distributing, or exhibiting any picture without the approval of the Production Code Administration, which had been given greater powers then ever before. Joseph I. Breen Office," is more commonly heard than "The Production Code Administration Office." A full appreciation of the types of cases upon which Breen and his office have to pass judgment may be gained only from a reading of the Code itself. Such a reading will make it quite clear that this form of precensorship would be considered quite inacceptable to the press.

The local censorship of newsreels, in particular, is inconsistent with the lack of censorship of television news and other newsreporting agencies. The theater newsreel is presently working under the handicap of time. News events reach us via television much faster and with more immediacy than through the theater newsreel, and in the future the latter may have to become a more editorialized, magazine-type presentation in order to service the public by getting behind the news on a thoughtful, less superficial level. Legally, however, the newsreel has been lumped with the entertainment film and has been subject to the same kind of censorship in some states, as, for example, Ohio.

Early in 1953, Senate Bill 159 was introduced by Ohio Senator Charles A. Mosher, in an attempt to do away with all film censorship laws in the state. The measure was withdrawn for lack of support, and in its place a second bill was introduced which was intended to eliminate only the censorship of newsreels. This bill was passed, and censorship of newsreels in Ohio was abolished in October, 1953.

Censorship of the motion picture takes many forms. It is found in federal laws such as those regulating the import and export of films, in state and local censorship rulings, and in the self-imposed censorship of scripts and films by the Production Code Administration. Special-interest groups in this country and in foreign lands where American films are shown may also voice disapproval of certain films which conflict with their own standards. And finally, there is a kind of censorship which grows from the fact that truth is hard to portray. There are artistic, technical, and human barriers which make it impossible to codify "good" and "bad," which make it difficult to present all side fairly and to please everyone with a completely objective and uncolored picture of the kaleidoscopic world in which we live. Dewey writes:

> Rigid codes that attempt to lay down definite injunctions and prohibitions for every occasion in life turn out in fact loose and slack. stretch ten commandments or any other number as far as you will by ingenious exegesis, yet acts unprovided for by them will occur.

When the Breen office rejects a film like Bicycle Thief as "indecent and unacceptable," how can the American film producer be scolded for not making the mature, realistic, and honest films we would have him make? when censors in an important southern city ban a picture like Curley because white children are shown playing with Negro children, how can we hope for more films which deal intelligently with our social problems?

Toward maturity

It would appear that the maturity we expect of the motion picture will have to exist also in the society of which the motion-picture industry is a part. Although we may expect standards in Hollywood which equal standards of morality the country over, we cannot expect them to be much better than those of the country as a whole.

We do not mean to speak of "maturity" glibly. It is not an easy goal to achieve. It is even somewhat hard to define. But certainly it is a quality of honesty, integrity, and respect for the dignity of human life and democratic living which can pervade a comedy, a tragedy, a western, or any other kind of film. Mature films will illuminate conduct, will enable us to live, for a moment, in close harmony and understanding with the lives of others. They will enable us to see ourselves as others see us. Such films will not necessarily all be great social comments. They may still be diverting. They may relax and amuse. Maturity requires only that they not be stupid, dishonest, or childish.

How, then, can we-as movie-goers-promote the production of such films? How can we proceed effectively in view of the monopolistic condition found in an industry which controls patents, production equipment, talent, and story material; an industry which had based its defense of shallow film stories on the appeal of such material to a mass audience which, it is claimed, wants nothing more than escape and amusement?

First, we must remember that, while we are part of a large, movie-going public, we are more importantly members of smaller groups. As a result of its tendency to look upon the American film audience as "the public," rather than as "the American publics," Hollywood has chosen to limit its market to younger, more immature members of our society. As members of more mature publics-parents and teachers groups, film councils, discussion groups, participants in adult-education programs-we must make our needs felt. We must not relinquish our right as consumers to demand what we want.

Our influence must be more than a boycott of poor films. It must include active support of good films and positive demand for better films. With the divorcement of exhibition from production and distribution, we may be able to deal more directly with the managers of our local theaters.

Many theater managers are genuinely interested in what the community thinks of their offerings. Some, for example, may be immediately open to the suggestion that there is an audience for good foreign films, for special showings of film classics, and for reshowings of really good current films, including documentaries.

Other exhibitors may not be easy to approach. Many theater operators are still close to the "peep-show" tradition, evaluating good and bad wholly in terms of present box-office returns. In such cases, actions speak louder than words. Film Festivals might be popularized so the general public can get a taste of the great diversity and rich content of nontheatrical films. Community groups, working through a local film council, may meet with exhibitors to make them aware of the kinds of pictures which the membership of these groups are willing to actively support and promote. Parents and teachers groups might enlist the support of local newspaper editors to get better publicity on good films. More responsible film reviewers are also needed. The canned reviews written by studio publicity departments and reprinted verbatim on the theater page of many newspapers must be replaced by critical evaluations which discuss the content of the film intelligently and give the public an honest account of what the picture is about.

Such action may cause the exhibitor to take a new look at his responsibility to serve the diverse needs of his community and he may, in turn, pass this reaction on to the producer in terms of a willingness to pay higher rental rates for the kind of films the local audience demands.

Group influence may also be brought to bear directly on the producer. The producer is the key man in the production of american films. It is he who selects the story, the screen writer, the director and the principle stars in the picture. He supervise the final editing and is responsible stars in the picture. He supervise the final editing and is responsible for bringing the picture meets all the requirements-financial, artistic, and administrative-during the production period. It is to the producer that, in the long run, we most direct our applause or our criticism. Good producers leave an unmistakable mark on their work, a stamp of their judgment in making such pictures as Home of the Brave, Boundaries, and Miracle on 34th Street.

The better Hollywood producers, sensitive to the nature of the times in which they live, are socially responsible. They are also shrewd showmen with good business sense. Many of them realize that the future of the industry depends on new insights into what the audience rally wants, instead of always falling back on the formula picture. Dore Schary describes how a producer successfully strikes out in a new direction in his case history of the production of The Next Voice You Hear:

> With The Next Voice, all we had to go on were the axioms that "messages" picture drive people away from the theatres, and religion is poison at the box-office. We would have both. Balancing these considerations was the conviction that we could make a whale of an interesting and exciting picture; that in the present distorted state of the world a lot of people needed the assurance and comfort that this story could bring, and that if you supply a real need you usually some-how get compensated for it. Also, any showman is bound to have in the back of his mind the tempting realization that it's often the gambling pictures which make the smashes: still fresh in my own mind was the success of battleground, the first to break through the latest of the recurring taboos against pictures about war.

Producers of first rank know that good pictures, mature pictures, can be good box-office prospects. They need to be supported in this belief. Their pictures need public support. The producer seeks it in the "sneak preview," he looks for it from the competent reviewer, and he wants it from the big audience. Schary, in writing about the audience reaction to The Next Voice as reported by comments written on preview cards, says:

We had gambled that audiences would accept a picture about decent people doing good things, had risked violating the axioms that message pictures drive people way from the theatres and religion is poison at the box office. In the space left open for comments, card after card asked, "Why don't you make more pictures like this?"

As teachers and parents, we can do something about influencing the kind of films that will be shown in our community. The audience is the final judge on whether a business is serving a public need. The exhibitor knows it. So does the wise producer. And the American public, with a constantly rising educational level, should and will become less and less easy to please. Here, the question of discrimination enters. This will be discussed in a later section. But it is certain that as we become more discriminating in the kinds of books and newspapers we read, the kinds of radio programs we listen to, and the kinds of television shows we watch, we will also develop, by a kind of affective expansion, an appreciation for better films.

We shall still need films which will carry the story to the poorly educated. One of the great powers of the medium is to transcend many of the barriers to communication with the unsophisticated and the illiterate. But we shall also need motion pictures designed for the highly literate and for the ever growing number of informed persons coming out of our high schools and colleges each year. Diversity of pictures is one of the important keys in the future of the industry. But this diversity must also include a recognition of the increasing maturity of the American public.

Many influences are at work on the movies. The competition of television is not the least of these. But unless the public reacts in a way to influence producers and exhibitors, and unless the public works through our schools and community groups to make its opinions felt, Hollywood's answer to television may simply continue to be the development of three-dimension, large-screen projection, and similar technical feats-and a continuance of insignificant themes amplified by these new devices.

Realistically, we cannot expect a sudden maturation of film fare from Hollywood. The sheer weight of the production process, the economic aspects involved, the toll of censorship in many forms, make the motion picture a conservative medium.

Also, new, fresh insights are hard to come by. Motion-picture producers, writers, and directors are only human. They express what they know and try to compromise as best they can with the financial, legal, moral, and artistic censorship which makes it difficult to tell the whole truth in any medium. There are too few film geniuses, and fewer still who are willing to break new ground at a time when new ideas are suspect. Experience with films like Grapes of Wrath, Home of the Brave, The Fight for Life and others which try to document the hard realities of our times shows that it often takes more courage to make social comment on celluloid than it does to do the same in a book or newspaper.

The making of a motion picture, like the development of an idea, is a complicated thing; for example, note the comment of the Senate Investigating Committee Report on the concentration of Economic Power in the motion-picture industry:

Any remedy or solution to the problems of the motion-picture industry in its relations with the consuming public will not be a simple one. it is a mistake to assume that any such cure-all as "divorcement of exhibition from production" or "restoration of competition in the production field" or any other single proposal will resolve all the difficulties to all the elements with an interest in this industry. Any single step might well ameliorate the effects of some of the undesirable practices of the industry as they affect the consumer, the exhibitor, or some other interested group. The motion-picture industry exhibits symptoms which are common to many of our great enterprise. Its problems are part of the larger problem of the development and direction of the American industry. More than anything else, perhaps, intelligent and sympathetic study is indicated.

The study indicated above must refer not only to the recurring "investigation" of personal conduct in Hollywood. It must include a serious study of the film "publics," of the potential market for films which fill the needs of special groups. It must take cognizance of the place of the foreign film, of the documentary, of films which interest "minorities" of a few million people. For example, a picture like The Four Poster might fail at the drive-in but do a land-office business in the specialized houses.

Such a study will, to be sure,analyze the danger points in Hollywood monopoly and consider carefully the trend toward control by the industry of the images which we see by television as well as on the motion-picture screen. It will assess the values as well as the iniquities of federal, state, and local censorship of films.

Through a study of the industry, we might find the "handles" by which to implement our desire for better films. We might find ways to get the co-operation of the exhibitor and to increase his respect for the community which his theater serves. We might, through our support of competent producers, encourage the production of films with real insight.

Even a superficial study of the motion-picture industry shows the value of re-runs of special films. Many good films are slow starters. Some way must be found to get such films featured as film classics. Film festivals, arranged through local film councils, may be effective in bringing to the attention of exhibitor and public alike the value of such pictures. We can teach motion-picture discrimination in our schools, clubs, adult-education programs and in our colleges and universities.

Finally, an intelligent study of the motion-picture industry must include a consideration of the film in the total pattern of mass communication. It must take into account some of the differences between film and press, radio, and other forms of communication described at the beginning of this chapter. It must include a study of the kind of world in which we live and the knowledge that what we "see" in a picture largely depends on how we look at the world and the other people in it.

The motion picture, then, will achieve its true role in mass communication only to the degree it becomes part of, and in turn reflects, our efforts as human beings to be a little more honest, more intelligent, more willing to evaluate our prejudices, fears, and hopes. This is maturity. And with the development of maturity, the role of the motion picture of tomorrow may possibly become what H.G. Wells describes as the role of the novel today:

> It is to be the social mediator, the vehicle of understanding, the instrument of self-examination, the parade of morals and the exchange of manners, the factory of customs and ideas, the criticism of laws and institutions and of social dogmas and ideas. it is to be the home confessional, the initiator of knowledge, the seed of fruitful self-questioning. Let me be very clear here, I do not mean for a moment that the novelist is going to set up as a teacher, as a sort of priest with a pen,

> who will make men and women believe and do this and that. The novel is not a new sort of pulpit... But the novelist is going to present conduct, devise beautiful conduct, discuss conduct, analyze conduct, suggest conduct, illuminate it through and through.

We are going to write, subject only to our own limitations, about the whole of human life. We are going to deal with political questions and religious questions and social questions. We cannot present people unless we have free hand, this unrestricted field.

We are going to write about it all... until a thousand pretences and ten thousand impostures shrivel in the cold, clear air of our elucidations. We are going to write of wasted opportunities and latent beauties, until a thousand new ways of living open to men and women.

6 The Motion Picture Business

A fundamental fact about motion pictures in the United States is that they are part of big business. Yet making a film is also an art, where the creative act costs money. Even the cheapest film represents a substantial investment on somebody's part.

See how many movies are advertised in your daily newspaper. In the course a year as many as 400 different films may be made available. Most are likely to cost more than $1 million to create. Some cost as much as $15 million.

Dealing with that kind of money is big business involving hundreds of deals, decisions, and compromises. Each of these affects the films that will eventually compete for the dollar bills that people pay at the local box office. This chapter examines the important financial and creative decisions that are made before a film gets to the local theater.

In the beginning is the idea

The first decision is, "What film to make?" Film ideas come from many source: novels, plays, biographies, historical events. Some film ideas are works of pure imagination. Among the most highly successful films, Love Story was adapted from a novel, The Sound of Music was adapted from a musical play which was based on a book that in turn told the true story of the Trapp Family Singers; Towering Inferno was based on two novels that had similar themes.

Everybody in the film industry is searching for ideas that can be turned into successful films. When someone begins to take these ideas seriously, they are called "properties" in Hollywood parlance. The search for properties is like prospecting for gold. One hit such as The Exorcist or The Godfather can make millionaires out of everyone who shares in the profits.

Looking for properties is like gold prospecting in other ways. Sometimes a hunch will turn up a field of gold, but a knowledge of the terrain is useful. Some people strike out for new territory, other look where there have been previous successes. A hit picture such as Easy Rider will start people looking for properties to turn into "youth pictures." When that vein runs out, as it usually does fairly quickly, other fields are dredged through. When someone strikes it rich with a Superfly or a Shaft, other people will search for properties with sensational black themes

Sometimes ideas are just lying around waiting to be used. The Sting was based on the knowledge many people had of confidence swindles since the publication of a popular book, The Big Con, more than 25 years ago. Butch Cassidy and the Sundance Kid was based on historical figures known to many people. Of the millions of people who came to maturity in the 1960s, only three of them turned their memories into American Graffiti.

Locating a possible property is only the beginning. If the property is a book, play, or screenplay written by someone else, the "rights" to make a film must be purchased from the copyright owners. These negotiations are typically the work of a producer trying to buy the rights from the owner.

The job of a producer is to bring together the elements necessary to the production of a film: the creative people, the technical people, the production facilities, and the financing to pay for all this. During the production of the film,, the producer is responsible for supervising the production; it is the producer's responsibility to deliver a completed film that can be shown in thousands of local movie theaters. One film may have producers, executive producers, associate producers; sometimes no one is actually called "the producer." Regardless of titles, someone must do the thins that a producer typically does.

There are different kinds of producers. Some are executives much like the executives of any other business. They make the major decisions and hire others to supervise the actual production. Other producers take a more active role in the production of a film. At best, they are creative collaborators; at worst, they are meddlers in the creative process.

A major part of the producer's work is dealing with agents. Agents are involved in virtually every part of the process of organizing a production; they represent writers, directors, actors, and even producers. Since they receive 10 percent of their clients' incomes, agents usually try to get as much money as possible for their clients. When a client is very much in demand an agent can ask and sometimes get as much as $2 million a picture for a particular star. Reports in 1976 said that steve McQueen was asking for $1 million a week for his services.

Sometimes, however, when agents can place several clients in one production, the agents might accept reduced individual salaries for their own overall benefit. Or when they represent a client much in demand, agents will use this leverage to place several clients in a single picture. At other times, agents become producers by putting together a property, a director, actors-all of whom they just happen to represent. Basically, agents are dealmakers; only occasionally are they concerned with the esthetic qualities of the films that result.

When a literary property is attractive-a "hot property" in the jargon-brisk bidding can push its price up into the hundreds of thousands of dollars. If the property does not attract much attention, a producer can sometimes purchase and "option" which gives the right to buy the work within some specified time. Depending on the relative bargaining positions of the producer and the original writer, it is sometimes possible to buy an option for as little as $500 or $1,000. The purchase price ,may sometimes be much higher than the cost of the option. It is sometimes possible to buy all of the film rights cheaply. The rights to A Clockwork Orange were originally sold by Anthony Burgess, the novelist, for a very small sum of money. He received no part of the millions in profits.

Part of the negotiations for rights may include negotiations for the author of the original work to write the screenplay; the rights to laws were sold for $150,000 plus an estimated $100,000 for a screenplay by Peter Benchley, who wrote the original novel. The reason for braking the price down this way is that the book publisher shares in the income from the rights but does not share in the income from writing the screenplay.

In recent year more films have been made directly from original screenplays. When the property is an original script, the producer is in a better position to judge the qualities of the possible film, and writers can maintain a greater amount of control over their work. Although an increasing number of successful films are based on original scripts, as many as 85 percent of the films produced come from other sources.

Publicity and promotion are basic reasons for buying the film rights to a successful novel or play. Hit plays and best -selling books carry with them built-in publicity that carries over to the film adaptation. Even people who never saw the stage productions heard of such long-running plays as The Sound of Music and Fiddler on the Roof through other media. While promoting the sales of a book, the author appears on many talk shows on television and makes personal appearances in bookstores; these activities are reported in newspapers and magazines along with personal interviews with the author. Even a title can be tantalizing. The movie rights to at least one book-Sex and the Single Girl-were bought and the title used on a picture that resembled the book in no other way.

And there are other reasons. A book or a play may just have a good idea that can be successfully translated into a film. A moderately successful book by Richard Hooker became a phenomenally successful film and later a television series under the title of M*A*S*H. A Clockwork Orange was first published as a novel and made into a good and successful film.

Since film is a different medium from plays or novels, it is necessary to have a screenwriter do an adaptation from the original property.

Adapting a novel or play to the screen is a complex task of dramatizing in visual terms the verbal narrative of the original. This may involve reorganizing the original plot so that it flows better as a film story, clarifying the storyline by eliminating subplots, inventing characters who were not in the original work, merging two or more characters into a single screen character, or changing locations. In short, writing an adaptation means doing what is necessary to tell the story on the screen while at the same time trying to maintain the qualities of the original.

The screenwriter is usually a "hired hand." In the best collaborations, the producer is a sympathetic, concerned sounding board for the writer; in extreme cases, the writer may work under the direct supervision of the producer, who will insist on seeing every page as it is being written. In any case, the producer has the final word; the writer is doing work that the producer wants dome. Working this way, the writer's creativity is restricted; the writer is always in some measure expressing someone else's view of the world. The work belongs to the producer who can do anything with it: change it, discard it, distort it.

Hollywood: old and new

This working arrangement has its roots in a period when most films were produced by big studios. Before the 1950s, the overwhelming share of motion-picture income in the United States went to seven studios-MGM, Paramount, Warner Brothers 20th Century-Fox, RKO, Universal, Columbia-and one distributor-United Artists. These studios were movie-making factories. They had on their payrolls all of the people needed to make about 350 to 400 picture a year: producers, directors writers, stars, feature players, camera and sound personnel, editor, designers, and dozens of other technicians. The studio heads approved every project and assigned the personnel, and the studio financed the production.

The studio system operated on the basis of a division of labor, using the specialized skills of various creative individuals, with the producer making the final decisions. For instance, there were some writers who specialized in plotting, others in character development, others in dialogue. Some writers specialized in gages; their skill was adding comic bits to otherwise completed scripts.

The big studios were efficient, but limited, operations. A corporation owned a studio and distributed its own films through theaters it owned. By interlocking arrangements, studios traded bookings with the theaters of other companies, each showing the films of its supposed competitors. The theaters had a guaranteed supply of films, and the studios had a guarantee outlet for their productions. Between them, the major studios skimmed the profits from motion-picture production and exhibition. The system discouraged new ideas and innovative talent, and made it difficult for truly independent producers to make pictures. Only films that were either very cheap or produced under the aegis of the major studios had a real chance of making any money-or even paying back their costs.

During the late 1940s, two important events occurred that were to change the studio system that had operated successfully for almost 30 years. Television was developing as a mass medium. Consequently people stated staying home instead of going out to the movies; motion-picture attendance decreased drastically. And in 1949, the Supreme Court ruled that the eight companies constituted an illegal monopoly.

The old system was dismantled. Theaters were sold by court order; no longer was there any guaranteed income for the studio. On land formerly used for motion-picture production were erected office buildings and shopping centers. Sound stages were sold or rented for the production of television series. Contracts with actors, writes, directors, and so on were not renewed.

What had earlier been complete, functioning motion-picture production organizations became financing. real estate, and film-distribution operations. Studio heads no longer exercise total control over the production of films. Producers, directors writers, and actors now make their own arrangements for motion-picture production. The only remnant of the old studio system is the production by some studios of television series.

For every film that is produced, hundreds of deals are discussed. Even before the script is completed, the producer begins to circulate the property among directors and actors; in the jargon, the property is being "packaged". Even the best script in the world is useless of on one can produce it; the ability to produce a script depends on being able to finance the production; and usually, the financing of the production depends on more than the script. The trick is to put together the most attractive package of script, director, and stars.

Packaging is a lengthy and complex process which is complicated by a mystique surrounding the production and financing of films; certain directors and stars are said to be "bankable". Bankable talent is believed to insure the success of a project at the box office.

Casting a picture with bankable talent is often used as a hedge against failure when other elements of the film call for substantial investment. But this only escalated the cost of the project; there is no guarantee of success eve when casting with so-called bankable talent. Each of the persons currently though to be bankable has been associated with pictures that were less than successful in the final accounting.

The notion of who or what is bankable it fuzzy. Jaws, one of the most financially successful films ever, featured no humans who were bankable, but Bruce the shark seems to have been preeminently bankable. The only clearly bankable actresses are barbra Streisand and liza Minelli. The actors believed to be bankable include Steve McQueen, Paul Newman, Robert Redford, and Burt Reynolds. Some directors and writers are thought to be bankable. The chances of financing are vastly improved if one of these persons agrees to work on the picture.

The filming of *Lucky Lady* is a revealing case study. The film was based on an original script written by Gloria Katz and Willard Huyck, who wrote the original screenplay for American Graffiti. Lucky Lady was a nostalgic picture made at a time when nostalgia seemed to be selling at the box office. But nostalgia in film production can be expensive. The story was set in the 1930s which increased the cost of costumes and sets; substantial parts of the scripts included sea-going action-scenes that are always costly to produce. Adding to the expense, if not the quality of the picture, were the stars: Burt Reynolds, Gene Hackman, and Liza Minelli.

The film was moderately successful, yet the several million dollars in box office income will probably still not be enough to return a profit on its estimated cost of $8 million. Some reviewers speculated that Lucky Lady would have been a better picture without the high-priced talent. Some films are like that; they cannot be made cheaply, yet well-known faces can detract from the story being told.

Producers who do not fall victim to the superstition of bankable talent merely attempt to get the best people possible for their project. This task is complicated by the many variables that enter into being willing and able to work on a particular picture at a particular time. There is the problem of scheduling; different people may have different commitments so that all members of the "perfect" package never are free at the same time. Schedules must be negotiated between and among numerous individuals and their agents and perhaps the people to whom they have conflicting commitments.

Compensation is a continuing problem. The producer receives a salary as part of a typical production package. After the costs of the production have been paid back, the producer shares equally with the financial backers in any profits. Parts of the producer's share of the hypothetical profits can be offered to other members of the package, in lieu of actual money "up-fort". Some elements of the package may insist on a share of the profits because they believe the property will be extremely profitable or because of their personal financial situation. Yet a producer may be unwilling to offer a percentage of the producer's share.

On the other hand, a producer's offer of points may be rejected because the project does not seem to be a profitable one or because profits are often difficult to calculate in a complex business deal. Instead of profit points, the demand might be made for percentage of box-office gross or film-rental gross, which are easier to determine. But this demand complicated subsequent negotiations for financing and distribution.

An actor's income tax liability can complicate negotiations. Robert Shaw, a resident of Ireland, who played the role of Quint in Jaws, had a tax problem. If he remained in the United States fewer than a specified number of days, as an alien he did not have to pay income taxes here. His time was running out; his agent insisted on a penalty clause in his contract for Jaws. If shaw became liable for taxes because of the shooting of the film, its producers would pay the tax.

Even the seemingly trivial question of how one's name appears in the credits can complicate negotiations. A player's or director's "billing" in the credits and advertising can be important in negotiations. Two players may demand that their names appear in top position in all billing; they may demand that their names appear in certain position in all billing. A director may demand that the top billing read "A Picture By..." But writers contest that claim and may demand that the phrase "A Picture By.." be used only when the director has also written the script. These kinds of demands are responsible for the very long credit titles that appear in many films and the increasing use of categories such as "starring", starring", also starring", "guest," "special guest star," and so on.

It sometimes seems as though more creativity is expended on these things than on the film itself. None of this has anything to do with the quality of the film, yet it is an unavoidable reality in contemporary film production.

When the package is more complete, the first stop of many producers is at one of the major film-distribution companies such as Paramount,

Universal, 20th Century-Fox, united Artists, Warner Communication Industries and Columbia pictures industries. Although these corporate descendants of the original integrated studios produce few theatrical motion pictures the way they did in the old days, they continue to be an important influence in the industry. Because of their assets, primarily the films in their libraries going back to the time when they were the major producers, these companies have access to very extensive bank credit.

In general, there are three ways that a distribution corporation finances film production. If the corporation has confidence that the production will be completed within the budget and will be profitable, the corporation may support the production from its own resources. This is an open-ended commitment. If the production runs over the budget, the corporation is responsible for the extra costs or the losses that may be incurred by ceasing production.

At a lower level of confidence, the corporation may agree to what is called a "negative pick-up". In this case, the corporation agrees to purchase the finished film at an agreed-upon price. A negative pick-up agreement with a major producer can usually serve the producer as collateral for a bank loan. Before a bank will release any money on a negative pick-up agreement, however, the producer must negotiate a completion bond which guarantees the bank loan. The cost of the completion bond cannot be part of the budget for the production; the producer must be prepared to pay this cost from other sources of financing.

At a even lower level of confidence, the corporation will not commit any of its resources to the production, but will agree to distribute the film if and when it is completed. A distribution agreement can sometimes be used as collateral along with a completion bond; it is more difficult to arrange such a loan and bond because repayment must depend on the box-office receipts of the film.

Each of these arrangement may be further contingent on the rental of sound stages and other facilities owned by the corporation. Thus, the corporation is in the position of making a profit on a production even if the film loses money. Moreover, depending on the degree of corporate commitment, there may be demands for changes in the script, casting, locales, and so on. Thus the producer is not truly independent; creative choices are limited by the financial arrangement that is made. Ultimately, these choices affect the film.

Producers who value their independence or fail to obtain distributor financial support can resort to outside financing. There are people and corporations that are willing to gamble on the possibility of sharing in a multimillion-dollar payoff. In various circumstances the income tax structure supports the gamble, with the government sharing in the loss. The investment, however, could return million of dollars in profits.

Dealing with outside investors causes its own

kind of problems. Nonprofessionals do not understand the intricacies of film production, and they may meddle in the production even more than a distribution corporation. Producers may find themselves with dozens of nervous partners; if any one of them backs out the whole project may collapse. Outside financiers require a great deal of "romancing," which takes energy away from the creative task.

The director starts work

while all of the telephone calls, office visits, long luncheons, and cocktail party lobbying have been going on, the director has perhaps already started to work on the picture. There are four creative phases in the production of a motion-picture: script, preproduction planning, filming, and editing. Under the old studio system, the director joined the production shortly before it was scheduled to start filming, was given a script complete with camera instructions, and told to "shoot as approved." In other words, directors then were responsible only for the actual filming while the total responsibility rested with the producer and the chief of production.

There are still some producers of the old school who hire directors to films the production while the producers maintain overall control. Ross Hunter, producer of Airport, and Dino Delaurentiis, who produced the recent remake of king kong, are reputed to be such producers. More typically in contemporary production, directors join the project early and participate in all of the creative phases. While the producer and the writer may have spent months working on the script, the director who will actually film the story can bring a fresh perspective that can be incorporated into the script.

In some cases, the director's tampering with the script is an exercise in personal vanity. Even under the old studio system, some directors managed to make films that were uniquely theirs; John Ford and Alfred Hitchcock are outstanding examples. It has since become a matter of pride for directors that their films are reflections of their personalities. This idea was given a name by French critics when they wrote of some of their films. The so-called auteur theory has become so influential that even run-of-the-mill directors try to claim the exclusive credit for the success of a film.

Genuinely gifted directors know that filmmaking is a profoundly collaborative art, and they welcome whatever help they can get. Director Francis Ford Coppola is himself a writer, yet he has collaborated with other writers in the creation of films such as The Godfather and Apocalypse Now. Other directors have been actors, editors, cinematographers, producers, television directors. Regardless of their backgrounds, all directors are storytellers whose instruments are the technical and human resources of film production.

How directors use these resources is not easy to describe briefly. There used to be a joke in the old days that the director was there to make sure that no one left before 5 o'clock. Like many cliches, it has a grain of truth. Shooting an ordinary, not very expensive, commercial film can cost between $25,000 and $30,000 a day. In an eight-hour day, this comes to about $50 to $60 a minute. At these prices there is no time for indecision. It is the director's job to make the most creative use of each minute.

Budgetary considerations affect everything in a picture. Take, for example, the visual and editing style of the film. Scenes where the camera moves during the shot are more time-consuming to photograph than static scenes. A scene shot as a single long take is cheaper than the same scene shot in several takes but it is more risky to shoot this way. If the desired effect is not obtained in the single take, it must be redone or used as "second". A scene shot with several takes can sometimes be improved in editing, but the single long take may be the more effective esthetic choice.

Good directors are very conscious of the cost factor and protect their projects by careful preplanning. Long before filming starts, they become intimately familiar with the nuances of the script, story, and characters. During this time the director develops a clear idea of the potential of the story to be told and a conception of how the story should be told by sounds and images.

Everything on the screen can convey meaning or evoke an emotional response. These responses can be manipulated from moment to moment in the unfolding of the story: the shock of surprise at one moment, the anxiety of suspense at another, the uncertainty of an ambiguous situation. The dramatic possibilities of each scene in the script are examined repeatedly and evaluated carefully.

During the preproduction period, the director consults with the director of photography. The job of the director of photography is to get on film the images conceived by the director. If the director wants as scene to be dark and foreboding, the director of photography will try to get it that way. If the director wants a scene to be light and airy but with a hint of disaster, that is what the director of photography will aim for. If the director wants a complicated shot with a lot of camera movement, the director and the director of photography will plan together how to execute the shot: Where will the actors be at different points in the action? Where will the camera be? How fast will they be moving? Will they move together or separately?

The more thoroughly scenes are planned, the fewer surprise there will be on the set and the faster the shooting will go. That is the whole point to the undertaking: to get the best shot possible, as quickly as possible.

Some directors plan the filming down to the last detail. Alfred Hitchcock is legendary for his meticulous planning. By using a series of sketches like a comic strip, Hitchcock knows before he starts filming what each action in the script should look like on the screen. Shooting a

Hitchcock film is a matter of translating these storyboards into strips of film.

Other directors use this techniques in planning visually complex sequences. Each shot in the big chase in The French Connection was carefully planned both for visual effect and safety. But in more static dialogue sequences, director William Friedkin says he likes to wait for the actual staging of the scene with actors before deciding on the particular composition to be used in depicting the action.

Before filming starts, the director is involved with dozens of large and small decisions. Where shall we shoot this scene, on location or on a sound stage? Is this the correct color for a costume? Who can we get for a small, but important, role? How many extras do we need for a scene on a big city street? How long will it take to shoot a crucial scene? How much additional time can we get if we don't go on location with this previous assignment? These are only partly administrative questions; the answers must come from the director's conception of the film. The incessant demand for compromise between esthetic and budgetary requirements is a fact of life for a director.

Shooting the film

If the project has been lucky, there may be a few days of calm before filming starts; the director can perhaps gather stength for the hectic period to follow. The next weeks and months will be a whirlwind of real and manufactured crises, with the director at the center trying to hold onto ideas conceived in the peace of the study.

To help in this job, there may be anywhere from 25 to hundreds of people on a typical film set. The camera crew consists of an operator and two assistants; the lighting crew of a gaffer, that is, chief electrician, an assistant, and several electricians who actually handle the lights. Both camera and lighting crews work under the director of photography. During filming, the director of photography is perhaps the busiest person on the set, and certainly the most important next to the director.

Another crew is responsible for the sound recording. There is a crew responsible for the set itself: grips, props, set dressers, carpenters. Yet another crew is responsible for the way that the actors and actresses look: wardrobe, hairdressers, makeup. And, of course, there are the stars, featured players, bit players, stunt players, and extras. The production staff of first, second, and third assistant directors, script supervisor, and production secretary schedule and administer the work of the other crews on the set. Another production staff under the unit production manager makes sure that everything is ready for subsequent days' shooting.

The first day of shooting can be a difficult time for the director. Until then, things could be changed; there was time to consider and contemplate possible effects. Once film starts rolling through the camera, the picture is committed; there is little opportunity and less time to change one's mind. The pressure is so intense that one well-known director is rumored to get sick to his stomach on the day he must walk onto a set and see "all those people waiting for me to say something."

Somehow something does get said. The players in the scene walk through it, practicing their lines, learning where they will have to move during the scene. The director works with them: advising them on the reading of a line, correcting an action, sometimes just watching. When the director is satisfied with the mood of the scene, the set is turned over to the gaffer and the lighting crew.

They begin to light the set; lamps are focused on stand-ins who walk through the actions that they have been the stars and featured players perform during rehearsal. The camera is moved into position and the first shot framed while the stand-ins walk through the action again and again, until the shot satisfies the director of photography. The director checks the shot. There are further technical rehearsals for the camera and sound crews.

While different specialists perform their jobs, the rest wait, gossip, do crossword puzzles, sleep, and sometimes study the script. The waiting can be enervating, yet all must be on the set when they are needed. When the scene is lit and the technical rehearsals finished, the assistant director calls for "the first team". The stand-ins are replaced by the actresses and actors who will actually perform the scene for the camera; they rehearse again, sharpening readings, refining movements.

The director checks the performance while the director of photography checks the lighting; the camera and sound crews follow the rehearsal through camera and microphone. An actor is reminded to "watch his marks"-actual marks on the floor that show where the actor must finish a movement to be properly frames in the image that will eventually appear on the screen.

The technical specialists indicate that they are ready; when the director is satisfied, a wry joke is sometimes uttered, "O.K., let's rehearse with film." The first shot will soon be completed. Actors and actresses are on the set; camera and sound are ready. At the assistant director's call," "Quiet on the set, this is a take. Roll sound," there is set in motion a well-practiced series of technical steps that lead to the director's instruction," "Action." The take is under way.

"Cut." Following the director's instruction to end the take, everybody stands by, waiting for the director's decision. Sometimes the take will be acceptable. Often the director will not be satisfied with the take. Did the actors and actresses reach an emotional peak too early in the scene? Is a particular action in keeping with the character? Does a facial expression tell too much-or not enough? Or perhaps, "it just doesn't feel right." Whatever the reason, additional takes of the same scene may be shot, sometimes as many as 40 or 50 times. A hundred takes are not unheard of.

All of this uses up time. A producer's representative is usually there to remind the director that "the clock is running." And other pressures exist. An actor may complain of "going stale"-losing the mood of the scene. Some directors were notorious for repeated takes of the same scene-William Wyler and George Stevens, for instance.

Was it worth it? One can never be sure. Multiple takes may have been an indulgence, but films from this period have a polish, a perfection, a poise that is lacking in many current films. Do repeated takes make a difference in the final film? Probably a single flawed take would not affect the overall presentation. What about two such takes? Or three? How many compromises can be made before the film's integrity is crucially damaged?

Contemporary productions film fewer takes of a single scene and make increased use of improvisation; the films are freer flowing, less predictable, more spontaneous. It may all be a matter of style, but the current style just happens also to be a less expensive way of shooting films. Directors who cannot shoot relatively fast find it difficult to get assignments.

Finally an acceptable take is filmed. The camera is moved, the lighting adjusted for the new angle, the whole process repeated. On an ordinary film, the process may be repeated more than 1,000 times. A thousand separate pieces of film will eventually be brought into a coherent whole. Meanwhile, in the maelstrom of filming, the director must retain the vision of how these pieces are supposed to fit together.

Ordinarily, putting the pieces together-the editing-is a continuing process that starts almost immediately after the first days shooting. At the end of the day, the film that has been exposed is sent to a film laboratory to be developed and printed overnight. Part of the daily ritual during filming is viewing the result of the previous day's shooting. Viewing the "rushes" or "dailies" enables the director to make preliminary judgments on the progress of the film. Often only part of the scene is shot from a particular angle. Running all of this together lends a peculiarity jumbles quality to what is supposed to be a coherent scene.

Finishing the film

Working with the director, the editor tries to make sense out of the apparently disordered mass of film. The editor is responsible for the selection of the pieces that make up the whole. The placement of a closeup in one part of a speech rather than in another can change the interpretation of the scene; the length of time a shot is allowed to remain on the screen will alter the pacing of the scene; an actor's performance can be affected by the way the pieces of the performance are put together.

Throughout the filming, the editor and the director discuss the sequences that have been shot, keeping in mind the context of the whole film. As the pattern of the film develops, the editor tries to incorporate the director's point of view in the way that the film is edited. Some editors do their job based on only general consultation with the director; other function as little more than technical assistants, following the director's instructions exactly. Usually editing, like other jobs in the making of a film, is part of a collaborative effort. By training and experience, editors understand, for instance, the possibilities of compressing dialogue and action, or how to emphasize a point by a judicious cut at the right moment. In other words, editors are skilled storytellers whose work is close to the work of a director; many skilled directors such as Robert Wise and Hal Ashby were once editors themselves.

Day by day as new scenes are photographed, they are edited and incorporated into the previously edited material. Sound effects are developed for eventual inclusion into the final film. Music is being composed. Edited portions of the film are shown and reshown, edited and reedited. Piece by piece the film begins to take shape.

Soon the picture and dialogue are edited into a complete rough cut, which has no music or sound effects. The music is recorded separately; another recording is made for the sound effects. Finally all of the separate recordings-dialogue, music, and sound effects-are mixed together onto one recording. The edited picture and sound track are printed by the film laboratory onto a single piece of film. The picture is ready for preview.

Until now the only people who have been seeing the film in the privacy of a studio viewing room are those who are close to the project. Their hopes and dreams are tied up in the success of the film. They have done the best they can. They think they have a good picture. Soon audiences will be making their own decisions. The preview is an attempt to judge what kind of decision audiences will make.

The preview is a long-standing ritual in making commercial films. Usually the picture is shown to a regular theater audience in a nearby town without any previous public announcement of the title. Part of the preview ritual is asking members of the audience to fill out brief questionnaires about their opinions of the film. These opinions are sometimes useful but the most important part of preview is what happens during the actual showing. A laugh at the right time-or the wrong one-says much to an experienced filmmaker. Even when the audience is not laughing, its sound can be revealing. A restless audience-shifting in their seats, scraping their feet, coughing-is a bored audience. An interested audience is much quieter. A gasp at the right moment says more about the audience' response than checkmarks on cards next to the words "Excellent," "Good," "Fair," "Poor."

The first preview is a moment of truth for a director. Depending on the audience's reaction, there is still a chance to change the picture through reediting, or more rarely these days, reshooting some scenes. The preview is the first-

and sometimes the last-time that the director's version of the film will be shown to an audience . Unless the director is established and influential, the film will may be taken away and reedited by others under the supervision of the producer. The story does not end there. If the financial backers are dissatisfied, they may take the film away from the producer to be reedited under the supervision of people who understand the film even less than the producer does.

Selling the film

The system that classifies pictures as G, PG, R, or X also plays a part in distoring artistic intention. By now it is widely understood that motion pictures can deal with a broad range of subjects, including some themes that are not fit for children. The rating system was introduced in 1968 ostensibly to make it possible to produce pictures of a wide range of maturity for different audiences. It did not make sense, the argument went, to force filmmakers to produce only pictures that were acceptable for children. The way it worked out, ratings became part of the strategy for marketing films.

Success in marketing films depends on the number and quality of theaters which play a particular film. Few theaters will play one that does not have a rating. Films exhibited in the United States are rated by a board of the Motion Picture Association of America, an organization of producers and distributors. If the producer disagrees with the rating, it can be appealed to another MPAA board, but this board usually supports the original rating.

In principle, filmmakers are free to deal with any theme in any way they wish; the board simply decides on the rating after the film is completed. In practice, filmmakers are "advised" by the board what changes are required to attain more favorable ratings. This advice rarely has anything to do with the artistic quality of the film. The filmmakers do not need to accept the advice, but refusal results in a more stringent rating which limits the possible audience.

When ratings were introduced, X ratings quickly became identified with "dirty" pictures in the minds of the general public, legislators, theater owners, and publishers. On the other side of the scale, children learn very early that G-rated pictures are bland; they want to see the more exciting PG films. Producers know the rules of the game: they include enough "mature" elements to warrant a PG rating, settle for an R if necessary, but avoid the X. Regardless of artistic quality, the market for X-rated films is severely restricted; advertising for X-rated films is limited is limited by newspapers, television, and radio; many theaters refuse to book X-rated films. And the key to success in the early stages of marketing a film is advertising and bookings.

Current film marketing operates on a boom-or-bust principle. Of the hundreds of films produced each year, only a dozen or so will be phenomenal successes; a few dozen more will be profitable; the rest will lose money. All theaters want to play a winning film; no one wants to have anything to do with a loser.

From the time the first contract for the production of the film was signed, plans for marketing the film were being made. The idea is to generate excitement so that everyone will want to see the film. Before that, the idea is to generate excitement to make exhibitors-the theater owners-think that everyone will want to see it.

Exhibitors are rarely interested in art. Films are a product that they rent for a percentage of the box-office income. Exhibitors get to keep only a small percentage of the admissions; and the more successful the picture, the lower the exhibitors' share of the box-office income. The exhibitors' main interest is in showing a film that will generate traffic through the lobby where the candy and popcorn are sold; many theaters make more money form the sale of popcorn than from their share of the admission price.

Producers and distributors, however, can get rich from a single successful film. Film rentals can accumulate to multimillion-dollar profits when a film plays in many theaters and plays return engagements. Once a picture has demonstrated its appeal to audiences, distributors can increase their share of the box-office dollar and still get more and more bookings. If a film has an extended run, people who do not ordinarily go to the movies are attracted to the theater. Success breeds success.

The important thing to understand about the making and selling of films is that there is no guaranteed audience. In the current market, each picture must attract its own audience. Relatively few people go to the movies regularly. For a film to be successful, it must attract those people who see films only sporadically.

No one knows why one film succeeds while another fails. The quality of the film has something to do with it, but some good films fail to attract an audience, and some apparently mediocre films cause lines to form outside theaters. Publicity has something to do with it, but there is no guaranteed way of getting it. The search for an answer to the enigma of success in film production has led over the years to an escalation of sex and violence in films. For many pictures these kinds of scenes appear to have less to do with artistic intention than an attempt to sensationalize the film. Each new picture, it seems, contains elements that are more bizarre than its predecessors.

The advertising for Taxi Driver reveals some of the current impulses in the production and marketing of films. One ad was headed in block letters: 3RD SHOCKING WEEK. A prominent part of the ad contained an alleged "Warning" which informed readers that the film "contains one of the Most Violent Scenes ever filmed". This was not mere advertising hyperbole, nor is the film a cheap attempt to exploit some people's morbid interests. Taxi Driver is a serious examination of alienation in modern urban society, written by

Paul Schrader and directed by Martin Scorcese, two of the brightest talents of the new generation of filmmakers. Whether the scenes made the picture better-more honest-is questionable. It is unquestionable, though, that they supplied a device for the promotion of the film, something to gossip about when speaking of the film.

Filmmaking is an art, but it is an art constrained by the fact that it is also a business. Even well-intentioned filmmakers are influenced in their creative endeavors by the need to recover large investments. At every stage in the commercial filmmaking process, every creative judgment is also a business judgment.

7 Current Issues

The issues that confront journalists tend to emerge slowly, often over a period of several years, and are not immediately recognizable. Most of the issues are the result of changes in our society, such as the civil rights movement and its leaders' demands for access to the media. Other issues, however, have arisen within the media themselves. For example: journalists are concerned about conflicts of interest and the practice of paying sources for their stories.

Persons who expect fast and easy solutions to the problems are likely to be disappointed. Some issues involve temporary aberrations-fads that quickly subside. But most are more lasting and more difficult to resolve; they may persist throughout our lifetime. The issues discussed in this chapter do not have two clear-cut sides that might be labeled "right" and "wrong". They involve complex issues, so that even the most intelligent and well-informed citizens may reach different conclusions about what needs to be done. Not every American will agree with the decisions made by journalists, but Americans should realize that journalists are at least aware of the issues, and that most are doing their best to resolve them.

Access to the media

The First Amendment was added to the U.S. Constitution to prevent the government from interfering with freedom of expression. At the time the Constitution was signed, government censorship appeared to be the only serious obstacle to free speech. persons with something important to say usually were able to find an effective outlet for their ideas. They might speak in the village square, hire someone to print a few hundred pamphlets, find an editor willing to publish their ideas, or, for a few hundred dollars, establish a newspaper of their own. Most cities had several newspapers, and the newspapers published a variety of conflicting ideas.

Conditions have changed. Towns have grown in size, and most now have only one newspaper. Yet people who have something to say must gain access to the media; other means of communication no longer are adequate. Individuals can still distribute pamphlets or speak from a soapbox, but few citizens will see and heat them.

The Commission on Freedom of the press warned that, because of these changes, protection from government interference no longer is adequate to guarantee that a person with something to say will have an opportunity to say it. The commission explained that American still have the legal right to speak, but that the freedom has lost its earlier reality. Speech alone has become inadequate; the mass media are necessary to amplify our voices. The commission concluded that the men and women who own and manage the media have become the most powerful censors in our society because they "determine which persons, which facts, which versions of the facts, and which ideas shall reach the public."

Critics have charged that the media favor the status quo and stifle the expression of unpopular opinions. When nearly 700 newspapers were offered an opportunity to publish portions of Unsafe at Any Speed, a book written by Ralph Nader, not a single newspaper accepted the offer. The book was critical of the automobile industry, a major advertiser. Minority groups have been particularly critical of the media, and groups unable to express their grievances in the media have staged demonstrations to attract more attention. The media, however, have always done a better job of reporting events than ideas, and groups, that want to publicize an idea or grievance are likely to be discouraged by the media's indifference to it. Journalists may not consider the idea very newsworthy and may ignore it not because of its unpopularity, but because they prefer stories that satisfy their more traditional definitions of news.

As a last resort, groups that want more publicity have tried to buy advertisements to express their ideas. Some media, however, have also rejected advertisements that advocated controversial ideas, such as the impeachment of President Nixon, the legalization of marijuana, the acceptance of homosexuals, and the boycott of local stores. Courts have upheld a newspaper's right to reject any advertisements that it considers objectionable, regardless of the topic. One case involved a movie producer who sued the Los Angeles Times for censorship because it altered an illustration and eliminated references to deviate sexual conduct in an advertisement for the movie The Killing of Sister George. The U.S. Court of Appeals upheld the newspaper's right to alter the advertisement and explained that the producer's objections "would violate the right of freedom of the press; that a newspaper publisher may not be forced to publish advertisements which, in its judgment, are in poor taste or offensive to its readers." The court declared that a newspaper is not a government agency, subject to regulation.

The debate over access involves a fundamental question: Does the freedom of the press guaranteed by the U.S. Constitution also protect citizens who rely upon the media for information? Because the Federal Communications Commission already requires radio and television stations to provide time for the expression of diverse viewpoints, the debate has focused primarily upon newspapers. Critics argue that the public will not be adequately informed if newspapers are allowed to deliberately suppress ideas they dislike.

Jerome Barron, a law professor at George Washington University, has suggested that the nation's courts reinterpret the First Amendment and give greater priority to the public's right to receive information uncontaminated by the bias of newspaper publishers. Barron says newspapers should be forced to provide space for individuals and groups that want to discuss significant ideas.

Barron argues that newspapers are quasi-public institutions, much like public utilities, and have certain responsibilities to the public. Because the U.S. Constitution prohibits the government from censoring speech, Barron believes that private citizens, including newspaper publishers, also are prohibited from censoring speech. Barron adds that the First Amendment was intended to encourage debate and to inform the public, not just to protect publishers' freedom to do as they please. He complains that the media are most likely to suppress ideas that are unpopular, so, "What happens, of course, is that the opinion vacuum is filled with the least controversial and bland ideas. Whatever is stale and accepted in the status quo is readily discussed and thereby reinforced and revitalized." To solve the problem, Barron has proposed that:

Public officials might be given the right to demand a retraction or the right to respond to criticisms printed in newspapers.

Groups denied access to newspapers might be allowed to appeal their cases to a court.

The groups' ideas might be published in paid advertisements or in columns set aside for letters to the editor.

Barron explains that, "A statute might impose the modest requirement, for example, that denial of access not be arbitrary but rather be based on rational grounds." Courts also might consider whether the material for which access is sought "is needed suppressed and underrepresented by the newspaper." Barron would not require the media to grant access to everyone, only to groups that represent a significant segment of their community. If several different groups wanted to express the same idea, Barron would require newspapers to grant access to only one of them. Despite Barron's arguments, which attracted widespread interest, courts have been reluctant to reinterpret the First Amendment, and the types of laws that he advocates have been declared unconstitutional.

A law enacted in Florida, for example, required newspapers which attacked a political candidates to "upon request immediately publish free of cost any reply he may make thereto in as conspicuous a place and in the same kind of type..." The law was upheld by the Florida Supreme Court, which commented, "The right of the public to know all dies of a controversy...is being jeopardized by a growing concentration of ownership of the mass media into fewer hands, resulting ultimately in a form of private censorship." Its decision was appealed to the U.S. Supreme Court and unanimously overturned.

Justices on the U.S. Supreme Court declared that the law violated the First Amendment, which prohibits any laws that abridge the freedom of the press.

Newspaper publishers have insisted that there is no need for a right of access in the United States and warned of the dangers that it would create. Ben Bagdikian, a journalist and frequent critic of the press, believes that: "Editors must decide what is news. This sounds arrogant, and of course it is. Who are we to decide what the world will see and hear? There is no really satisfactory answer. We are frail human beings, and we don't have any magical powers or special wisdom. But there is no alternative." While commenting on the same issue, another journalist added that, "No editor can or should be required to print the views of those he disagrees with except as he needs to make his case or as he feels compelled by conscience to do. Freedom to publish must include freedom not to publish."

Barron also fails to deal with the practical problems that would arise if his proposals were adopted. For example: How could newspapers create enough space to publish more diverse viewpoints? The New York Times already receives 38,000 letters a year and publishers about six percent of them. Clifton Daniel, associate editor of the Times, has estimated that, if all letters were published, they would completely fill at least 135 weekday issues of the Times, leaving no space for the news.

Newspapers have adopted other, less drastic remedies to encourage the expression of diverse ideas. Newspapers attempt to balance their editorial pages by publishing the columns written by both liberals and conservatives. News stories routinely quote the spokesmen for all sides in controversial issues. Typically, The New York Times has a rule "that anyone who is accused or criticized in a controversial or adversary situation should be given an opportunity to comment before publication." The Times also has a policy of accepting controversial advertisements about social and political issues, even though they might offend some readers. Newspapers also are trying to publish more letters to the editor. While he was published of Newsday, Bill Moyers "ordered his editorial page staff to concentrate on letters that offered criticism of the publication's editorials." Newspapers have expanded their editorial pages, and some encourage experts from other institutions to discuss significant issues conforming their communities.

Checkbook Journalism

CBS News paid H.R.Haldeman $50,000 to appear on two special hour-long television programs after President Richard Nixon resigned. Haldeman, who had been Nixon's chief of staff, was interviewed by Mike Wallace and showed some amateur movies that he had shot at the White House and on presidential trips. The payments renewed a furor that had been simmering for years-the practice of paying persons involved in the news for their stories. James Reston of The New York Times warned that CBS was "introducing the unequal principle that news belongs to the outfit with the biggest payroll." The practice of buying exclusive news stories however, has a long history.

After reaching the North Pole on April 6, 1909, Commander Robert E. Peary sent a coded message back to The New York Times, which sold the story to other newspapers throughout the world. Peary received $12.000 as his share of the profits. Charles A. Lindbergh earned more than $60,000 from the sale of a story about his flight across the Atlantic in 1927. Lindbergh was from St.Louis, but the St. Louis Post-Dispatch refused to buy his story; its managing editor said he would not "gamble on a man's life for the sake of a piece of newspaper promotion." Two reporters for The new York Times became convinced that Lindbergh would succeed, and they persuaded the Times to buy Lindbergh's story if he succeeded in flying from New York to Paris, Flying alone in a plane named. "The Spirit of St.Louis," Lindbergh landed at Le Bourget field outside Paris at 10 P.M. on May 12. His story, under his byline, appeared in the Times the next morning. Other newspapers that wanted to publish Lindbergh's personal account of the flight had to buy it from the Times.

Checkbook journalism is not confined to the United States. The competition between the newspapers in London is particularly fierce, and the stories they have published have been more scandalous than any seen in the United States. In 1963, for example, London newspapers reported that John profumo, the British minister of war, had slept with Christine Keeler, a prostitute who had also shared her bed with a Soviet military agent. A Sunday paper, News of the World, paid Miss Keeler 23,000 for her story; its publication ruined profumo's career. Six years later, News of the World announced that it had paid Miss keeler an additional 21,000 for the right to publish excerpts from her memoirs, which had just been published as a book. The story's renewed publication was particularly damaging for profumo, who was trying to redeem his reputation through employment as a social worker in London.

Critics charged that News of the World was exploiting sex and vice for commercial purposes. One critic observed that, "This is not the work of journalists but of money-grubbers." Despite their criticism, other newspapers defended News of the World's right to publish the story. They said the paper's action, however regrettable, involved a matter of taste, and that each newspaper must decide such issues for itself. Journalists also warned that government action to-prevent the publication of such revelations would be more harmful than the revelations themselves. The Daily Mail explained, "Free speech means what it says. It means freedom for silly or tasteless words as for the wise and noble. It is not for the law to decide questions of taste. Every journalist must argue that out with his own conscience.

In the United States, Life magazine obtained an exclusive contract with space program's astronauts. The first seven astronauts were named in 1959, and guidelines established by the national Aeronautics and Space Administration allowed them to sell their "personal" stories. Their "official" stories were considered public property. To eliminate the possibility that the astronauts might compete with one another for the sale of their stories, it was agreed that all seven astronauts would sign a contract with the same company and share the proceeds. Life, the only serious bidder, offered each astronaut about $25,000 a year-nearly 2.5 times his military salary. Other journalists objected, but without success. The managing editor of The Washington Post complained, "The story of what the Mercury astronauts do in Project Mercury belongs to the public, It cannot be sold by anyone to anyone".

When President Nixon left the White House, both CBS and ABC declined to bid for the exclusive television rights to his memories. NBC reportedly bid $300,000 but broke off the negotiations because Nixon's agent demanded more than twice that much. Former talk show host David Frost subsequently announced that Nixon had agreed to tape four 90-minute programs with him. Frost, backed by a consortium of international investors, reportedly agreed to pay Nixon $600,000, plus a percentage of the programs' profits, which were expected to total $2.5 million. It is believed that the former president earned a total of about $1 million. A special network of 155 television stations broadcast the programs in the United States, and the first attracted 50 million viewers, making it the most popular news interview in television history. In New York and Los Angeles, for example, it attracted a 42 percent share of the television audience. As the programs continued, however, they attracted fewer and fewer viewers. All four programs were also sold to broadcasting stations in other countries.

Proponents believe that checkbook journalism encourages people who have been involved in the news to reveal more information about their stories. But even many of the proponents add that the public should be told about the payments that celebrities receive for their stories. Columnist Patrick J. Buchanan said CBS's interviews with Haldeman were interesting and informative. Buchanan added, however, that CBS made a mistake "in not fully informing its audience of all the details, and all the conditions of the contract with Haldeman." Shana Alexander, a columnist for Newsweek, commented that, "Personally, I thought Mike Wallace's interviews were good tough reporting, loaded with news and worth every cent". She observed that, "Nobody gives you information for nothing... If someone doesn't tell you his story for cash, he does it for publicity, or creditability, or an alibi; to make himself look good or his enemy look bad, to sell his record or hawk his new book or get his kid a job."

Other journalists are more dubious about the benefits of checkbook journalism. When a newspaper or magazine buys a story, it usually obtains the exclusive right to report that story and, as a consequence, most Americans may never have an opportunity to see it. Journalists have been particularly critical of government officials who sold their stories. Because the officials are paid by the public, many journalists insist that every citizen should have a right to receive their stories, and that the officials do not have a right to sell them. In other cases, checkbook journalism may inhibit critical reporting. After Life magazine bought the astronauts' story, for example, it rarely criticized NASA, the space program, or the astronauts. Because stories that contain starting revelations attract the highest bids, checkbook journalism also encourages sensationalism. As just one example, a book written by a White House electrician aroused widespread interest solely because it charged that President Kennedy had enjoyed swimming nude with attractive young women.

Checkbook journalism also seems to reward criminals, and critics feat that the payments may encourage criminals to commit even more bizarre crimes. The Macmillan Company paid $250,000 for the english-language rights to the memories of Albert Speer, who served as minister of arms and munitions for Adolph Hitler. While he was being taken to jail after shooting George Wallace in 1972, Arthur Bremer asked FBI agents. "How much do you think I'll get for my autobiography?" Bremer had only $1.35 in his pocket when he was arrested, but Harper's magazine paid $15,000 for the right to publish portions of his diary, and the entire diary was later published as a book.

Competition between the media has encouraged

checkbook journalism. Also, the media can afford to pay larger amounts for new, exciting, or exclusive stories, and the higher payments are inducing more persons to sell their stories. McCall's magazine paid $1 million for a single story-Robert Kennedy's account of the Cuban missile crisis. The stories often require little effort, since celebrities can hire ghost writers to do most of the work for them. Checkbook journalism undoubtedly will continue as long as it is popular and profitable. The American public seems to welcome the information that it receives and rarely objects to the practice. Few persons suggest that the practice should be outlawed, simply that the media exercise more discretion, particularly while dealing with convicted criminals. The National New Council, an organization concerned with the media's fairness and accuracy, also recommends that, "If compensation beyond actual expenses is made to any person for information aired or published by a news organization, that fact should be disclosed. A prefatory note or on-the-air statement immediately preceding the article or program should be published or broadcast".

Discrimination in the media

Against racial minorities

Discrimination against racial groups, particularly blacks, has been common. Movies are implied that blacks are lazy, backward, and inferior to whites. For years, they portrayed blacks almost exclusively as laborers, servants, shoe-shine boys, and elevator operators. Newspapers, which refer to whites by their last names, used blacks' first names. They also mentioned the race of blacks charged with crimes. Today, however, the practices have disappeared from all but a few newspapers. An individual's race and religion no longer are likely to be mentioned unless they are clearly relevant to the story.

Black leaders have criticized the media in both the North and the South. Charles Evers has called the police and newspapers the two worst enemies of blacks in Mississippi. Evers has complained that television newspeople in the South have gone around "trying to find the wrong and evil and worst part of blacks, and that's how they show us on the 6 o'clock news". Black columnist Carl T rowan, who once headed the U.S. Information Agency, observed that, "If you were a black, you almost had to rape or murder someone, generally white, to make the newspapers." Rowan adds that, "For years, the two best-known Africans were Tarzan and Jane". Evers further charges that reporters have twisted stories about blacks. During a speech in Nashville, he said, "If the whites don't stop beating and mistreating us and burning our churches and killing our brother and sisters, we're going to shoot back." According to evers, a newspapers headline reported, "Evers Says Negroes Will Shoot whites."

Systematic studies have documented many of these complaints. Helen Tatro of Indiana University examined the stories that five newspapers in the Deep south published about blacks in 1950, 1960, and 1970. She found that the proportion of stories that newspapers published about blacks remained relatively stable; 1.7 percent in 1950, 2.3 percent in 1960, and 2.7 percent in 1970. Most of the stories concerned just three topics; crime, politics, and education. Fifty-five percent of the stories that the newspapers published about blacks in 1950 involved crime, compared to only 4 percent of stories about whites. By 1970, the figures for blacks had declined to 24 percent but still was considerably higher than the 3 percent for whites. Tatro concluded that individual stories published by the newspapers were not biased, but that the newspapers presented an unfavorable image of backs because the types of stories they published were not representative of all the activities that blacks engaged in. A somewhat similar study in Orlando, Florida, found that 30 whites and 52 blacks were arrested for serious crimes during a 10-day period, but that the local newspapers reported the arrest of only 7 percent of the whites, compared to 25 percent of the blacks. Viewed from another perspective, the newspapers reported 25 percent of the crimes in which a white was the victim-but not a single crime in which a black was the victim.

The studies support charges that the media report policies news but fail to report stories about the normal life of nonwhites; their births, academic achievements, marriages, careers, and religious and social activities. Yet the media routinely report the activities of whites.

The riot that devastated Watts in August of 1965 greatly altered the media's policies. Because the media had failed to develop any sources in the area, editors did not know whom to contact and were unable to immediately learn what was happening and the reasons behind the riot. White reporters were attacked, and the media had not yet employed any blacks who might have safely entered the riot area. For years, the blacks in Watts and elsewhere in the United States had been ignored and mistreated by the media. Now, when the media suddenly approached them, they reacted with distrust and hostility.

The National Advisory Commission on Civil disorders, appointed by President Johnson to investigate the riots, found that the media made a real effort to provide a balanced, factual account of the disorders. The media, however, exaggerated the amount of damage caused by the riots and the extent to which the riots were confrontations between blacks and whites. The commission considered another of its findings far more important-the fact that the media had 'failed to report adequately on the causes and consequences of civil disorders and the underlying problems of race relations." The commission added.

> They have not communicated to the majority of their audience-which is white-a sense of the degradation, misery, and hopelessness of living in the ghetto. They have not communicated to whites a feeling for the difficulties and frustrations

> of being a black in the United States. They have not shown understanding or appreciation of-and thus have not communicated-a sense of black culture, thoughts, or history.

The commission also said journalists had ignored the fact that a large portion of their audience is black and that journalists had contributed to the divisions that exist between blacks and whites because the failed to show blacks engaged in normal activities. In short, the commission reached the same conclusion as the other studies mentioned in this chapter; it found that the media have not always reported the daily activities of both blacks and whites.

Journalists hope that the employment of more nonwhites will help resolve the problem, but progress has been slow. In 1972, the American Society of Newspaper Editors estimated that 40,000 persons in the United States were employed as newspapers reporters, writers, photographers, and editors, but that only 300 were nonwhites. Newspapers have lagged behind even the other media in their employment of nonwhites. In 1975, the journalism Council reported that about 8.6 percent of the persons employed in the broadcasting industry were nonwhite, compared to only 3.2 percent of the persons employed by newspapers.

The task of finding qualified nonwhites had aroused heated debates. Some media, particularly radio and television stations, have begun to offer nonwhites on-the-job training. And schools of journalism now offer special scholarships to attract more nonwhites. In 1975, the School of Journalism at the University of California in Berkeley announced the establishment of an intensive summer program to train nonwhites to work for newspapers. Fifteen students-blacks, Chicanos, and other persons from ethnic minorities-will be selected each summer and guaranteed jobs after they graduate. The program is financed by private funds, including gifts from foundations and news media. It is only one many such efforts. From 1968 to 1974, a similar program at Columbia University helped about 225 nonwhites find jobs with the media. According to some estimates, the constitute one-fifth of all the nonwhites now employed by the media. Many editors, however, are reluctant to establish special training programs for nonwhites, and some whites complain that the programs are discriminatory, since similar programs are not offered for them.

Women object to being called "girls" and to the use of their first names in news stories. The media rarely call men "boys" or use their first names. When Mildred Caroon, who had served in the WACs for 30 years, was promoted to the rank of brigadier general, a headline in the Chicago Tribune read. "She Takes a Whack at Being General," and a caption added, "All Girl in Outlook." Few newspapers would be that frivolous about a man's promotion.

Women also have charged that the media, particularly newspapers, are preoccupied with the bodies of women and frequently describe their clothes, dimensions, hair, eyes, makeup, and voice. For example, a story about a woman involved in politics described her as a "petite housewife" and a "mother of three." Women responded that the comments were irrelevant to her candidacy, and that the media rarely mention a man's size of his family. Other stories have reflected an even more blatant sexism. A newspaper in Massachusetts published a photograph that showed a half-naked woman on the hod of a car, and it commented that, "The hood ornament is a custom accessory." Few newspapers would call any man an "ornament." Newsweek magazine praised Fire in the Lake, a best-selling book written by Frances FitzGerald. Newsweek, however, also commented that, "Frankie Fitzgerald, a tall..31-year-old blonde, may appear to be an unlikely personality to unravel the complexities of the war in Vietnam." Women asked why she is an unlikely personality: because she is a woman, or because she is young and beautiful?

Sexist advertisements are even more common. Advertisements for a major airline have whispered: "Fly Kathy... I'm Kathy. And I'm going to fly you like you've never been flown before." Other advertisements proclaimed: "Candy For Her-Cigars For Him."

Television programs have perpetuated the unfavorable stereotypes of women. One study found that most of the women who appear in the television programs broadcast for family audiences are married and seldom work outside their homes.

Women who do work are subservient to men, and wives are subservient to their husbands. Some have been shown asking, begging, or tricking their husbands into giving them money and then being forced to tell their husbands how they spent it. The study found that, with only a few exceptions, women shown on the television programs looked alike: tall, thin, attractive, and nicely dressed. The men on some comedy shows appeared to be stupid and bungling, but overall, the programs showed men more favorably than women. Men occupied roles of prestige and leadership; they were capable, strong, intelligent, and held prestigious jobs as engineers and business executives. Women were subservient, dependent, and less rational; unmarried women spent much of their time trying to attract a man.

Not all the criticism directed at the media are deserved. The media are more likely to mention men than women in news storied because other institutions have failed t place women in positions of authority-positions likely to create news. In other instances, the media were simply reflecting societal norms, which also viewed women primarily as wives and mothers. The worst abuses have already been corrected. Pay differentials between men and women are being eliminated. In response to a suit filed by its employees, Newsweek magazine agreed to give women more jobs as writers and more opportunities for promotions. Newsday, a paper on Long island, has begun to hire and promote more women and has revised its stylebook to prevent sexism and racism in news stories. The Boston Globe reexamined its policies following charges that it discriminated against women in its news stories and advertisements. Women employed by the Globe complained about the newspaper's ridicule of the women's liberation movement, the use of women in photographs for sex interest, the use of the word "girl" in place of "woman," bizarre references to women's underwear, and advertisements that clearly exploited women as sex objects. A sympathetic article published in the newspaper responded: "It is often difficult for males to see what all the fuss is about, but it comes down to one simple things; women want to be treated as individuals, not with some special peculiar reference to sex or appearance... All they're asking for is respect, one human being to another. It is not an unreasonable request."

The popular culture debate

Another issue-the media's impact upon cultural standards-involves a philosophical debate that is more likely to arise in the nation's classrooms than in its news-rooms. Some scholars fear that the mass media are lowering the nation's cultural standards. Because there is little conclusive evidence to support or refute their charges, the issue may never be resolved to everyone's satisfaction. It is primarily an elitist debate but involves an issue of considerable significant: the media's impact upon our minds.

The scholars believe that industrialized nations such as the United States have several different types or levels of culture. The best, "elite culture," is distinguished by its seriousness, traditions, and contributions from earlier generations. Elite culture is created by skilled artists and rarely appears in the mass media. It includes great works of art, literature, music, philosophy, and scientific theory. Lower levels, often called "brutal" or "mass culture," are often physical rather than intellectual. They have little intellectual content and include most games and spectacles, such as football, boxing, and racing. The scholars complain that, like chewing gum, mass culture is manufactured for a profit by technicians and merchants. The public remains passive because mass culture does not require its active participation. Its critics insist that mass culture can never be good because it sinks to the level of the most ignorant members of society; it excludes no one, regardless of how crude their tastes might be. The following paragraphs summarize their arguments.

Properly used, the media could elevate cultural standards to unparalleled heights. The commission on Freedom of the Press believed that, "These agencies can facilitate though and discussion. They can stifle it. They can advance the progress of civilization or they can thwart it. Despite the media's potential, they are being used to entertain rather than to educate and uplift. They transmit mass culture to everyone, including the elite, and corrupt their tastes.

Most of the programs on television-soap operas, comedies, quiz shows, and detective stories-are boring and superficial. They encourage escapism and erode self discipline. Television programs also suggest that viewers can achieve success through passive absorption. "By the time a child graduates from high school, he will have spent 15,000 hours in classrooms, but 18,000 hours in front of a television set. "If the average person continues to watch television at the present rate, that person will devote nine years of his life to the tube by the time he is 65 years old. If television and all the other mass media were not available, people would devote more time to the improvement of their minds.

The media occasionally transmit high culture to the masses, but they cheapen it. The media condense, simplify, rewrite, and popularize. They mix the good and bad until the public no longer can tell them apart. Instead of raising the level of mass culture, the media corrupt high culture.

Mass culture also poses a variety of other danger. It political systems by creating a passive audience that can easily be manipulated. The media, particularly television, tranquilize rather than arouse. They deaden people's senses and stifle creativity. Audiences become uncritical because they cannot respond; they learn to accept whatever is offered. The media "drug us beyond any hope of redemption."

Other scholars reject the notion that mass culture is harmful. They believe that the media play only a minor role in the determination of culture standards, and that the nation's cultural standards are rising rather than declining. The following arguments summarize their views.

Cultural levels are determined primarily by families, schools, churches, and communities-not the media. There is a particularly strong correlation between educational and cultural levels; persons who have attended college are most likely to enjoy cultural pursuits. Critics also exaggerate the media's flaws and minimize their contributions. Much of their content is mediocre, but when the media do something good, their programs have a tremendous impact; they reach an audience of millions. "A single performance of Hamlet on a national network reaches more people than all the performances in theaters from Shakespeare's day to our own."

Americans are becoming more active and spend more time and money on leisure activities than ever before. There is no evidence to support the charges that mass media make people passive. New sports such as water skiing and scuba diving have emerged, and old sports such as tennis are attracting millions of new participants. At the same time, cultural institutions have been multiplying at an unprecedented rate. There are more than 1,200 symphony orchestras and 1,500 local theater groups in the United States. Attendance at museums, concerts, operas, and libraries also has been increasing, and Americans buy millions of paperback books every year. Some paperbacks have little value, but others have made the world's finest literature available to the masses at a price they can afford.

The media's critics have distorted history. Their arguments imply that mass culture has replaced something good. Yet mass culture is better for the masses than anything they had before. They have never preferred elite culture and rarely had access to it. They never spent their spare time reading pieces of literature, visiting art galleries, or attending theaters. In the past, the masses were mistreated, poor, and illiterate.

There is no way to resolve the debate conclusively. Too much rests upon assumptions rather than verifiable fact. It is too difficult to compare the cultural standards that prevail today with the standards in Western Europe hundreds of years ago. Much of the criticism has arisen because intellectuals misunderstand the media. persons with first-rate minds have always considered the mass media superficial, inadequate, and sensations. Because intellectuals constitute a small minority and because the types of programs they want would not interest many other persons, the media can never satisfy the intellectuals' demands. Intellectuals who prefer programs that possess more cultural merit must learn to look elsewhere for them. The truly mass media, particularly television, are not an appropriate vehicle for them.

Conflicts of interest

Because conflicts of interest endanger the media's credibility, the media are reexamining and banning practices that used to be common. Rules are in a state of transition, and practices that are accepted by some media are cause for firing at others.

Journalists agree that they should not accept money from the persons they write about, but many accept other kinds of gifts, often called "freebies." Reviewers receive free theater tickets and books. Free trips, called "junkets", are common. Fashion writers receive trips to New York, and sports writers receive trips to games in other cities. The athletic teams they cover also may pay for their meals, hotel rooms, and drinks. When it began to manufacture Mustangs, the Ford Motor Company offered the editors of newspapers a free airline ticket to Detroit, a night's lodging, and the loan of a new Mustang. CBS News forbids its reporters to go on junkets, but the CBS television network gives television critics lavish trips to Hollywood and New York. The critics are introduced to television starts, given rides abroad luxurious yachts, and fed gourmet meals.

Companies that sponsor the junkets expect favorable publicity, and they usually get it. Norman mark, a radio-TV critic for the Chicago Daily News, has estimated that the television networks get twice as much publicity from the junkets as from newspaper advertisement that cost an equal amount. Newspapers published more than 200 stories after a four-day junket sponsored by ABC, and a press agent estimated that a good junket would provide 600 stories about the network's fall season. Gratitude and busy schedules discourage independent or critical investigations by journalists who go on the junkets. newspeople also may fear that, if they are too critical, they will not be invited back.

The junkets' proponents respond that the main issue should be the public's right to know. They explain that smaller newspapers often cannot afford to send their own reporters to distant cities, and that junkets help the newspapers obtain stories that corrupt any journalists, since they have been trained to remain objectives. Journalists who accept the junkets and other gifts also have said that most of the gifts are insignificant, often small tokens of appreciation for their work-and that they would be less susceptible to accepting any of the gifts if they were better paid and could afford to buy the items for themselves.

Other conflicts arise because of journalists involvements in groups that they may be asked to report on. Some editors, particularly those on small newspapers, encourage their employees to become involved in community affairs; to join the Kiwanis, Lions, or Rotary Club, and to help the Cancer Society or Salvation Army. Robert E.Lind, managing editor of the Connellsville Daily Courier in Pennsylvania, even pays for his staff members' dues, meals, and other expenses. On the other hand, Terry Smiley, news editor of the North Hills News Record in Pittsburgh, has said that reporters "don't have to belong to anything to do a good job." Smiley warns that reporters who get too involved risk losing their ability to write objectively and effectively.

Colurnnist Jack Kilpatrick opposes blanket policies, since different journalists have different responsibilities. Kilpatrick explains, "I would see nothing much that is wrong and much, in fact, that is right in a publisher serving as a member of the board of directors of the local symphony orchestra, but I would see a good deal wrong in the music critic's serving on that board." However, even Kilpatrick's proposals involve some dangers. If a publishers serves on the symphony's board of directors, for example, readers may question his music critic's freedom to criticize the symphony's performances.

Conflicts of interest, however, are becoming less common. Richard Hardwood of *The Washington Post* has observed that, "It is rather generally accepted among newspaper people that financial corruption is probably sinful, that editors and reporters ought not take money or other things of value from people and organizations that are in the news. On some newspapers, the acceptance of a bribe-for that is what it is-is a firing offense. Fifty percent of the newspapers that responded to a recent survey said that now prohibit the acceptance of gifts by members of their staffs. A new code of ethics adopted by the Society of professional Journalists, Sigma Delta Chi, prohibits the acceptance of anything of value. Other rules are even more restrictive. Media executives have explained that journalists occupy a unique position, and that their obligations to readers are more important than their enjoyment of some personal rights which may have to be sacrificed.

The *Courier-journal* and the Louisville Times of Kentucky have adopted a detailed code "to protect the newspapers' integrity". The newspapers' editors believe that, "It is absolutely essential that our newspapers, which claim always to be neutral and far in their handling of news, are believed by others to be neutral, fair, and untainted by outside influence." The code forbids any professional work for any other companies or organizations in the Louisville area. Newspeople employed by the papers cannot prepare publicity material for organizations that hope to deal with the newspapers; they may not appear on radio or television stations in the area for pay; and they may not hold any public office or accept any political appointments. Work for a politician or political organization, either paid or voluntary, is forbidden.

Reporters object to some of the restrictions. When the Denver Post announced that it did not want its employees to accept any more gifts, tickets, or junkets, the employees objected, and the post agreed to let them decide for themselves whether they should accept anything of value. Journalists also objected when the Madison Capital Times adopted a code that prohibited everyone, including the publisher, from accepting free tickets and gifts. The paper warned that employees could be fired for violating the rules. The code adopted by the Capital Times did not ban outside activities, but required staff members to notify the newspaper's editors if their outside activities might conflict with their jobs. A complaint filed with the national Labor Relations Board charged that the code changed working conditions at the newspapers and that it should be required to consult the Newspaper Guild. The Guild, which represents the newspaper's employees, did not necessarily want to defend the practice of accepting freebies, but if insisted that it had a right bargain over codes of ethics which happened to involve freebies. The newspaper's executives responded that ethical matters were too important to the risked at a bargaining table and that their right to adopt the code was protected by the first Amendment. The NLRB ruled that the Capital Times could adopt the code of ethics without consulting the union. However, the NLRB added that the Capital Times would have to negotiate with the Guild in regard to the penalties for violating the code "since the suspension and discharge provisions of the Code of Ethics directly affect employment security."

Young reporters also have challenged the media's traditional standards of impartiality and noninvolvement. The reporters insist that restriction imposed upon their activities abridge freedoms guaranteed by the U.S. Constitution, including their freedom of speech. Because reporters lack access to their newspapers' editorial pages, many say the only way they can express their opinions is by signing petitions, joining demonstrations, and devoting their time to the issues they consider important. Reporters have said that some issues, such as the war in Vietnam, are so important that they have a moral duty to act-and that the duty is more important than their obligations to their employers. They deny that their activities will compromise their accuracy and fairness.

Thus, more than ever before, journalists are becoming aware of the danger that conflicts of interest pose to their integrity as professionals. The media already have begun to adopt strict codes of ethics intended to halt the acceptance of freebies and to limit reporters' involvement in stories they may be asked to cover. However, it would be unrealistic to expect all the media to act. Too many philosophical differences remain. Also, some reporters oppose the policies, which they believe infringe upon their freedoms.

Although important, the topics discussed in this chapter reflect just a few of the issues confronting the media. As journalists have become more conscious of the issues' significance, they have intensified their efforts to resolve them. Newspapers, for example, provide more space for the expression of diverse ideas, and all the media are more hesitant to pay individuals for their exclusive stories. When the stories are published, the media are more aware of the need to inform the public about the payments. The media have begun to employ more women, to pay them equal salaries, to promote them as rapidly as men, and to treat them more fairly whenever they are mentioned in news stories. Because of threats to their creditability, the media are trying to eliminate conflicts of interest, and many now ban the acceptance of favors that used to be common.

Even as these issues are resolved, however, new and seemingly more serious issues will inevitably arise. So thee will always be problems and reasons to question the media's performance. The issues can play a beneficial role, however, since they force the media to reexamine their traditions and adapt to society's changing needs.

8 Administration of Educational Media

The media program in a school includes all of the media services to the school, the administration of the collection, and uses of media, both book and nonbook materials. All are coordinated in the library media center under the direction of the librarian or media specialist. To make effective use of media, whether in a school on the elementary or secondary level, or in the university, administration must be well-planned and coordinated. To effectively use materials they must be organized and cataloged. There must be a carefully planned and balanced program of learning resources. The concept of the media center or learning resource center provides for integrated use of all media. In education, the secondary schools have led the way in this approach to learning. Many of the community colleges are moving toward the concept of integrated media use, but he four-year program is changing more slowly, and in many colleges the audio-visual department is entirely separate form the library.

Edgar Dale has said that "every classroom can have the best in instructional materials now produced" but even if the school's instructional materials are less than excellent, they must be well-organized and administered for effective use. The library is the center of the program and must lead the way to effective use of educational media. A fine, attractive learning resources center is not the only answer. Teachers must be led to, informed about, and must make use of book and nonbook resources to be found in the center. The program of the media center must be planned also to meet the varying and different needs of students.

It is the responsibility of the school librarian or media specialist to formulate the objectives of the specific media program, the sum total of all services and learning involved in the center. This must be based upon full and effective participation in the school's curriculum planning. One objective must be to stimulate and guide students and teachers in the uses of media. Another of the objectives of the media center must be to provide the opportunity for creative uses of media, to recommend and suggest to students appropriate uses of all media as they work in the center or library.

It is necessary that teachers be involved in the selection of media as well as in utilization. To effectively use media as in integral part of the classroom instruction, teachers must know what is available, have previewed the materials, and have access to the needed equipment and materials.

Most of the media program will be implemented outside the center itself, to facilitate and enrich the instruction in the classroom.

"The educational program of the school is strengthened in direct proportion to the quality of the school's library service," said the 1960 Pennsylvania Governor's Committee on Education. The statement is as valid today as it was then. Today the media specialist or librarian in a teacher in the best sense of the world. His responsibility extends far beyond organizing and maintaining a materials collection. He works directly with teachers and students to achieve educational excellence.

Media in curriculum design

There are a variety of definition of educational technology or educational media. The Random House Dictionary defines *technology* as "The application of knowledge to practical ends, as in a particular field: educational technology." The U.S. Office of Education has established a National Center for Educational Technology. In our schools and libraries we are most concerned with *media*, many resources which are used in teaching and learning. Hence the name educational media.

The Department of Audiovisual Instruction Commission on Definition and Terminology has this definition: "Educational technology is that field of educational theory and practice primarily concerned with the design and use of messages which control the learning process." The term audiovisual communication was the label formerly used.

The Presidential Commission on Instructional Technology offer the following: "*Educational technology* is a systematic way of designing, carrying out and evaluating the total process of learning and teaching in terms of specific objectives, based on research in human learning and communication, and employing a combination of human and non-human resources to bring about more effective instruction."

Whichever definition is chosen, the important aspect is that education is a systematic process within the framework of educational technology or educational media, a process with a purpose. The purpose of curriculum design is to bring about more effective learning, to solve educational problems, to design effective instruction. Curriculum development must be systematic if students are to learn to the maximum. We are a goal-oriented society. Whereas most curriculum planning has traditionally been concerned with concept, design for learning in the classroom and school to day is based upon objectives. Educational technology is concerned with curriculum design emphasizing objectives, as well as with methods, materials and evaluation. A Maugham Lee, writing in *Audiovisual Instruction*, states that "Instructional development seems to hold the greatest promise yet for a way to improve instruction and promote more efficient learning in our increasingly complex and technological society, and without compounding the very problem that we are trying to solve."

The purpose of *design* as a funtion is to

translate general educational technology theory and research, as well as subject-matter content, into specifications for learning resources. Design is not as broad a term as development; development includes production and evaluation functions as well as design.

Students enjoy mediated instruction; they do learn and their varying needs can be met through the use of many media. But media must be a part of planned instruction, and we must have clearly stated objectives.

This bibliography emphasizes the importance of design in the curriculum, and the place media has in learning in our schools. We will "manage" learning as we consider planning, controlling, organizing and uses of media. It is the teacher and his new concept of teaching and learning that will change education. It is not the machine but how and why media are used that is important.

System evaluation

Educational evaluation must be based upon definition. A precise use of terms must be arrived at before evaluation begins, or before the evaluative instrument is devised. The basic terms given here are from the *Dictionary of Education.*

Checklist: A prepared list of items that may relate to a person, procedure, institution, building, etc., used for purposes of observation and/or evaluation, and on which one may show by a check mark or other simple method the presence, absence, or frequency of occurrence of each items on the list.

Criterion: A standard, norm, or judgment selected as a basis for quantitative and qualitative comparison.

Evaluative criteria: The standards against which a person or group a procedure may be checked; the factors considered by an accrediting agency in analyzing the status of an educational institution to determine whether it shall be accredited.

Evaluative method: The procedure in a study that has evaluation as its chief purpose and that in most cases includes some definite fact finding, through observation, and that involves the careful description of aspects to be evaluated, a statement of purpose, frame of reference, and criteria for the evaluation, and the degrees or terms that are to be employed in recording judgements.

Inventory: In the field of evaluation, a test or checklist used to determine the subject's or examinee's ability, achievement, aptitude, interest, or likes, generally in a limited area.

Rating scale: A device used in evaluating products, attitudes, or other characteristics of instructors or learners.

School survey: A study or evaluation of a school, a school system, or any part thereof; may be fact finding, or may indicate the strong and weak features as judged by definite criteria; commonly concluded with suggestions for needed changes and/or recommendations for more desirable practices.

Standard: A goal or objective or criterion of

education expressed either numerically as a statistical average or philosophically as an ideal of excellence; any criterion by which things are judged.

Librarians and teachers work together when selecting resources to support the program of the school. A librarian must be knowledgeable of the educational program of a school This is a time-consuming task but important as one aims to provide educational media for the total school program. He must consult with the administration as well as with individual teachers; he must analyze course content and know textbooks well, and must analyze course content and activities to be included in each unit plan. He must know his students, their needs, interests, goals, abilities and concerns. He must match materials with needs; offer services designed to make those materials effective teaching resources in the school.

Evaluation involves definition, decision-making, values and criteria, administrative levels and the research model.

Learning theory

The items listed in this chapter deal basically with education and learning as related to educational technology. There are references which discuss the major theories of learning in the twentieth century. Emphasis is upon books which attempt to answer the question of what is known about the process of learning which can be used to design better education in our schools and for individual students. A good background reading before progressing to other books in the bibliography is Robert M.W. Travers' *Essentials of Learning: An Overview for Students of Education.* An excellent book of background readings which analyze selected factors underlying the process of individualized learning is R.A. Weisgerber's *Perspectives in Individualized Learning.*

An excellent film-which shows the work of Howard Kendler of New York University, Tracy Kendler of Barnard College, Kenneth Spence of the State University of Iowa, Harry Harlow of the University of Wisconsin and B.F. Skinner of Harvard-is *Learning about learning.* The film is available form State University Film Service, 1400 Washington Avenue, albany, New York 12203. It shows the different strategies employed by these men in developing new theoretical concepts about man's ability to learn, and demonstrates the effect of their theories and work upon methods of instruction in schools and colleges.

Instruction and learning encompass many processes, many that are not included in learning theories specifically. Instruction involves such considerations as stimulating recall, guiding the learning, gaining and controlling attention, aiding remembering, providing feedback and assessing outcomes. Ultimately, it is the learner who performs such functions. Carefully designed combinations of media best serve the teacher and the school to achieve the kind of learning that is most effective.

Robert Glaser, in a number of reports issued through the Learning Research and Development Center, University of Pittsburgh, stressed the concept of learning as education for individuals. The University of Pittsburgh Learning Research and Development Center is an important source for up-to-date information on individualized instruction and learning.

In this bibliography, basic background readings on learning are included to provide students of education with an overview of current knowledge. Emphasis is upon research taking place in the field of learning, and the implications of that research for educational planning. The need for further research, as it affects knowledge in learning theory, is emphasized.

9 Improving the Media

If the media are to improve, they will have to improve themselves. No one else can do it for them. The public can help by being an alert, discriminating audience and by expressing its views. But audiences dissatisfied with the media's performance rarely have been able to force them to change It takes a major issue to arouse the public and, when an issue does arise, the public is likely to be divided. It also is difficult to organize a diverse group of newspaper readers or television viewers and to find an effective means of influencing the media's policies. A few citizens' groups have been effective, particularly in their most recent efforts to reduce the amount of violence shown on television, but they appear to be a rare exception.

One of the more effective efforts was led by the National Citizens Committee for Broadcasting. After conducting a 13-week study of prime-time violence, the NCCB reported that NBC was America's most violent network, followed by ABC, then CBS. More importantly, the NCCB listed the 10 advertisers that sponsored the most violent programs on television. The leading sponsors of violence included Chevrolet, Whitehall Labs American Motors, Sears, and Kodak. Stung by the unfavourable publicity, the advertisers immediately began moving their commercials other programs, and the three networks announced plans to reduce the amount of violence in their programs.

Like the public, the government also is unable to do much to improve the media. Its ability to act is limited by the First Amendment. Government officials cannot censor the media or force them to publish any specific stories. The government's primary responsibility is almost entirely negative-to refrain from interfering with the media's content. The temptation to act may be enormous. Private citizens who feel helpless to change the media by themselves may turn to the government for help, and government officials may sympathize with their demands. They must, however, resist the temptation to act. Freedom has always involved some risks, since it is inefficient and may be abused. But freedom is an essential part of our democratic heritage and should be cherished rather then be subject to any additional limitations.

Acting on their own, many of the media already have adopted a variety of policies to improve their performance. Other media, which are more satisfied with the status quo, have done nothing. Some of the differences, however, have arisen because of philosophical conflicts. The remedies adopted by one journalist may seem inadequate or dangerous to another. The media also differ in their capabilities. Some have more resources-larger budgets, more manpower, and more space than others and consequently can afford to be more innovative.

Remedies adopted by the media

Correction of errors

Journalists have begun by improving their systems for the correction of errors. In the past, news media often ignored their own errors unless the victims were influential members of their communities or threatened to file a successful lawsuit. Corrections were small and scattered throughout the inside pages of newspapers. Largely because of a growing dissatisfaction with their performance, newspapers have begun to publish more corrections, often in the same places where they published the original error. Other newspapers now publish all their corrections in a regular column that appears in the same place every day. But because the correction of a single fact rarely is as newsworthy as the original story, corrections continue to be brief. Most are only one or two paragraphs long and consequently are not as noticeable as the original error. When newspapers publish the corrections, they usually title them: "Corrections," "Setting the Record Straight," or "We Beg Your Pardon." An exception, the Boca Raton News, labels its corrections, "Dumb Things We Did."

Some newspapers also mail accuracy forms to the persons mentioned in their news stories. Each accuracy from usually includes a copy of the story and asks whether the facts in the story and its headline are accurate, whether the story is fair, and whether it contains all the necessary information. Other papers publish the accuracy forms in their news columns so that every reader, not just the persons mentioned in news stories, can evaluate their adequacy. The accuracy forms are not very popular because they require a considerable amount of work and often fail to provide much useful information. Editors who have stopped using the forms have explained that they received few significant complaints. The accuracy forms may be used primarily because of their public relations value; they help convince readers that journalists are committed to accuracy and are willing to correct their mistakes. Or, editors may use the forms only a few weeks each year.

Action lines

Actions lines, established primarily by newspapers and television stations, are rather common. Anyone with a question or problem can call the action lines, and their reporter will try to solve the dilemma. They publish or broadcast the most interesting stories, usually in a question-and-answer format. The first action lines appeared more than 30 years ago and were intended to help citizens who encountered a problem while dealing with the government. Today, the action lines devote more attention to consumer problems. Like politicians, merchants are sensitive to adverse publicity and more likely to respond to the media's inquiries than to complaints from private individuals. Many of the calls received by action lines are from customers dissatisfied with merchandise they purchased by mail. When they move out of an apartment, renters often complain that their damage deposits were not refunded. Consumers also complain about defective merchandise and inadequate warranties.

Action lines refuse to handle some types of problems, particularly medical, legal, and tax cases. On smaller papers, the actin lines may be written by a single reporter. A larger paper, the Plain Daler in Cleveland, has assigned one editor, four reporters, and a secretary to its "PDQuickline." The Chicago Tribune sends a van, called the "Action Express," wherever problems arise.

The action lines help establish rapport between the media and the public, ideally, the public will learn it can turn to the media for help, and the media will become better acquainted with their audiences' problems. If the media receive several complaints about a single problem, they may investigate it more thoroughly and prepare a lengthy story about it.

Advisory boards

Newspapers as well as radio and television stations have asked citizens in their communities to serve on advisory boards that meet a regular intervals to comment on their performance. Some advisory boards also consider complaints received by the media. The boards may be composed of prominent citizens or a cross section of the communities' residents: men, women, Youths, union, members, merchants, whites, blacks, and so fourth. Typically, the Milwaukee Journal invites a dozen persons to community relations dinners once a month to discuss the newspaper's performance. Some media, however, have discontinued the practice because few citizens are well acquainted with the media and able to suggest any practical way to improve their performance. Also, it is difficult to select a group that accurately represents everyone in a community.

Ombudsmen

Perhaps two dozen newspapers in the United States have appointed ombudsmen, usually experienced editors, to investigate complaints about their performance. Until the ombudsmen were appointed, persons dissatisfied with a newspaper's performance might call a newspaper and complain, but they often would be referred to the reporter or editor responsible for the error. The journalists might be reluctant to admit that they made a mistake, or they might consider the mistake unimportant.

Ombudsmen serve as impartial arbitrators. They now receive and investigate the complaints and are empowered to publish any corrections that they consider necessary. In many cases, the ombudsmen also read the comment on their newspapers' performance even before receiving any complaints. On larger newspapers, it is full time job.

The Courier-Journal and Louisville Times appointed the nation's first ombudsman in 1967. Readers in Louisville, Kentucky, are encouraged to call the ombudsman at any time, day or night, and he receives almost 3,000 calls a year. Most callers want to voice a complaints, but some offer suggestions, and a few praise the papers. The Washington Post appointed its first ombudsman in 1970. One of the Post's editors explained. "We were being robbed or our one essential asset, without which no reporter or newscaster can operate, which is public confidence, or, to use the more fashionable word, `credibility." The ombudsman at the post receives complaints, personally monitors the performance of the newspaper, prepares critiques of its staff, and writers a regular column that is published on the editorial page. The column, titled "The News Business," Sometimes criticizes the Post and other news media, but it also discusses current issues of interest to the public. The Los Angeles Times publishes the articles written by its press critic, David Shaw, at the top of the front page. Saw has criticized the newspaper's reporters and editors. Despite his criticisms of other journalists, Shaw says that he has never had a story significantly changed or killed by the Times. Other ombudsmen have been appointed by newspapers in Omaha; Minneapolis; Salt Lake City; Milwaukee; Greenville, Mississippi; and Grand Rapids, Michigan, for example.

One survey that involved 134 daily newspapers, primarily those that have circulation of 100,000 or more, found that only eight employed a genuine ombudsman. The survey included at least one newspaper from every state. Most editors said they had not yet considered the idea, that other persons on their staffs already performed the tasks normally assigned to ombudsmen, or that they did not have enough money or employees to appoint one. Few , if any, ombudsmen have been named by the broadcast media.

Investigative reporting

Increasingly, the media are trying to free experienced reporter from routine stories so they can investigate significant issues that require more time and expertise. Investigative reporting involves virtually all the media, from radio to books. The best example involves Carl Benstein and Bob Wood ward, whose stories in *The Washington Post* contributed to the resignation of President Nixon and to the conviction of nearly 20 of his top aides. Before it ceased publication, Life magazine investigated organized crime and political corruption in the United States, and one of its stories caused Abe Fortas to resign from the U.S. Supreme Court. Similarly, television documentaries have discussed the Pentagon's use of publicity, the plight of migrant workers, and hunger in America.

Investigative reporting, called "muckraking" during earlier periods in the country's history, seems to arise at regular intervals. It is uncommon during periods of general contentment and propriety, such as the 1920s and 1950s, but reemerges during periods of turmoil. When new problems arose during the 1960s, Americans began to question the nation's social, political, and economic systems, and the media joined in their reexamination of the nation's major institutions. The growing popularity of television, which threatened to capture the other media's audiences and advertisers, also encouraged the revival of investigative reporting. Newspapers no longer were first with the news, and picture magazines such as Look and Life could not present visual images as effectively as television. The older media had to reevaluate their roles, and several began to engage in investigative reporting, which they can do more effectively than television. Television stations are handicapped because they have less time and smaller staffs. Also, they must comply with the Fairness Doctrine and, because they are licensed by the federal government, can be more easily intimidated.

Investigative stories often require months of tedious work but can have a dramatic effect. A group of small weeklies, the Sun Newspapers in Omaha, Nebraska, revealed that Father Flanagan's Boy Home, better known as "Boys Town," has become rich by requesting contributions that tit no longer seems to need. Boys Town, which is located near Onaha, was founded in 1917. The newspapers' editors which is located near Omaha, was founded in 1917. The newspapers' editors noticed that Boys Town has stopped its physical expansion in 1948 but continued to solicit money twice every year. Even though Boys Town claimed that it "receives no funds from any church, state, or federal government," the editors learned that Boys Town was receiving some money from both the state and federal governments. The discovery encouraged the editors to question the town's other claims. Members of the staff at Boys Town complained about the institution's conservative attitudes, tight budget, and low salaries. State educational records revealed that Boys Town, which had been designed that 50 million letters had been mailed from a post office at Boys town in a single year. The editors calculated that it cost no more than $5 million to operate the institution for one year, yet experts estimated that the town's fund drives raised at least $15 million. Public records from the Internal Revenue Service in Washington eventually revealed that the town's annual income actually totaled $25.9 million, and that its net worth has risen to at least $191 million. As a result of a 3.500 word expose published by the newspapers, Boys Town canceled its fund raising activities and announced taut it would use some of the money it has accumulated to establish an institute for the treatment of speech and hearing defects in children and a national center for the study of child development. The Sun Newspapers received a Pulitzer Prize foi their work.

Consumer reporting, and offshoot of investigative reporting, exposes business practices the exploit the public. One of the most active newspapers in the field, the ST. Peterburg Times, regularly compares the prices at area stores. It also evaluated the claims made by advertisers and found that several failed to keep their promises. Other stories in the Times have discussed unsanitary conditions in supermarkets, investigated conditions in local nursing homes, exposed the sale of swampland by real estate swindlers, and complained about the high price of Cokes at a local sports stadium.

Investigative and consumer reporting appear to be growing in popularity, yet both practices have aroused some opposition. Critics say that investigative reporting already has been carried to an extreme-that reporters have become irrationally suspicious of everything they are told, rely too heavily upon anonymous sources, and are more concerned with winning prizes that exposing social evils.

Before he retired as president and general manager of the Associated Press, Wes Gallagher complained: "Too many readers are beginning to look upon the press as a multi-voiced shrew, nitpicking through the debris of government decisions for scandals but not solutions." Stephen Hartgen, a reporter and educator, has added that investigative reporting focuses too exclusively on abuses. "The result is to give the reader and viewer a narrow, simplistic view of what is wrong with American institutions, and what actions are needed to correct the faults." Hartgen adds that investigative reporters focus on the abuses that are easiest to expose, and that not of their stories are "one-shot affairs." He explains that investigative reporters expose problems, then move on to new issues. They generally fail to follow up on their stories and, as a result, their stories fail to result in substantive changes.

Other factors-particularly cost-also discourage investigative reporting. Stories are expensive, likely to offend some readers and advertisers, and involve the risk of ruinous libel suits. Even if the media can win the libel suits field against them, their legal costs may be prohibitive.

The media's more conscientious editors can avoid many of the problems, caused by investigative reporting. They may be able to hire talented investigative reporters or give their regular staff members some additional training. Editors also can instruct their reporters to pursue more meaningful topics, and they can conduct follow-up investigations to determine whether the problems they exposed have been corrected. Larger papers are better able to withstand the threat of libel suits, but any paper can take some elementary precautions that will at least reduce the risks that it will be sued for libel. The risks can never be totally eliminated, however.

Attempts at self-regulation

The rise of self-criticism

The Commission of Freedom of the Press believed that more self-criticism would help improve the media, but it found that most journalists ignore one another's errors. Rober Maynard, who has served as an ombudsman for *The Washington Post,* agrees that, "We have virtually no internal quality control; we scrutinize others with vigor, as well we should, yet we do little exposing of our own weaknesses and failures."

Self-criticism seems to have become slightly more common during the 1970s. Journalists dissatisfied with the media's performance have established about two dozen "journalism reviews" to evaluate their content and policies. Journalists in Chicago established the first journalism review in 1968 because they were unhappy believed that Mayor Richard Daley tried to minimize the problem of police brutality during the riots that accompanied the convention, and that the men who controlled the city's media supported Daley. The journalists were infuriated because many of them had been singled out and attacked by the police. A federal commission found that at least 49 journalists were "hit, maced, or arrested, apparently without reason by the police." Forty of the journalists were clearly identified; they wore helmets marked "press" and had tied badges around their necks. The equipment used by 10 of the journalists was deliberately smashed.

The journalists established the *Chicago Journalism Review* to fight "news management, news manipulation and assaults on the integrity of the working press." The new publication began to criticize the media's content and policies. Following its example, other journalism reviews soon were established in Denver, Philadelphia, St. Louis, Providence, and Honolulu, for example.

Most of the journalism reviews are small and are concerned with all the media in a specific geographical area: not just newspapers, but also radio and television stations, magazines, and movies. One of the best, MorE, is published in New York City but seeks a national audience. The pretentious idea, a review of Arizona journalism, reported that salaries paid by news media in the state ranged from a low of $66 at one radio station to a high of $250 at another. The *Twin Cities journalism Review* criticized the practice of interviewing persons whose relatives have died "before the blood barely congeals." In St. Louis, a journalism review complained that the half-hour newscasts broadcast by television stations contain no more than 13 minutes of news.

A few schools of journalism also have criticized the media. The School of journalism at Columbia University has published the *Columbia Journalism Review* since 1961. It is a well-documented, highly professional magazine, and it publishes articles written by some of the nation's most prominent journalists. The University of Wisconsin at Milwaukee has produced a series of television programs that evaluated the performance of newspapers and radio ad television stating in the area. Topics ranged from criticism of the media's election coverage to discussions about violence in children's programs. Most schools, however, are hesitant to become involved in criticism. It is often expensive, time-consuming, and likely to offend the local media. Also, many schools simply do not consider it one of their more important priorities.

Criticism also appears in countless books and in a variety of periodicals, primarily those published for journalists, such as *The Quill* and *Nieman Reports.* Few of the truly mass media vigorously criticize one another. An exception, the Wall Street Journal, often described other periodicals and discusses problems that confront the media. Its best articles have been compiled in a book titled *The Press.* Informed criticism also appears in magazines such as The Nation, Harpers' and the Atlantic.

Codes of ethics

The media have adopted a dozen or more codes of ethics, but few of the codes have had much impact upon their performance. All the codes in effect today are voluntary; none can be enforced. Most were adopted to protect the media from criticism rather than to improve their performance. Whenever they have come under attack, the media have adopted new codes to appease their critics. The codes are discussed in college classrooms and at a few of the annual conventions held by journalists but rarely are posted or even mentioned in the media's newsrooms.

Newspaper Codes. The American Society of Newspaper Editors adopted its first code, The Canons of Journalism, on April 23, 1923. For years, the Canons were the only code adopted voluntarily, without any public pressure. They declared that newspapers should act responsibly and should be truthful, sincere, impartial, decent, and fair. The Canons of journalism did not prohibit anything; rather, they told newspaper editors what they should do. They reflect the belief that people are rational, intelligent beings-that they should be given raw facts as fairly as possible and should be allowed to reach their own conclusions about those facts. However, the Canons' provisions were vague, and even the most sincere journalists might reach different conclusions about their meaning and the types of stories that should be reported.

The ASNE repeatedly rejected attempts to enforce the Canons of Journalism. In one case, Frederick Bonfils, co-publisher of The Denver Post, learned about the Teapot Dome scandal during President Harding's administration but accepted a bribe of at least $250,000 to suppress stories about it. When the ASNE learned about the bribe, it considered expelling Bonfils but soon abandoned the idea. Instead, the ASNE decided to encourage editors to voluntarily comply with the Canons of journalism. Its members were divided over the issue, and they feared that any attempt to enforce the Canons and to expel Bonfils would split the society. In 1929, the society considered a new proposal to strengthen the Canons of Journalism, but it too was defeated.

Movie Codes. Codes adopted by the movie, broadcast, and comic book industries are based upon newer and more pessimistic theories about humans. All of their codes reflect the belief that human are weak, irrational, and in need of protection. They forbid the dissemination of immoral or controversial material that might corrupt persons who use the media.

The Motion Picture Association of America adopted an elaborate code that was enforced and obeyed for almost 30 years. The code was intended to regulate the content of movies so they would be approved by government censors and would not antagonize pressure groups. Religious and civic groups had begun to criticize movies almost as soon as they became popular; most of the groups feared that movies would harm the public's moral values. Beginning in 1909, the State of New York adopted a law forbidding children under 16 from attending a movie unless they were accompanied by an adult. Other cities and states established boards of censorship, and movies had to be approved by the boards before they could be shown in some areas.

To appease its critics, the movie industry adopted its first code in 1930. The code, however, established minimum standards of acceptability, not responsibility. It told producers what to avoid, such as sex, profanity, and brutality, so their movies would be approved by the censors. A few years later a Catholic group known as the National Legion of Decency forced the movie industry to begin enforcing the code. New provisions specified that companies which subscribed to the code could be fined up to $25,000 for serious violations.

Despite the movie industry's attempts at self-regulation, Catholics threatened to boycott movies that they considered indecent, and the National Legion of Decency began to rate movies and to publish its findings. The ratings ranged from "acceptable for all audiences" to "condemned for all viewers." Producers fearful of offending the group avoided controversial topics. So for years, the National Legion of Decency influenced the content of movies produced in the Unites States.

The movie industry's code of ethics was obeyed, at least temporarily, because of a highly unusual set of circumstances. Producers and distributors cold be fined of violating the code, and they were afraid that controversial movies might not be approved by government censors. Also, most theaters were controlled by holly wood's major producers and distributors, and they refused to show movies that violated the code. The industry's self-censorship, though, may have caused more harm than good, Many persons feel that it encouraged producers to create a world of fantasy that offended no one. During the 1930s, Hollywood produced hundreds of westerns, comedies, musicals, and love stories. It produced little serious drama.

Movie producers began to ignore the code during the 1950s, and flagrant violations became common during the 1960s. In 1952, the U.S. Supreme Court ruled that movies are protected by the freedom of speech guarantees of the First Amendment, and its decision prohibited further government censorship, except in cases of outright pornography. Because of the need for more realistic guidelines, the old code was abandoned, and movies released in the United States since November 1, 1968, have been reviewed and assigned one of four ratings: G, suitable for general audiences; PG, all ages admitted, parental guidance suggested; R, restricted to persons over 17, unless accompanied by a parent or adult guardian; and X, no one under 17 admitted. The 17-year age limit was suggested; individual communities might raise it to 18. Movies not submitted for review are given an automatic X. The new code, which has undergone some slight modifications, is designed to prevent very young children from attending movies intended for adults. Parents can consult the ratings to help decide whether a particular movie is suitable for their children. The new code does not place any restrictions upon adults.

The code's enforcement varies from one theater to another; enforcement is least strict at drive-in theaters. But several other problems have also arisen. Parents have objected because they have been unable to take their own children to X-rated movies which they believe possess some artistic merit. In an attempt to appeal to the public's prurient interests, some theaters emphasize the fact that all the movies they show have X ratings. Also, the new code is concerned primarily with sex, not violence. Violent movies such as laws are generally rated PG.

The new system's success depends upon the cooperation of parents and children, but studies have found that few persons seem to consider the ratings before they attend a movie. Sixty-five percent of the parents and 70 percent of the high school students interviews for one survey said they had heard about the movie code and knew its purpose. However, only 39 of the 110 parents who were contacted could name a movie that their teenagers has seen recently, and only 19 knew the movie's rating.

Broadcast codes: The National Association of Broadcasters has adopted separate codes for the radio and television industries. Each code forbids profanity, obscenity, vulgarity, and sexual material. The NAB adopted the television code in 1952, but not every television station subscribes to it, and stations that do not cannot be forced to follow its guidelines. The NAB awards a Seal of Approval to stations that obey the code, and the stations often flash the seal on the screen when they come on the air in the morning and again when they go off the air at night. The only penalty for violating the code is the loss of the Seal of Approval. Because the NAB depends upon its members for revenue and moral strength, it has not been zealous in its attempts to enforce the codes. Radio and television stations may be regulated more effectively by advertisers, who are hesitant to sponsor programs that might offend the public.

The comic book code: The comic book industry adopted a more successful code in 1954. The public had begun to mount a vigorous campaign against unnecessary violence, horror, sex, torture, and sadism, and congressional investigators blamed comics for increases in the rate of juvenile delinquency. Unlike newspapers, the comic book industry was afraid of government regulation, since the Fist Amendment did not clearly protect its publications. Ninety percent of the companies that publish comics now belong to the comics Magazine Association and adhere to its code. Each publisher submits his material for review; excessive amounts of obscenity, nudity, horror, and violence are prohibited. Comics also are expected to respect law and order, marriage, the home, and religion; good must always triumph over evil. The comics magazine Association, however, is powerless to deal with publishers who do not voluntarily subscribe to its code.

The journalists' code: The Society of Professional journalists, Sigma Delta Chi, voluntarily adopted a new code of ethics at its national convention in 1973. The code declares that journalists must seek the truth and have a responsibility to "perform with intelligence, objectivity, accuracy, and fairness." They should accept "nothing of value," because gifts and special favours might compromise their integrity. The code also recommends that might cause a conflict of interest. It concludes: "Journalists should actively censure and try to prevent violations of these standards, and they should encourage their observance by all newspeople. Adherence to this code of ethics is intended to preserve the bond of mutual trust and respect between American journalists and the American people."

A journalist critical of the society's code complained that, "There is an inherent weakness in written codes of ethics. They imply that any act which is not obviously in violation of the code must be ethical." The journalist added that persons, since they may act out of fear of punishment rather than consideration for other people "Ultimately," he concluded, "the individual journalist will act ethically to the extent that he himself if an ethical, thinking person."

Despite their problems ad limitations, codes of ethics undoubtedly are better than nothing at all. The codes at least force journalists to think about and to publicly acknowledge their responsibilities and to formulate guidelines for the attainment of their goals.

The establishment of press councils

Press councils in Great Britain

Although many journalists refuse to cooperate with them, press councils are being established to help improve the media's performance. Most of the organizations in the United States are modeled after the British Press Council, which has become the most famous and perhaps not successful in the world. In 1946, the British government appointed a commission to investigate the country's press. Government officials were disturbed a commission to investigate the country's press. government officials were disturbed by charges that the media were biased and by the growth of newspaper chains and monopolies. The British commission, which issued its report in 1949, recommended that journalists establish a press council. Journalists opposed the idea and failed to act until the House of Commons threatened to establish a government council. To avoid the government agency, journalists finally established the British Press Council, but they ignored several of the commission's recommendations, including the suggestion that the press council should represent both the press and the public. British journalists named 25 persons to serve on the press council,

---

Code of ethics

The Society of Professional journalists, Sigma Delta Chi, believes the duty of journalists is to serve the truth.

We believe the agencies of mass communication are carriers of public discussion and information, acting on their Constitutional mandate and freedom to learn and report the facts.

We believe in public enlightenment as the forerunner of justice, and in our Constitutional role to seek the truth as part of the public's right to know the truth.

We believe those responsibilities carry obligations that require journalists to perform with intelligence, objectivity, accuracy, and fairness.

To these ends, we declare acceptance of the standards of practice here set forth:

- *Responsibility*: The public's right to know of events of public importance and interest is the over riding mission of the mass media. The purpose of distributing news and enlightened opinion is to serve the general welfare. Journalists who use their professional status as representatives of the public for selfish or other unworthy motives violate a high trust.

- *Freedom of the press*: Freedom of the press is to be guarded as an inalienable right of people in a free society. It carries with it the freedom and the responsibility to discuss, question, and challenge actions and utterances of our government and of our public and private institution. Journalists uphold the right to speak unpopular opinions and the privilege to agree with the majority.

- *Ethics:* Journalists must be free of obligation to any interest other than the public's right to know the truth.

1. Gifts, favors, free travel, special treatment or privileges can compromise the integrity of journalists and their employers. Nothing of value should be accepted.

2. Secondary employment, political involvement, holding public office, and service in community organizations should be avoided if compromises the integrity of journalists and their employers. Journalists and their employers should conduct their personal lives in a manner which protects hem from conflict of interest, real or apparent. Their responsibilities to the public are paramount. That is the nature of their profession.

3. So-called news communications, from private

sources should not be published or broadcast without substantiation of their claims to news value.

4. Journalists will seek news that serves the public interest, despite the obstacles. They will make constant efforts to assure that the public's business is conducted in public and that public records are open to public inspection.
5. Journalists acknowledge the newsman's ethic of protecting confidential sources of information.

- *Accuracy and objectivity*: Good faith the public is the foundation of all worthy journalism.

1. Truth is our ultimate goal.
2. Objectivity in reporting the news is another goal, which serves as the mark of an experienced professional. It is a standard of performance toward which we strive. We honor those who achieve it.
3. There is no excuse for inaccuracies or lack of thoroughness.
4. Newspaper headlines should be fully warranted by the contents of the articles they accompany. Photographs and telecasts should give and accurate picture of an event and not highlight a minor incident out of context.
5. Sound practice makes clear distinction between news reports and expressions of opinion. News reports should be free of opinion or bias and represent all sides of an issue.

6. Partisanship in editorial comment which knowingly departs from the truth violates the spirit of American journalism.

7. Journalists recognize their responsibility for offering informed analysis, comment, and editorial opinion on public events and issues. They accept the obligation to present such material by individuals whose competence, experience, and judgement quality them for it.

8. Special articles or presentations devoted to advocacy or the writer's own conclusions and interpretations should be labeled as such.

- *Fair play*: journalists at all times will show respect for the dignity, privacy, rights, and well-being of people encountered in the course of gathering and presenting the news.

1. The news media should not communicate unofficial charges affecting reputation or moral character without giving the accused a chance to reply.

2. The news media must guard against invading a persons right to privacy.

3. The media should not pander to morbid curiosity about details of vice and crime.

4. It is the duty of news media to make prompt and complete correction of their errors.

5. Journalists should be accountable to the public for their reports ad the public should be encouraged to voice its grievances against the media. Open dialogue with our readers, viewers, and listeners should be fostered.

- *Pledge*: Journalists should actively censure and try to prevent violations of these standards, and they should encourage their observance by all newspeople. Adherence to this code of ethics is intended to preserve the bond of mutual trust and respect between American journalists and American people.

---

and all 25 were associated with the media, including the council's chairman. The press council floundered for 10 years, then was reorganized. In 1963, five private citizens were added to it, including a lay chairperson, and the changes increased its effectiveness.

The British Press Council uses the principle of common law, which its members believe is more flexible that a written code. When the council hears a case, it rules on the basis of tradition and its past decisions. Its past decisions also provide guidelines that editors can consider whenever a problem arises. The British Press Council does not have any legal power. It cannot suppress a newspaper or fine its editor. It cannot force witnesses to testify, punish them for perjury, or subpoena any records. Its only weapon is publicity. Newspapers in Britain have voluntarily agreed to publish the council's decisions, including decisions critical of their own performance. The British Press decisions, including decisions, critical of their own performance. The British Press Council, however, is concerned only with newspapers. It does not consider the performance of radio or television stations.

About 75 percent of the press council's decisions have favored the press. When the council does rule against an editor, the editor cannot appeal the decision; cases end with the council's decision. Because of their promise to do so, editors are morally obligated to publish the decision in their newspapers. The council has heard more than 2.000 cases, and only five newspapers have refused to publish the results.

Despite their initial opposition, recent surveys have found that 86 percent of Britain's newspaper editors now like the press council. Journalists have found that the council protects as well as criticizes the press. In addition to investigating the public's complaints, the press council guards against legislation that might interfere with newspapers' freedom. Moreover, it is free of government controls and cannot threaten newspapers' freedom or economic stability.

The Press council has ruled that a newspaper had the right to publish a poem which called God an "utterly incomprehensible idiot." It also declared that a reporter had a right to pose as a patient while writing about quack doctors, and it explained that investigative reporting serves the public interest. In other cases, the press council: (1) Warned two government agencies that they were violating the law by refusing to let newspaper reporters attend their meetings. (2) criticized officials who had lied to a reporter about an outbreak of infection in a hospital, and (3) warned government officials against marking documents "confidential" in order to avoid infavourable publicity.

He press council also criticized a newspaper that published the photograph of a 2-year-old girl drinking from a bottle of liquor. It censured newspapers for identifying the victim of a rape and for publishing the photograph of a reformed criminal. The council has declared that newspapers have an obligation to select a representative sample of letters that express different viewpoints, and that newspapers cannot omit key ideas, destroy their meaning, or cut out parts of a letter without the permission of its author. The press council also has tried to draw a lone between newsworthy photographs of tragedies and photographs that exploit human suffering.

Press councils in the United States

About a dozen press councils have been established in the United State, but most have served a single city or state. Many journalists have been reluctant to cooperate with them. Journalists have also resisted other attempts to monitor their performance. In 1952, for example, some evidence suggested that newspapers slated their news stories in favour of the Republican party's presidential nominee, General Dwight D. Eisenhower. The Society of Professional Journalists. Sigma Delta Chi, voted to investigate the charges, and two foundations agreed to finance a systematic study of the papers' performance. Because it would be difficult to judge the performance of newspapers in a campaign that had already ended, the researchers suggested studying the performance of newspapers during the 1956 election instead. Newspaper publishers objected to the study, and the Society of Professional Journalists was forced to abandon it.

During the late 1960s, the Mellett Fund, a private foundation, financed the establishment of experimental press councils in six cities in the Midwest and on the West Coast. Researchers who helped organize the press councils found no evidence that they threatened the freedom of the press. Journalists in the six communities were apprehensive when the councils were established but soon began to consider them a valuable asset. The press councils made journalists more conscious of their responsibilities and served as a valuable public relations tool. They gave private citizens and opportunity to express their complaints, and they gave private citizens and opportunity to express their complaints, and they gave the journalists an opportunity to explain their policies. Newspapers in the six communities changed only slightly after the press councils were established. Their biggest problem was the apathy of other journalists and the public.

In 1971, the Minnesota Newspaper Association established a press council to serve the entire State of Minnesota. The council has 18 members; half represent the news media and half represent the public. The Minnesota council is modeled after the British Press council. It has no legal power; its only weapon is publicity, and its effectiveness depends upon the cooperation of newspapers in the state.

The National News council, which now serves the entire country, bean work on August 1, 1973, but even today, few Americans seem to be aware of its existence. The Twentieth Century Fund, a foundation in New York, helped found the National News Council because it was concerned with the growing concentration of news organizations in the United States and their apparent unresponsiveness to public pressure and criticism. During the first there years of its existence, the news council acted on 72 complaints. It upheld the media in 41 cases and found them at fault in nine. The remaining cases were dismissed or solved during the investigative process.

William Arthur, the council's executive director, believes that," the biggest problem encountered has been public unawareness of the council's existence." During its first years, the council did not handle any cases of major significance, and many journalists refused to cooperate with it. Arthur Ochs Sulzberger, publisher of *The New York Times,* has explained: "As see it, we are being asked to accept what we regard as a form of voluntary regulation in the name of enhancing press freedom. We respect the good intention of the fund, but we believe the operation of such a council would not only fail to achieve its purposes but could actually harm the cause of press freedom in the United States." Similarly, the New York Daily News commented: "We don't care how much the fund prates about its virtuous intentions. This is a sneak attempt at press regulation, a bid for a role as unofficial news censor." John S. Knight, editorial chairman of the Knight Newspapers, has added that, "Editors are accountable to their readers, not to a group of self-appointed busybodies with time on their hands...any self-respecting editor who subscribes to meddling by the National News Council is simply eroding his own freedoms".

Journalists also fear that the press councils may penalize the most courageous media in the United States, since their stories about controversial issues are most likely to provide complaints. Critics have insisted that there is little need for a press council in the United States because most journalists are doing a good job and regularly correct their errors. Because the media are already under attack, journalists are also hesitant to support another organization that will add to the criticism.

A committee that evaluated the National News Council after its first two years of work concluded that the council "provides a public sounding board for criticism of individual newspaper stories or television or radio broadcasts which vary from the truth either by deliberate slating or form want of fair procedures." The committee added that the council can held deflate unfair criticism by careful investigation and documented findings of fault or exoneration. It called the council's first year "a sound if not spectacular beginning." Noting that the council had been handicapped by the opposition of important media and by the fact that toto few persons were aware of its purposes, procedures, and findings. The committee estimated that it will take a minimum of 10 years before anyone will be able to make a sound evaluation of the council's permanent usefulness.

Education and professionalism

Perhaps the best way to assure the improvement of the media is through education and increased professionalism. In the past many journalists do not attend college. Instead, they went directly to work for a small-town newspaper, radio station, or television station. After several years, and if they showed exceptional ability, they moved to larger media outlets, usually located on one of the major cities. Today the majority of young reporters have a college degree. A re recent study found that 86 percent of the reporters now employed by newspapers have attended college; 58 percent have an undergraduate degree; and 8 percent completed graduate school and received at least a master's degree.

Although it is now generally agreed that journalists should have a college education, the type of education needed for journalism is still controversial. Most editors look for reporters with a degree in journalism. Some editors, however, prefer apprentice reporters who have majored in history, law, sociology, or political science, for example. These editors believe that capable individuals can be taught all the journalistic skills they will need in a few months of on-the-job training, and that their journalistic skills they will need in a few months of on-the-job training, and that their college majors will provide them with some expertise in a needed area. On-the—job training, however, involves some risks. First, of course, it is costly for the newspaper or television station, since it usually takes several months at best before a trainee is productive. Second, a trainee may find after several months on the job that he or she does not enjoy the work or is not talented enough to succeed and thus will leave before the employer can get a return on his or her investment. In addition to providing knowledge, colleges also provide a screening process for the industry. Journalism students can discover whether or not they are suited to the field while still in school and can move to another field to endeavor without any loss to the industry.

All most schools, journalism students are encouraged to obtain a broad liberal arts education. To be accredited by the American Council on Education for Journalism, programs must offer students a mix of about 25 percent journalism courses and 75 percent liberal arts courses. A former president of the Association for Education in Journalism has explained it this way: "This concept rests on the idea that future newsmen need to know not only how to write and edit but enough to ask intelligent questions and to understand most of the answers." Some schools also encourage students to minor in another area, such as political science; others do not. Students have also been encouraged to work for their college newspapers or radio and television stations. At many schools, special internship programs offer students an opportunity to spend a full quarter working for the media on a full-time basis and to receive credit toward their degrees.

Linked to education is the concept of professionalism, which may also improve the media by raising journalistic standards. Most experienced journalists already believe they are "pros" because they are though-minded objective reporters who do not allow their personal opinions to influence their work. Within the limitations of this notion of professionalism they may be right, but generally a profession requires much more.

Sociologists, who have devoted considerable attention to the question of professionalism, have observed that most professions involve skills that require lengthy training. On-the-job training or vocational schooling is inadequate. A professional person requires formal education, usually at a professional school in university. His or her skills are based upon a systematic body of theory which must be mastered before the skills themselves can be developed. Professions, sociologists say, also develop distinctive values and norms that guide the behaviour of their members, and usually require that public service be placed head of personal gain. Generally professional organizations are empowered to discipline their members when they violate these norms of behaviour.

Although most journalists have begun or receive a formal education in their field, they are strongly opposed to the idea of empowering an organization to enforce a set of professional norms.

In journalism, attempts to require every practitioner to accept a particular set of values and perform in a specified manner would have a chilling effect upon their freedom of expression and would curtail their enjoyment of freedoms guaranteed by the First Amendment. Even more serious conflicts would arise if a professional organization attempted to screen and license applicants and denied some entry to the profession-in essence, denied them the right to write and speak for the media. As a consequence, journalists question the sociologists' criteria for professionalism; too many of the criteria are inappropriate for their work.

Journalists are aware of the media's flaws, and many are striving to improve their performance. Few media are likely to try all the remedies discussed in this chapter. Yet change is always slow, and the pioneers in a new field are always few in number. Moreover, the reluctance of journalists to adopt some of the innovations is understandable. Many genuinely question the need for certain innovations. Some fear their cost. Other are philosophically opposed to remedies such as the National News council, which they view as a threat to their autonomy.

Differences in the media's efforts can be viewed as both strength and a weakness. Not all the media will improve as rapidly as the public might like, and some may not improve at all. But the differences also mean that the media will retain their diversity; their content and policies will never be identical.

10 Freedom of Access to Broadcasting

What is the purpose of broadcasting? What functions do radio and television perform for individuals and for society? Only with a clear understanding of the part these media play in present-day life can we appraise their success of failure or take appropriate action with regard to them.

The services broadcasting performs for individuals or groups depends upon their own interests or purposes. If you consider radio and television from the standpoint of a listener or viewer, broadcasting may provide you with (a) entertainment, (b) information and education, and (c) advertising. If you approach broadcasting as an entrepreneur or businessman, it may serve two functions, (a) to bring a return on an investment, to earn a profit, and (b) to render a service to the public. Finally, if you approach broadcasting from the standpoint of the role it plays in the political order, you are apt to consider its primary function, in terms of its relationship to the dominating philosophy of government, i.e., as authoritarian, libertarian, communist, or socially responsible.

Importance of broadcasting in contemporary society

Certainly, as a responsible citizen, you cannot ignore the values of broadcasting. It plays a larger part in the lives of Americans than the other mass media. About 97 per cent of American homes are equipped with radio receiving sets, and a majority of homes have more than one. Furthermore, about two-thirds of American automobiles are radio-equipped. As for television, a similar situation is fast approaching. In so-called "saturated" areas in which television service has been provided for four or more years, the percentage of homes with television receiving sets is already in the 80's. And with lifting of the "freeze" on the construction of new television stations, we may expect similar coverage in the remainder of the country in the next five years or so.

As a result of ready access to broadcasting, Americans spend more time exposed to radio and television than they spend in any other voluntary activity. What this does to them and what they can do about it will be considered in later chapters. Every responsible citizen should understand the functions of broadcasting and appreciate its influence in present-day society. Anyone with educational responsibilities should be especially alert to the potentialities of broadcasting for the enrichment of learning experiences.

Indeed, broadcasting plays an important role

in most nations and in an important instrument in international policy. In other which prevails in the United States. In Russia and other Communist controlled countries, it is a vital arm of the state. In the underdeveloped countries of the Middle East, Asia, and Latin America, it is beginning to be used deliberately to inform and instruct the masses of people in the rudiments of health, sanitation, agriculture, home skills, and citizenship.

As an agency for crossing international frontiers, whether this be considered "psychological warfare" or a "campaign of truth," radio has no equal. The United States, with its official "Voice of America" and its private "Radio Free Europe" and "Radio Free Asia," wages only a small part of the war of words. The Soviet Union spends several times as much money and effort on its foreign broadcast propaganda as does the United States. The British, too, have pioneered in international short-wave and have continued to broadcast on a large scale during the cold war. Even the small nations recognize the importance of voicing their particular views and versions of world events, so that the ether is crowded with competing propagandas.

How broadcasting serves the listener-viewer

The most common motive for turning on the receiving set is to be entertained. Life in the United States is tense and fast-moving, and relaxation is essential. Because of the accessibility of radio and television, they have become a primary means of release the relief. Moreover, when a set is owned, broadcasting is the cheapest form of diversion. Reading, sports attendance, movie-and neighbors require an immediate outlay of cash. But the receiving set has only to be turned on, and a wide selection of entertainment is at once available.

Most Americans seek entertainment at times because they are lonely. The United States is becoming increasingly a land of urban people, and one notable characteristic of city life is loneliness. Entertainment provided by radio and television provides a sense of companionship and an escape form solitude. Studies of social maladjusted boys and girls indicate that these youth devote large amounts of time to listening and viewing in a conscious use of these media to "forget my troubles" and to find companionship in the broadcasting activity.

American broadcasting provides a wider range of entertainment than any of the other mass media. It is the common man's theater, his music hall, his vaudeville house, his circus tent, and his medicine show. He can view football, baseball, and basketball, as well as wrestling and boxing. He can travel around the world without moving from his easy chair. And all of this with a minimum of effort on his own part. While he cannot literally have anything he wants when he wants it, he can find a surprising range of offerings available to him because of the competition among four national networks in both radio and television, supplemented by offerings from near-by independent stations.

But this is by no means the whole story. The informative or educational role of broadcasting is both effective and important even though the listener or viewer is interested primarily in entertainment. He depends upon radio or television to keep him up to date on the news. He listens to or views the national political conventions, the presidential inaugurations, the United Nations in sessions, the proceedings of investigational committees, and the workings of his local traffic court. He garners his political opinions from his favorite commentators and listens to a sampling of campaign oratory. He depends upon broadcasting for weather forecasts and market reports. The farmer receives guidance on when to plant and spray and how to overcome a variety of crop pests. The housewife gets tips on everything from home decoration and child care to the serving of leftovers. Important audiences follow forums and debates on political and social issues, take "tele-courses" in a variety of academic fields, listen to talks on myriad subjects, learn the workings of community organizations and institutions, and pick up new angles and tips on the pursuit of hobbies and leisure-time activities.

A third function performed by broadcasting is to provide the consumer with information about goods and services and with incentives to desire them. Radio and television have become prime means of selling the stream of products pouring forth from American farms and factories. It is doubtful if the listener-viewer often turns consciously to his receiving set for advertising.

Indeed, he is frequently annoyed by its length, its blatancy, and its continual intrusion. Nevertheless, it profoundly affects him. He frequently buys the products that he sees and hears about, and his desires for new goods and services are whetted by the appeals that are made to him.

Advertising has a unique relationship to the medium of broadcasting. In the United States it is the principal means of financial support for commercial radio and television stations, and well over 95 per cent of American stations are commercial. Moreover, this has a profound influence upon the nature of programs to be found on radio and television stations as will be shown in chapter ix. Sponsors and the advertising agencies are not only responsible for the sales massages but usually determine the content of the sponsored programs themselves. Seldom do stations or networks try to enlist they confine themselves to selling time and facilities for program reduced, typically, to making a selection meets his requirements. Since sponsored network programs are made available on a larger number of stations, the programs with the largest following and the largest influence are those furnished by sponsors rather than by the broadcasters themselves. In no other medium does the advertiser exert such a direct influence.

The function of broadcasting for the entrepreneur

From the standpoint of the owner and operator of a broadcast station in the United States, except in the case of noncommercial stations, broadcasting is a business. A radio or television station represents a sizeable investment and is expected to bring a fair return. If the station is owned by a corporation, the management has a financial responsibility to the stockholders to see that the total operation is a profitable one. In this respect, operation of a broadcast station is no different than publishing a newspaper or managing a motion-picture theater.

But whether he likes it or not, the manager of a radio or television station must perform another function. He is licensed to operate on a frequency or channel belonging to the United States, and the condition of his license is that he must operate in the "public convenience, interest, or necessity." Unlike any other medium, the number of broadcast stations is limited by the nature of the medium, and the licensee is a privileged person who has been selected on the basis of evidence that he will serve the public better than the other applicants. He pays nothing for his license and is entitled to exploit it commercially as he sees fit so long as he serves the public adequately thereby.

Thus, the broadcaster has to serve two masters-profit ad public service. Much of the time he can serve the two concurrently, but sometimes he must make a choice of one or the other. And the choices he makes affect the nature of the programs offered to the public. If he has a high sense of public responsibility, the station may become not only a source of entertainment but also an important agency of the community, reflecting its problems and resources and providing a means of public enlightenment. If, on the contrary, he is motivated more largely by the desire for quick and easy profits, the station may become only a purveyor of mass entertainment, directed always to the lowest common denominator of taste.

The Federal Communications Commission, the independent agency set up by Congress to issue licenses and regulate broadcasting, his a primary responsibility for seeing that broadcasters perform in the public interest. But since the Commission's staff cannot keep track of more than three thousand radio and television stations, in addition to many other primary responsibilities, the existing machinery has been severely taxes. As a result, the Commission's influence has largely been exerted through a body of rules and interpretations which have developed through the years as guides to broadcasting practice.

This brings us to the role broadcasting plays in American democracy. And, because broadcasting is a product of the twentieth century, it had to find itself within a society which has already developed concepts of "freedom from government interference," "freedom of the press", and other manifestations of libertarian theory which did not always fit the new medium as it grew in size and complexity. To appreciate broadcasting's present role in our democracy, it is important to view its function as an evolving one, growing out of a body of trial and error, influenced by the currents and eddies of changing opinion, and still far from being completely defined. Furthermore, the citizen, alert to the problems involved, can, in concert with other active citizens, be influential in shaping this role. For broadcasting, by its very nature, requires orderly regulation, and the nature of this regulation is determined by the congress and the creature of the Congress, the Federal Communications Commission. Both are subject to the mandate of the people either directly or through public opinion.

The development of broadcasting in the united states

Radio, as initially developed by physicists and engineer, was conceived as a means of point-to-point communication, not as "broadcasting." Its uses previous to 1920 were for ship-to-shore contact, for military communication in World War I, and as a means of conveying messages to specific receivers. What little regulation the law provided was administered by the Secretary of Commerce who was empowered to issue licenses to all applicants who qualified. This served mainly to keep track of the wave-length and power of each station and to assure their operation only by American citizens as a protection of national security against foreign intrigue. Few foresaw the development of radio as a medium of mass communication.

Early "broadcasts" were more or less accidental. A lonely engineer played phonograph records to a friend at another station and was overheard by amateur eavesdroppers who had constructed their own receivers. Similar incidents occurred as the interest of the people in this amazing new invention stimulated the buying of radio parts and the building of simple crystal sets. Soon the radio manufacturers caught on to the new development and began sending out broadcasts of records, news read from the newspaper, and similar impromptu programs, as a means for stimulating the sale of parts and, later, entire receiving sets. And so, almost spontaneously, a mass medium was born.

As the number of receivers increased, the number of transmitting stations also increased. Business of all kinds from department stores to insurance companies acquired broadcasting licenses as did churches, labour unions, farm organizations, and schools and colleges. While the sale of time had not yet become a means of support, radio was recognized as a medium of great influence which could be utilized advantageously by its owner. Public opinion on this matter in the early 1920's is indicated by the following statement:

The emphasis throughout this early period was on the use of radio by commercial companies solely to create public good will. This policy was emphatically approved by the then Secretary of Commerce, Herbert Hoover, who said in 1922, "It is inconceivable that we should allow so great possibility for service, for news, for entertainment, for education, and for vital commercial purposes to be drowned in advertising charter. The First Annual Radio Conference held that year recommended "that direct advertising in radio broadcast service be absolutely prohibited and that indirect advertising be limited to the announcements of the call letters of the station and of the name of the concern responsible for the matter broadcasted.

Under the prevailing interpretation of libertarian theory, a medium of mass communication-in order to participate in a search for truth-must be kept free from government control. Likewise as broadcasting began to develop into a profitable business with the support of advertising, it seemed proper, too, to protect it from government interference. Radio as a mass medium seemed destined to follow the pattern of the press" private initiative and competition, unregulated by government. Robinson has noted the joint efforts of government and the radio industry to achieve this objective:

The Secretary of Commerce and Labor, under the broad power granted to him, attempted to keep abreast of the rapid development which took place in the art of radio broadcasting. He held radio conferences; he assigned frequencies to stations; he refused to grant licenses to those whom he did not consider qualified; and he specified the time during which an individual broadcasting station could operate. It was however, an era characterized by self-regulation. The leading executives and engineers attended the annual conference in Washington, made suggestion for the rapidly expanding business, which in turn were usually adopted by the

Secretary in the form of regulations. This regulatory period prior to the Radio Act of 1927 was marked by a rapprochement between the government and the radio industry. To a large extend the Federal authorities maintained a hands-off attitude and the principle of laissez faire predominated.

But this period of self regulation for broadcasters became an increasing headache for broadcasters and listeners alike. The practice of laissez faire, which had operated so well with the press, did not take into account the peculiar nature of the broadcast medium. The spectrum upon which radio operated was a limited one, and, as the number of stations increased, three became fewer desirable frequencies and increasing problems of interference. Stations, which in the early 1920's were of low power, began to increase their power so as to overcome interference from rival stations, only to have their competitors do the same. Finally, to make the situation even more difficult, the regulation that did two Federal court decisions and an opinion by the Attorney General in 1926, which held that the Secretary could not refuse licenses nor specify frequencies or times of operation. The result was a scramble for frequencies and much confusion.

Freedom from government regulation in broadcasting had thus developed a situation from which no one gained anything. It became perfectly clear to broadcasters and listeners alike that government regulation was imperative if the medium was to function with any degree of effectiveness. The libertarian theory, interpreted as freedom from government interference, had proved itself unworkable when applied to broadcasting. It needed to be reinterpreted of it was to be applied to radio.

The Radio Act of 1927 established the basic pattern of regulation under the Interstate Commerce Clause of the constitution. When this was later challenged, Judge Wilkerson ruled as follows:

> It does not seem to be open to question that radio transmission and reception among the stations are interstate. To be sure, it is a new species of commerce. Nothing visible and tangible is transported. There is not even a wire over which "ideas, wishes, orders, and intelligence" are carried. A device in one state produces energy which reaches every part, however small, of the space affected by its power. Other devices in that space response to the energy thus transmitted. The joint action of the transmitter owned by one person and the receiver owned by another is essential to the result. But that result is the transmission of intelligence, ideas, and entertainment. It is intercourse, and that intercourse is commerce.

The basic problem before Congress was the kind of broadcasting system that should be created. Should it be government owned, a pattern being adopted in some foreign nations? Should it be completely a private system with the government confined to policing the wave-lengths? Or should it be a system in which private stations become trustees of the public domain, with responsibilities as well as privileges? These were the basic questions faced by the Sixty-seventh Congress.

The role of broadcasting as prescribed by congress

The Radio Act of 1927 and the subsequent Communications Act of 1934 were strongly influenced by existing libertarian theory. Although complete laissez faire had been proven unworkable, radio was regarded as a new medium for conveying information and points of view to be tested in "the market place of ideas." Hence, it was not to be government owned and operated. In addition, the private operators were to be free from government censorship. Sec. 326 of the Communications Act not only makes this clear but at the same time recognizes the minimum limitations upon freedom in terms of customary morality:

> Nothing in this Act shall be understood or construed to give the Commission the power of censorship over the radio communications or signals transmitted by any radio station, and no regulation or condition shall be promulgated or fixed by the Commission which shall interfere with the right of free speech by means of radio communication. No person, within the jurisdiction of the United States shall

> utter any obscene, indecent, or profane language by means of radio communication.

Thus far radio was to follow in the pattern of the press-private operation, no government censorship, no limitation by a government agency of the right of free speech. But more basic questions remained. Who should own the air, the medium over which the broadcasting takes place? If the ownership lies in the government, then what responsibilities should be laid upon those entrusted with the privilege of using their public domain? How could the concept of the market place of ideas be maintained when the number of possible stations is limited by physical properties inherent in the nature of the medium?

Both the Radio Act and the later Communications Act state unequivocally that all broadcasting channels belong to the government. Sec. 301 of the latter Act states:

> It is the purpose of this Act, among other things, to maintain the control of the United States over all the channels of interstate and foreign radio transmission; and to provide for the use of such channels, but not the ownership thereof, by persons for limited periods of time, under licenses granted by Federal authority, and no such license shall be construed to create any right, beyond the terms, conditions, and periods of the license.

From the two basic premises that the number of stations is limited and that a license is a privilege to use a channel belonging to the United States, Congress went on to state the general principle that a station is licensed to serve "the public convenience, interest, or necessity." And the debate leading to the enactment of the law indicates clearly that this public takes precedence over any private interests. For example, Congressman White stated:

> We have reached the definite conclusion that the right of all our people to enjoy this means of communication can be preserved only by the repudiation of the idea underlying the 1912 law that anyone who will, may transmit an by the assertion in its stead of the doctrine that the right of the public to be served is superior to the right of any individual to use the ether the recent radio conference met this issue squarely. It recognized that in the present state of scientific development there must be a limitation upon the number of broadcasting stations, and it recommended that licenses should be issued only to those stations whose operation would render a benefit to the public are necessary in the public interest, or would contribute to the development of the art. This principle was approved by every witness before you committee. We have written it into the bill. If enacted into law, the broadcasting

privilege will not be a right of selfishness.
It will rest upon an assurance of public
interest to the served.

While Congress placed upon each station licensee the responsibility for operation in the public convenience, interest, or necessity, it defined the implications of this order for the handling of broadcasts by candidates for public office. The lawmakers recognized that radio was becoming a powerful medium for affecting public opinion and that it might well be influential in determining the results of electrons. They provided, therefore, in the now-famous Sec. 315, for equal opportunity in the use of a broadcast station is not require to make its facilities available to any candidate, but if it does offer opportunity to any candidate, it must afford equal opportunity to all other candidates for the same office. To further safeguard the freedom of speech of candidates, they added that "such licensee shall have no power of censorship over the material broadcast under the provisions of the section.

So much for the basic law governing broadcasting. Stations are granted licenses to serve the public interest by broadcasting on channels belonging to the United States. This public interest overrides private and personal interests. The government regulatory body is precluded from censorship, and all candidate of public office must be treated equally.

Its role ad developed by the FCC

But the actual establishment in practice of the

modified libertarian theory has been a gradual development through the years. Through rule-making procedures and through the adjudication of disputes, the Federal Communications Commission has built up a body of rules and principles that govern all broadcast stations. As an independent regulatory body, it legislates within the limitations imposed upon it by Congress and the Constitution. It also acts as a judicial body in choosing among competing applicants for licenses or in deciding disputes involving alleged violations of the law or regulations. It also as an administrative body and must, on its own initiative, seek out the facts and hail the parties before it. Its actions are subject to review by the courts.

Running through this body of rules and principles will be found a continuous concern with freedom of expression. As a former chairman of the commission, Wayne Coy, stated:

> This goal of the widest possible freedom of speech on the air, including the principle of the utmost fairness, is based on the mandate of Congress as expressed in the communications Act that licenses must operates in the public interest.

This concern with freedom of the air stems, of course, from the First Amendment to the Constitution of the United States and the eighteenth-century philosophy out of which it grew. But broadcasting is a recent development and was certainly not envisioned by the founding fathers. Only by interpretation can the First Amendment be applied to broadcasting. So far as speech and the press are concerned, this amendment reads: "Congress shall make no law abridging the freedom of speech, or of the press..."

Here the founding fathers were clearly trying to safeguard the individual's right to say what he pleased, but it would be naive, indeed, after the experience of the 1920's to interpret this to mean that Congress, or its creature, the commission, cannot prevent anyone from owning a broadcast station. As the Supreme court put it, when the National Broadcasting Company challenged the authority of the Commission to issue the network regulations:

> We come, finally, to an appeal to the First Amendment. The Regulations, even if valid in all other respects, must fail because they abridge, say the appellants, their right of free speech. If that be so, it would follow that every person whose application for a license to operate a station is denied by the commission is thereby denied his constitutional right of free speech. Freedom of utterance is abridged to many who wish to use the limited facilities of radio. Unlike other modes of expressions, radio inherently is not available to all. That is its unique characteristic, and that is why, unlike other modes of expression it is subject to governmental regulation.

Neither can freedom of speech be construed to mean that every one has the right to speak over radio or television. There is not enough time on all the stations to give all of the nation's millions their chance to be heard. It is simply impossible to apply the freedom-of-speech principle literally to the field of broadcasting.

But the act of broadcasting has been held to be the act of publication. Perhaps, then, we should interpret this amendment in terms of freedom of the press. Indeed this point of view has been put forward vigorously by a former president of the National Association of Radio and Television Broadcasters who argued that "radio should be as free as the press." Here, again, the essential distinction between publishing and broadcasting makes the parallel inoperative. First of all, the number of possible stations is limited while the number of publishers is not. While economics may limit the number of newspapers, it is still possible for anyone who wants to publish his views to issue a handbill or tract to spread his views as best he can. But there is not parallel opportunity in broadcasting. There is a limited number of broadcasters and each has the responsibility to determine who shall and who shall not be heard.

In the second place, broadcasting is a privilege. It involves using channels belonging to the United States and is extended only to those who pledge themselves to operate in the public convenience, interest, or necessity. No such requirement is binding upon publishers. Therefore, while publishers can print what they like and say what they please through their pages, broadcasters have their personal freedom of expression limited at the point at which this violates the public interests.

How, then, can the First Amendment be interpreted to apply to broadcasting?

Here the basic libertarian theory has become the guide. Democracy is an effective system because the judgements of the many are superior to the decisions of the few. But the functioning of democracy is dependent upon an enlightened citizenry. Such enlightenment takes place only when there is a free flow of ideas and opinion unimpeded by interference either by government or vested interest. Furthermore, the nation's security is assured only when the citizen has access to all conflicting points of view, for, in the market place of ideas, the good will ultimately be chosen.

It is the principle of "unimpeded access" that has been applied to broadcasting. Freedom of speech has become the right of the listener or viewer to have access to all significant ideas and opinions. Broadcasters are to ensure this access through the application of fairness. Only thus will the public interest be served.

Let us examine some of the steps that have been taken in developing this principle of fairness.

In one of the early cases of refusal by the Commission to renew a broadcast license, the precedent was established that station could not be used for personal attack upon religious, civic, and governmental groups. The station was licensed to the Trinity Methodist Church, South in Los Angeles, but was actually owned by its minister, the Reverend Robert Shulter. Complaints had been registered with the commission, at the time of hearing on the renewal of license, to the effect that Mr. Shuler had on numerous occasions attacked the Catholic Church, the Jews, labour unions, and certain city bureaus. Mr. Shuyler's defense was not an offer to prove the truth of these attacks but merely a statement that "these were his sentiments." The station was deleted by the Commission, and this action as upheld in the courts as neither censorship on the part of government nor a denial of free speech.

In another case in which a license renewal was refused, the Commission held that it was not in the public interest to permit a station to operate for the personal advantage of the owner, Dr. John Richard Brinkley. Dr. Brindley had aroused the ire of the medical association by making diagnoses over the air, often prescribing one or more of his own patent medicines. It was held that such practices were against the interest of the public health. The court, on appeal, upheld the Commission. This case indicated that the Commission considered the public interest violated when stations were used in pursuance of private interests without regard to the welfare of the total community.

The Commission went much further in defining the rules of fairness in the Mayflower case. For more than a year a Boston station, before the Commission for license renewal, had broadcast editorials urging the election of various candidates for public office or supporting one side or another of controversial questions. Section 315 was not an issue since it was not the broadcasting of candidates themselves which was questioned but rather so-called editorials supporting a particular candidate or viewpoint. The resulting decision became binding upon all stations.

Under the American system of broadcasting, it is clear that responsibility for the conduct of a broadcast station must rest initially with the broadcaster. It is equally clear that with the limitations in frequencies inherent in the nature of radio, the public interest can never be served by a dedication of any broadcast facility to the support of his own partisan ends. Radio ca serve as an instrument of democracy only when devoted to the communication of information and the exchange of ideas fairly and objectively presented. A truly free radio cannot be used to advocate the causes of the licensee. It cannot be used to support the candidacies of his friends. It cannot be devoted to the support of principle she happens to regard most favorably. In brief, the broadcaster cannot be an advocate.

Freedom of speech on the radio must be broad enough to provide full and equal opportunity for the presentation to the public of all sides of public issues. Indeed, as one licensed to operate in a public domain, the licensee has assumed the obligation of presenting all sides of important public questions, fairly, objectively, and without bias. THe public interest-not the private-is paramount. These requirements are inherent in the conception of public interest set up by the Communications Act as the criterion of regulation.

This decision by the Federal Communications Commission stood without challenge in the courts until it was modified on june 1, 1949, after a hearing held on the commission's own initiative on the issue of "editorializing."

Protection against monopoly

As the libertarian theory developed, it was, of course, affected by current issues and trends. As industrialization increased in the United States and combines and trusts appeared, these accumulations of economic power appeared to threaten man's freedoms in way similar to the threats by autocratic government in the past. Trust-busting became popular and monopoly was considered dangerous per se. Broadcasting came into being at the time of greatest sensitivity to "bigness" and "monopoly." It was only to be expected, therefore, that the Communications Act would contain provisions to prevent monopoly. Sec. 311, for example, directs the Commission to refuse a station license to any person "which has been finally adjudged guilty by a Federal court of unlawfully monopolizing or attempting unlawfully to monopolize, radio communication or to have been using unfair methods of competition.

The Commission has, likewise, been sensitive to the dangers of monopoly as this affects radio communication. In the first place, it has limited the power of radio stations. Concerned with the lack of adequate coverage of certain rural areas in the United States, the FCC at one time had granted Station WLW in Cincinnati an experimental license providing for 500 kilowatts power in contrast to other clear-channel stations which had a ceiling of 50 kilowatts. The Cincinnati station enjoyed this advantage for several years, much to the distress of other radio stations in the area. It was alleged that sponsors could buy time on the one station more cheaply than they could buy time on the one station more cheaply than they could buy time on the score or more other stations required to cover the same territory. It was also pointed out that such power constituted a concentrated control over the content of radio communications. When the Commission failed to act promptly on these complaints, the Congress itself took action in the form of a resolution expressing the judgment that power in excess of 50 kilowatts was not in the public interest. The FCC promptly revoked the experimental grant of superpower and reduced the station to 50 kilowatts.

In the late thirties the Federal Communications Commission began a study of the monopoly of radio communication as related both to networks and to local areas. This study revealed that 90 per cent of the nighttime broadcasting power was utilized by stations affliated with only two network companies, the National Broadcasting Company, which operated two networks, and the columbia Broadcasting system. Independent stations and those affiliated with the Mutual Broadcasting System were characteristically of low power and coverage, even though they represented a considerable percentage of the total number of stations then holding licenses.

The commission found that the contracts between the networks and their affiliated stations were so exclusive as to bar a station from carrying any network programs except from the affiliated network even though it had the available time and the other network was willing. Furthermore:

It found that some stations had a contractual right to keep neighboring stations from broadcasting those programs which they rejected, thus depriving listeners in that community of particular network programs. It found that the networks optioned the choice hours of most of its stations, thus handicapping the affliated stations in the development of programs to serve local community needs. The time under option vastly exceeded the time used by the networks.

The Commission thereupon issued, in May, 1941, new regulations governing chain broadcasting. The practices cited above together with other restraining practices, were banned. The National Broadcasting Company was ordered to divest itself of one of its networks. It was ordered that no one person or company could own more than one station of the same type in the same coverage area. The commission said:

> We believe that these regulations will foster and strengthen network broadcasting by opening up the field to competition... Radio broadcasting is competitive industry. The Congress has so declared it in the Communications Act of 1934 and has required the fullest measure of competition possible within physical limitations. If the industry cannot go forward on a competitive basis, if the substantial restraints upon competition which we seek to eliminate are indispensable to the industry, then we must frankly conceive that broadcasting is not properly a competitive industry...We believe, however, that competition, given a fair test, will best protect the public interest. That is the American system.

The report of the Commission was appealed to the Courts but was upheld by the Supreme Court and went into effect in 1943.

The rules of the FCC make another provision to prevent a possible monopoly of broadcasting communication. The number of stations of the same type that can be owned by a person or company is limited to no more than five television stations, six FM stations, or seven AM stations.

While monopoly, as so far considered, is economic as well as in terms of the content of communications, the commission has not been blind to the possible dangers of the latter. Is it in the public interest to permit joint ownership of both radio stations and newspapers? The Commission conducted a hearing on this question in 1941. It was revealed that of some 800 standard broadcast stations, approximately 200 were owned to the extent of 50 per cent or more by newspaper interests, and 48 others were to some extent controlled by newspapers. Even more alarming, from this point of view, was the fact that in 90 communities the sole radio station was controlled by or associated with the only newspaper.

The Commission did not adopt any general rule as a result of this hearing. Indeed, through the years, it has blown hot and cold on the subject. As a general policy, however, when the Commission is considering two competing applications, it gives preference to the nonnewspaper application, other things being equal.

Public service responsibilities defined

In the more than twenty-five years of broadcasting growth up to 1946, the obligations involved in serving the "public interest" had never been defined. The various rules and decisions of the Commission, together with the basic communications Act, made it clear that, to obtain and continue to hold a broadcast license, the station must operate in the "public interest, convenience, or necessity," and that this involved putting the public's interest ahead of the interest of the licensee, presenting controversial material so as to provide access to important points of view by listeners,using "fairness" in such presentation, and having an over-all well-balanced service. What constituted a "well-rounded program service" was particularly vague.

In 1929, the old Federal Radio Committee had declared that it should consist of "entertainment, consisting of music of both classical and lighter grades, religion, education, and instruction, important public events, discussion of public questions, weather, market reports, nd news and matters of interest to all members of the family." In 1934, the National Association of Broadcasters, in congressional hearings, declared that public service "necessarily includes broadcasting of a considerable proportion of programs devoted to education, religion, labour, agriculture, and similar activities concerned with human betterment. "And stations generally have, in practice, recognized the principle started by William S. Paley, former president of the Columbia Broadcasting System, that time should be made available to recognized public groups. He testified in 1934: "We hold our license by serving the public interest, convenience, and necessity. And only by adequate co-operation with all public spirited groups can we be deemed to perform the conditions of our contract."

Contrary to popular belief, the Federal Communications Commission has never specified a fixed amount or percentage of time to be devoted by stations to programs serving the public interest. Neither has it specified an amount or percentage of time to be devoted to sustaining programs in contrast to commercially sponsored programs. Such suggestions have been made to the Commission through the years both by members of the Congress and by other influential persons, but the Commission has taken the position that individual circumstances vary so widely from station to station that such a fixed requirement would have little meaning. Rather, the Commission has insisted that the performance in the public interest by a station can best be judged by inspecting its over-all programming.

Finally, however, on March 7, 1946, the Commission did attempt to indicate more exactly the types of public service performance by stations which would be considered as a basis for reviewing licenses. This was the famous "Blue Book," a report by the Federal Communications Commission which was titled: *Public Service Responsibility of Broadcast Licensees.*

In this bulletin the Commission stated that there were "four major issues currently involved in the application of the `public interest' standard to program-service policy; namely, (a) the carrying of sustaining programs, (b) the carrying of local, live programs, (c) the carrying of programs devoted to public discussion, and (d) the elimination of commercial advertising excesses."

While the Commission did not attempt to fix any proportion of time to b devoted to sustaining programs, it asserted that such programs have "an integral and irreplaceable part in the American system of broadcasting." Sustaining programs are those for which the station receives no remuneration. Such programs cannot be omitted from a station's offerings or even the seriously reduced in quantity if the station is to serve the public interest. This is because sustaining programs serve five important functions:

1. To secure fo the station or network a means by which, in the over. all structure of its program service, it can achieve a balanced interpretation of public needs.
2. To provide programs which by their very nature may not be sponsored with propriety.
3. To provide programs for significant minority tastes and interests.
4. To provide programs devoted to the needs and purposes of non-profit organizations.
5. To provide a field for experiment in new types of programs, secure from the restrictions that obtain with reference to programs in which the advertiser's interest in selling goods predominates.

"But," said the FCC, "while networks and stations alike have traditionally recognized the importance of the sustaining program as an integral part of the American system of broadcasting, there is evidence to suggest that such programs are disappearing from the program service of some stations, especially during the best listening hours.

From the annual reports of stations and networks to the Commission, in which program structures for January, 1945, were analyzed, certain tabulations were made by the Commission. After pointing our certain weaknesses in the data supplied by the stations, the FCC suggested that the following conclusions seemed warranted: First, the largest stations carried a considerably smaller percentage of sustaining programs than the smaller stations, and, second, the proportion of time devoted to sustaining programs during the best listening time from 6.00 to 11.00 p.m. was lower than during other hours. Even more striking was the death of network sustaining programs. Examples were cited to indicate "the failure of American broadcasters to provide nation-wide distribution for even outstanding network sustaining programs.." This situation was declared to result from two factors: "first, he failure of the networks to supply sustaining programs in quantity during the best listening hours and, second, the failure of some stations to carry even those network sustaining programs which are offered."

The second factor to be used in judging performance in the public interest was the carrying of local, live programs. Such programs are the means by which stations can provide for local interests, activities, and talent. The Commission pointed out that assurances by an applicant that he will use local talent, deal with civic matters, report local news and market reports, and cover civic and political activities have contributed to favorable decision on many applications. In the Supplemental Report on

Chain Broadcasting, the commission noted that it "has been the consistent intention of the Commission to assure that an adequate amount of time during the good listening hours shall be made available to meet the needs of the community in terms of public expression and of local interest." Furthermore, the Commission cites there examples to suggest "that local programming may also be good business policy and may contribute to the popularity of the station."

Using January, 1945, as a basis, the "Blue Book" reports all stations averaging 12.7 per cent of their time on the air devoted to local commercial programs and 7.0 per cent of their time given to local sustaining programs. here, again, during the "good hours" of 6.00 to 11.00 P.M., nonnetwork, nontranscribed programs were considerably rare.

The Commission quotes figures indicating that stations paid $3.30 for salesmen for every $1.00 paid for writers, and that the average station employed less than one-third of a full-time musician and less than one-sixth of a full-time actor. It concludes with regard to local programming:

> Such figures suggest, particularly at the local-station level, that few stations are staffed adequately to meet their responsibilities in serving the community. A positive responsibility rests upon local stations to make articulate the voice of the community. Unless time is earmarked

> for such a purpose, unless talent is positively sought and given at least some degree of expert assistance, radio stations have abdicated their local responsibilities and have become mere common carriers of program material piped in form outside the community.

The third factor, suggested in the "Blue Book" as a standard of public interest programming, was the carrying of programs devoted to public discussion. In discussing this elements, the Commission noted that there were many complex problems involved and that their solution rested, under the Communications Act, primarily upon the broadcasters themselves. "Probably no other type of problem in the entire broadcasting industry," the report asserts, "is as important, or requires of the broadcaster a greater sense of objectivity, responsibility, and fair play." The Commission is required periodically to review a station's operation, to determine whether it has operated in the public interest. The station's establishment of sound policy with respect to news, information, and the discussion of public issues is a major factor in operation in the public interest, says the report.

The quantity of time which a licensee makes available for the discussion of public issues is an important part of over-all program structure. BEcause "any vigorous presentation of a point of view will of necessity annoy or offend at least some listeners," there may be a temptation for broadcasters to avoid discussion programs. This, is

Commission stated flatly, would "thwart the effectiveness of broadcasting in a democracy." The Commission, therefore, concludes that:

> The public interest clearly requires that an adequate amount of time be made available for the discussion of public issues; and the commission, in determining whether a station has served the public interest, will take into consideration the amount of time which has been or will be devoted to the discussion of public issues.

The final factor to be used in judging station performance in the public interest was started in the report to be the "elimination of commercial advertising excesses." While recognizing the value of advertising as the only source of revenue for most american stations and the role it plays in the distribution of goods and services the Commission notes that this "does not mean that broadcasting should be run solely in the interest of the advertisers rather than that of the listeners. Throughout the history of broadcasting, a limitation on the amount and character of advertising has been one element of "public interest."

The Commission indicated that there has been a steady increase in the amount of time devoted to advertising from the beginning of the regulation, in 1927, to the date of the report, in 1946. Furthermore, a study of the actual practices of stations in Washington, D.C., indicated that the NAB standards were "as honored in the breach as in the observance." The Commission further noted certain problems "to stimulate further research." listing (a), length of individual commercials, (b) number of commercials, (c) piling up of commercials, (d) time between commercials, (e) the middle commercial, (f) the patriotic appeal, (g) propaganda in commercials, and (h) intermixture of program and advertising. This, the Commission states, is not to b e taken "as an exhaustive list of advertising excesses." Indeed, "it is not the intention of the Commission to concern itself with advertising excesses other than an excessive ratio of advertising time to program time..."

Presumably, then, this ratio of advertising time to program time is the factor is the factor the Federal Communications commission will consider in judging station performance in the public interest.

In concluding the report, *Public Service Responsibility of Broadcast Licensees,* the Commission indicated that it would implement these standards by making certain changes in application forms for new stations and for license renewals, and in annual reports and statistics, so that it can make judgements as to the observance, proposed or past, of these standards by broadcasters as the basis for licensing.

Further refinements of "fair play" in treatment of controversy

The principle of "fair play" in the treatment of controversial matters, in order to afford free access to varied points of view on the part of listeners and viewers, has undergone a number of refinements, in the last few years, through cases which have come before the Commission.

In the WHKC case, in 1945 a columbus Ohio, station had its renewal application set for a hearing because a CIO Union had protested its inability to buy time to present labour's case on he air. The station defended this practice on the ground that it gave time free for the presentation of controversial matter, and refused to sell time to any party to a dispute, except, of course, for political talks during a compaigan. In so doing, the station declared, it was following a provision of the Code of the National Association of Broadcasts which was designed to promote fairness by making it impossible for interests with greater financial resources to have a preponderant influence.

The labour group started that, on the free time provided the local of the Untied Automobile Workers, their talks were subject to stringent censorship on the part of the station. In addition, since the UAW believed that it could not make its views known through the newspapers, it was in the public interest for time to be provided for the airing of labour views, time for which the UAW was willing to pay. The UAW also attempted to show that the over-all program balance of the station favored industry and business, not only because certain commentators were biased in this direction but also because the commercial programs were sponsored by business and industry- as sort of tacit endorsement-while labour and professional groups were prohibited from buying time.

In reviewing the license at the request of both parties after Station WHKC had promised to afford unions a reasonable opportunity to be heard, the Commission asserted the general policy that licensees had the "affirmative duty" to make provision of the airing of the important viewpoints of those involved in controversy of public importance in the community. This opened the gates to the selling of time to labour organizations.

In the Scott Case, in 1946, the issue was whether a station must give time to a view point generally opposed by an overwhelming majority of listeners, when the station regularly gave time to the contrary, but generally approved, point of view. The petitioner, Robert Harold Scott, was self-professed atheist. He filed a petition with the FCC, asking for the revocation of the licenses of three California stations because they refused to give him time to discuss atheism while regularly carrying religious programs which attacked atheism.

The Commission denied the petition but issued a general opinion concerning the aiming of unpopular viewpoints.

Every idea does not rise to the dignity of "public controversy," and every organization, regardless of membership of the seriousness of purposes, is not per se entitled to time on the air. But an organization or idea may be projected into the realm of controversy by virtue of being attacked. The holders of a belief should not be denied the right to answer attacks upon them or their belief solely because they are few in number.

The fact that a licensee's duty to make time available for the presentation of opposing views on current controversial issues of public importance may not extend to all possible differences of opinion within the ambit of human contemplation cannot serve as the basis for any rigid policy that time shall be denied for the presentation of views which may have a high degree of unpopularity. The criterion of the public interest in the field of broadcasting clearly precludes a polity of making radio wholly unavailable as medium for the expression of any view which falls within the scope of the Constitutional guarantee of freedom of speech.

As was suggested previously, the Mayflower Decision, which in effect barred all editorializing on the part of broadcast stations, was revised in 1949, after an extended hearing on the Commission's own motion, to permit expression of editorial viewpoints as long as equal opportunity was afforded for reply. It has been argued that the Mayflower Decision prevented stations from engaging in activities aimed at civic betterment and that the station licensee did not have the same freedom to voice his own viewpoints that other representatives had.

In reviewing the whole matter, in this opinion, the Commission stated its philosophy of the right of the public to be informed. Because of the importance of disseminating news and ideas on vital public issues, the Commission has expected licensees to devote a reasonable percentage of their time to such programs.

And we have recognized, with respect to such programs, the paramount right of the public in a free society to be informed and to have presented to it for acceptance or rejection the different issues which are held by the various groups which make up the community. It is this right of the public to be informed, rather than any right on the part of the government, any broadcast licensee, or any individual member of the public to broadcast his own particular views on any matter, which is the foundation stone of the American system of broadcasting.

Thus the licensee must operate on a basis of over-all fairness, "making his facilities available for the expression of the contrasting views of tall the responsible elements in the community on the various issues which arise." He should avoid the assumption that he must insure fair presentation of all sides before allotting time to a controversial matter, however, because, in may instances the "primary `controversy' will be whether or not the particular problem should be discussed at all; in such circumstances, where the licensee has determined that the subject is of sufficient import to receive broadcast attention, it would obviously not be in the pubic interest for spokesmen for one of the opposing points of few to be able to exercise a veto power over the entire presentation by refusing to broadcast its position."

Fairness, in such circumstances might require not more than that the licensee make a reasonable effort to secure responsible representation of the particular position and, if it fails in this effort, to continue to make available this facilities to the spokesmen for such position in the event that, after the original programs are broadcast, they then decide to avail themselves of a right to reply to present their contrary opinion.

But the broadcasters responsibility goes even further. They have an affirmative duty generally to encourage and implement the broadcast of all sides of controversial public issues over their facilities, over and beyond their obligation to make available on demand opportunities for the expression of opposing views. It is clear that any approximation of fairness in the presentation of any controversy will be difficult if not impossible of achievement unless the licensee plays a conscious and positive role in bringing about balanced presentation of the opposing view-points.

With this as a background, the Commission concluded that the presentation of public discussion by a station "may include the identified expression of the licensee's personal viewpoint as part of the more general presentation of views or comments on the various issues, but the opportunity of licensees to present such views may not be utilized to achieve a partisan or one-sided presentation of issues." Stations are free to editorialize, but only if they give equal opportunity for opposing viewpoints.

Reservations for educational stations

The most recent development, affecting the public interest in the field of broadcasting, wa the action of Federal Communications Commission in the final television allocation report of April 14, 1952, reserving 242 out of more than 2,000 television channels throughout the United States and possessions for the exclusive use of noncommercial educational television stations. This was a recognition of the fact that the use of broadcasting for educational purposes was of prime importance in the public interest and that the AM radio situation, in which education was largely dependent upon the granting of free time by commercial broadcasters, had not worked out satisfactorily. Because educational institutions require more time to marshall their resources in order to undertake the construction ad operation of such stations. the Commission reserved channels for this use. In effect FCC recognized "the right of access" of viewers to programs of information and education which were not available in sufficient quantity or at convenient times on commercial stations and set aside channels upon which noncommercial educational stations might at a later time be built in order to ensure such programming.

Thus, in the very structure of television in this country, there is a clear recognition of the priority of education in the public welfare. It is too important in broadcasting to be delegated to such free time as commercial licensees may be able and willing to provide. Education s to be given time in which to develop plans for utilizing this most effective tool directly through stations which they own and operate.

The Commission arrived at this decision after extensive hearings in which 76 witnesses appeared, all but five of them supporting the general case of organized education. On the basis of the record, the Commission concluded:

> That there is need for noncommercial educational television stations; that because educational institutions require more time to prepare for television that commercial interests, a reservation of channels is necessary to insure that such stations come into existence; that such reservations should not be for an excessively long period and should be surveyed from time to time; and that channels in both the VHF and UHF bands should be reserved.

The Commission sees these educational stations not only as making contributions to organized education but also as supplementing commercial programming.

We conclude that the record show the desire and ability of education to make a substantial contribution to the use of television. There is much evidence in the record concerning the activities of educational organizations in AM and FM broadcasting. It is true and was to be expected that education has to utilized these media to the full extent that commercial broadcasters have, in terms of number of stations and number of hours of operation. However, it has also been shown that many of the educational institutions which are engaged in aural broadcasting are doing an outstanding job in the presentation of high-quality programming and have been getting excellent public response. And most important in this connection, it is agreed that the potential of television is much greater and more readily apparent than that of aural broadcasting, and that the interest of the educational community in the field is much greater than it was in aural broadcasting. Further, the justification for an educational station should not, in our view, turn simply an account of audience size. The public interest will clearly be served if these stations are used to contribute significantly to the educational process of the nation. The type f programs which have been broadcast by educational organizations, and those which the record indicates can and would be televised by educators, will provide a valuable complement to commercial programming.

The movement to develop, build, and operate these educational stations has been furthered not only by educators but by citizens generally. Like the struggle for free public schools a century ago, the present effort has enlisted men and women from all walks of life who see in educational television a potential or raising the level of citizenship and improving the day-to-day living of both adults and children.

The pattern of support for these stations differs widely from one community to another. In some, one educational institution-a university or a public school system-is to become the licensee with programming support from other institutions and organizations. In other communities, public and private institutions of common school an college level go together to form a nonprofit corporation to operate the station. Taxation is the financial support in some situations; foundations and private philanthropy, in others; while will other will depend upon community fund-raising campaigns and various combinations of sources.

What is to be noted, however, is that the special provision by government for educational television is establishing a new pattern of broadcasting and that citizens have become involved to a degree that is unprecedented. While commercial stations are not relieved of their educational responsibilities by the provision of educational stations, we can expect that the educational function of broadcasting will be greatly increased for the average viewer. Many minority interests and needs, not heretofore met by this mass medium will be catered to. Serious and informative programming will be available at hours when the greatest number of viewers is available. In short, education in the home through television will become a reality. Surely this, too, extends the freedom of unimpeded access to information and education which is the heart of the libertarian theory.

Broadcasting functions to bring consumers entertainment, informative and educational material, and advertising. To the businessman it offers an opportunity for profit and an obligation to serve the public interest. In our society, broadcasting has evolved rom a practically unregulated medium to a social instrumentality charged with heavy responsibilities through the privilege of governmental license. The concept of libertarian theory as meaning protection of a medium form the tyranny of government has developed into a concern for protecting listeners and viewers in their right of access to all important points of vie, with a government agency made responsible by Congress for ensuring that stations thus operate in the public interest. The rules of fairness, by which stations operate, have evolved gradually from a series of public concerns over monopoly, controversial issues, editorializing, program standards, and finally, educational stations. Certainly the end is not yet. Citizens can play an important role in determining the functions which broadcasting will serve in the future.

11 The Future of Educaitonal Broadcasting

Variety

Broadcasting is a major form of educational publishing. It provides, in Britain at least, a massive amount of educational material which by and large increases the nation's stock of educational resources, since it is funded separately from the education budget. The length of this book is in part testimony to the extremely wide range of purposes, target groups and contexts for which broadcasting has been used, both in the formal and non-formal education sectors. Furthermore, television and radio are heavily utilised in British schools.

To some extent, though, the variety of educational broadcasting merely reflects the wide variety of educational needs in the public at large. For broadcasting to succeed, it must actually meet those needs, not only by providing programmes but also by enabling real learning to take place. This requires learners' needs to be accurately identified in each of the many contexts in which educational broadcasting is used. It also required choice of appropriate programme formats to meet those learning needs, which will vary from context to context; too often, programme formats have been chosen irrespective of learning needs.

Successes

Differences within a medium are far more important than differences between media. Thus a well-designed television programme is more likely to be effective than a poorly designed book, while a poorly designed television programme will be far less effective than a well-designed lecture. Given the talent and resources that have gone into educational broadcasting, it is not surprising that there are numerous examples of extremely effective uses of broadcasting in education, in all sectors. Many children from poorer homes have learned pre-reading skills before attending school from programmes specially designed for the purpose; teachers in schools in Britain use television and radio extensively, and there is evidence of television and radio helping in the development of language skills and pupils' understanding of other races; broadcasting has been used effectively for in-service teacher training and for recruiting to personal tuition large numbers of adults with reading difficulties; television has proved to be a unique and valuable resources for multi-media distance education, and has been used as a catalyst for the reform of whole national school curricula, resulting in major improvements in academic performance; broadcasters have initiated badly-needed educational development which conventional educational agencies had hitherto ignored or neglected; most of all, broadcasting has brought education to many who otherwise would not have had it.

Weaknesses

However, on balance, broadcasting has tended to be a marginal educational activity. For it to be used successfully very demanding conditions have to be met, and meeting these has often proved to be impossible. Within the formal education sector, more recording and playback equipment, improved training of teachers and major changes in the way lessons and curricula are designed, are all necessary if television and radio are to be used as effective learning resources rather than as a weak form of enrichment. Broadcasting's real potential for meeting special needs in schools has been largely unexploited because the broadcasters are not expert in these areas and have not used their advisers to the full. In developing countries, while the introduction of direct teaching by broadcasting has led to improved educational provision, it has had little impact on their wider political, economic and social problems, which can really be resolved only by radical political, economic and social reforms. While broadcasting has helped a little then, it is no substitute for more radical action.

In non-formal education the huge educational potential of general broadcasting is chained within the prison of copyright and royalty restrictions. Furthermore the shunting of educational broadcasts to minority channels and unsocial hours limits their effectiveness. This is a particular difficulty for basic adult education which needs access to its target audience through the more popular channels. Broadcasting has generally proved ineffective educationally in non-formal education unless combined with substantial non-broadcast support services. Although i recent years thee has been an increase in truly co-operative projects between broadcasters and other agencies providing the support services, too often partnerships, where they have existed, have been unequal ones, with broadcasters setting the agenda and timing and the other agencies scrabbling in the wake.

In distance education, the role of broadcasting has never been central in terms of teaching, and in recent years difficulties with transmission arrangements, small student target groups, the ephemeral nature of broadcast material and technological development in non-broadcast audio-visual media, have all combined to promote a shift away from broadcasting to other media, even in those few distance educations which use broadcasting extensively.

The basic problem is that broadcasting is a weak instructional medium. It is difficult for students to master skills or acquire deep understanding through broadcasting alone, and difficult for teachers to integrate broadcasting with other learning activities.

Broadcasting as a profession

In judging effectiveness one must ask: 'By whose criteria?' Broadcasting as a profession has its own standards and criteria for judging success, and these criteria have been developed as a result of organisational and institutional pressures unique to broadcasting. Professionalism in broadcasting allows the potential or richness of the medium to be fully exploited, but at a price. Producers have a different approach to teachers. Educators see viewers and listeners as students for whom a broadcast is only one, relatively minor event in a much broader learning context; for a producer, the programme is the centre of attention. This is not to argue that broadcasters' criteria and approaches are better or worse, more right or more wrong, than those of teachers. However, educational broadcasters, many of whom started out as teachers, are to some extent caught between these different professional ideologies, and one will therefore find a spectrum of approaches in any educational broadcasting department. On balance, though, I believe that the technological pressures of creating broadcast programmes, the full-time commitment of educational producers to programme making, and the organisational milieu in which they work, clearly identify them as broadcasters rather than teachers.

Future trends

There are several clear trends emerging in media development, each of which will have implications for educational broadcasting.

Educators have more audio-visual media to choose from. Broadcasting is therefore facing increasing competition from other sources for teachers' and learners' time. Both broadcasters and teachers then will need to identify and fully exploit the unique teaching strengths of broadcasting if it is to continue to be used. Broadcasting can no longer be considered a comprehensive teaching medium in its own right.

Media are converging. Technological developments are bringing together print, the telephone, the computer and video, into integrated systems that combine the strengths of each medium. Such developments have major implications for professional boundaries. Broadcasting skills will not necessarily carry over to the design of computer-assisted learning programmes, not to overall instructional design. Indeed, computer programming and television production require very different approaches and ways of thinking, and tend to attract different kinds of people. Thus training and skills in one are may inhibit an individual's ability to work in another. Successful integrated teaching will require a genuine team approach, drawing on the separate skills of different professions and the expertise of the teacher. Currently, the existence of independent, professional broadcasting organisations, with their own career structure and methods of rewards separate from the educational system, is a major obstacle to a fully integrated team approach. Broadcasting is not a superior instructional medium to which others must pay obeisance. For this reason. I see independent non-broadcast, multi-media production companies who contract consultant staff willing to work together as equals, becoming increasingly more influential in education during the 1980s and early 90s. It will be a measure of their flexibility if broadcasting organisations are willing to enter into such arrangements as one amongst equals. If not, they will find they are losing audience to such independent non-broadcast companies.

Because of the rapid expansion in the range of media available to educators, there is an urgent need for practical guidelines on media selection and use. This is an old chestnut in educational technology. Many attempts have been made in the past by academic to develop theories of media selection, based primarily on pedagogic considerations. All have failed miserable to come up with a theory that can be applied in practice. The difficulty is in finding a practical set of guidelines which can at the same time take account of all the different contextual factors found in education. Also, most previous attempts have concentrated almost entirely on pedagogic factors. Although these are important, so too are factors such as cost, accessibility, convenience for both learners and teachers, and academic control. Further development of this issue is beyond the scope of this book; it is sufficient here to note that educators are now being forced to choose between a wide range of media, and this will require the unique characteristics of broadcasting to be clearly differentiated from those of other media if a rational choice is to be made.

Current developments in media allow for alternatives very different from the mass media model of education fashionable in the 1960s and 1970s, a model which led to such radical but different innovations as the Open University and the EI Salvador ETV school reform. More diverse, smaller and less centralised models are now possible. This could mean a move away from large national systems of audio-visual production and distribution for education, to more diversity of provision and more local initiatives. There will be much greater opportunities for 'do-it-yourself' production of audio-visual materials by teachers, or for buying audio-visual materials from sources other than broadcasting organisations. New media allow local schools and colleges to develop their own on-campus, and, more significantly, off-campus multi-media course at reasonable cost. With enrolments of full-time students steadily dropping in a number of countries, local, off-campus teaching using low-cost audio-visual media will become increasingly important. This development will affect not only the use of educational broadcasting but even more so large centralised distance teaching systems, such as the Open University.

The spread of technology, particularly to the home, is likely to increase educational differences within society. Not everyone will be able to afford to be connected to a cable system and to erect a dish aerial for satellite transmission and to buy or rent a video-cassette machine and a video-disc machine and a computer and a telephone, nor will everyone be able to afford the purchase of the software that will carry the educational material. What we will see is a much greater variety of technological equipment in people's homes with potential educational uses. Those in most need of further education and training the unemployed and the less well educated, who tend to have lower incomes-are the least likely to benefit from home learning through the new media since they are likely to have a more limited range of home equipment. How does one get through to these people, to promote the opportunities for further education and training that are available outside the home? Here surely remains a vital role for broadcasting since, together with the postal service, broadcast television and radio will for many, many years be the only media that can reach into every home.

Future advantages of broadcasting

Where do these developments leave broadcasting? I believe there are several major reasons why broadcasting should continue to play a major role in education.

Access

Broadcasting reaches the parts that other forms of education do not reach. In the United Kingdom and North America, 98 per cent of homes have television sets, and 97 per cent one radio set least. About 80 per cent of the United Kingdom population watch television at least some time during each day, and just over half listen at least once a day to the radio. The average time each adult spends watching television in Britain is between two to three hours per day. In many developed countries, more than half the population will be watching television at the same time during some parts of an evening.

Access to television and radio in developing countries is less universal, particularly regarding television. According to Katz and Wedell, there was less than one radio set for every ten people in fifty-four developing countries in 1976, despite a massive and continuing expansion of radio ownership over the previous twenty years in such countries. Nevertheless, there is now only a handful of countries without any form of broadcast television service. There is no country in the world without widespread geographical coverage by radio, and in all but the poorest countries, a high proportion of households have at least one radio receiver. Many bars and cafes in poor urban areas have television sets, and in Latin America and the Middle East, television coverage is wide-spread. Neither television nor radio demand literacy skills, and for most countries these media offer the most effective way of accessing the bulk of the population.

Recruitment to education

Broadcasting has the capacity to reach people who are uninterested in or disenchanted with conventional educational provision, even if local courses are available. There is a good deal of accidental or unplanned viewing and listening. At certain times-in particular early evening and weekend mornings in Britain-millions of people will be randomly accessing television; not switching on because they know a particular programmes is on at that time, but just waiting to see what comes on. Broadcasting can therefore ply the role of recruiting agent for education, either attracting and holding the audience through the intrinsic interest of the programmes themselves, or leading viewers to pursue the subject further, through purchasing accompanying books, contacting agencies, or enrolling in local classes or correspondence schools.

Convenience

For working adults, time is at a premium. Study has to be fitted into their leisure time, outside working hours. For many people then, it is attractive to be able to study in the comfort of their own homes, without the cost and inconvenience of travel to schools or colleges which may be miles away.

Motivation

Broadcasting clearly has the ability to make education interesting and enjoyable, when it is used well. It provides a break from the normal school routine. For adult learners, independent study, especially starting back to study for the first time, requires considerable motivation. Through the variety of techniques used to appeal to audience, broadcasting can provide a real stimulus to learning.

Consciousness-raising

Broadcasting can help to raise general awareness of problem or situations about which the general public were previously ignorant or apathetic. Thus,as well as the primary target group for a set of programmes, there is often a secondly target audience; the general public, local or national politicians, leaders of industry, whose awareness of a problem may be raised by the programmes. It is claimed for instance by some broadcasters that the British television programmes 'The Chips are Down' was mainly responsible for alerting the British government to the real significance of microchip technology. This may say more about the British government than about broadcasting if it is true, but certainly causal viewers can have their awareness raised by such programming.

Comparative cheapness

broadcasting can be the cheapest way to get large quantities of audio-visual learning materials to large numbers of people scattered throughout the country. This is particularly important for schools. Even if schools have an abundant provision of video-recording and playback equipment, broadcasting and local recording is the cheapest way to distribute large quantities of audio-visual material. This applies also to computer-based audio-visual media which can be broadcast within a radio bandwidth.

Improving the general cultural milieu

Educational broadcasting can be multi-purpose, not only in raising awareness but also in presenting an alternative source of programming to that available on the general service, an alternative sometimes desperately needed. For those who otherwise would be left with a choice between Nationwide, Crossroads and a rock music programme, an Open University programme on the economics of oil-pricing can provide a welcome alternative. The cultural argument for educational programmes only holds if the programmes are comprehensible to a general public and available at times when most people are able to watch them.

Needed improvements

Having set out some of the special advantages of broadcasting for education, there is still much that needs to be done to make it more effective:

Increased access to general programming for educational purposes

It should be permissible to record selected general broadcast programmes and series, so that they can be used in schools and colleges and for adult education courses. This means easing copyright and royalty agreements on general programmes for strictly non-profit, educational purposes, Support materials for schools and adults using pictures and materials from selected general programmes and other sources should also be prepared, either by the existing publication departments in broadcasting organisations, or by external agencies with particular interest in the series. Broadcast announcements before and following the programmes should be made indicating the availability of support materials and permission to record for educational purposes. The value of such general programmes and series would be enhanced if there was liaison between the production team and appropriate educational agencies or voluntary organisations from an early stage. Easing copyright and royalty restrictions would not mean loss of income for artists and performers in general programmes since at the moment no income is generated by educational users, unless programmes are available for purchase, which many are not.

Production of integrated, multi-media packages

Serious considerations needs to be given to the appropriateness of current broadcast provision to schools. Continuous broadcast programmes of a set length are not necessarily the best way to use television or radio. Self-standing programmes, even when recorded on cassette, are difficult to integrate with other teaching activities. More useful to teachers will be integrated multi-media packages with varying combinations of print, video, microcomputer material and audio-cassettes. This requires broadcasters to join with other agencies in the design of such components, as equal members in a team.

Improved teacher training in media

Improved and extended training of teachers in the use of media is becoming desperately urgent. Saunders carried out a thorough study of training for use of broadcasting in schools provided by eleven initial teacher-training centres and a variety of in-service courses in five countries in the south of England. She found that training was on the whole inadequate and misdirected. Teachers after training frequently used broadcasting incompetently and unimaginatively, yet broadcast materials is if anything being used more than ever. Cassettes offer greater opportunities for more effective use as integrated components in a carefully planned curriculum. The range of media available is rapidly widening, and teachers will need to know not only how to use the different media available but when and why the should use each medium. Teacher training in this area needs to be more widely available and better designed.

Improved co-operative arrangements

This is perhaps the most important and certainly the most difficult area for improvement. Robinson provides an excellent account of the development of partnership. His account shows increasing co-operation and a genuine willingness on the part of educational broadcasters to work with other agencies. The BBC and the IBA have for many years had advisory panels for schools and adult education. There are examples in this book of highly successful co-operative ventures. But nevertheless there are wide-spread criticisms of broadcasting arrangements from other agencies wishing to make full use of the promotional opportunities of broadcasting. Too often other agencies are consulted too late after all the major decisions have been made by the broadcasting organisation. Too often the approach of broadcasters is paternalistic and condescending. This kind of criticism can be found from teachers, programmes advisers, voluntary agencies and even from academics at the Open University where the partnership arrangement is formalised. Such tensions are inherent in the way broadcasting is structured, financed and controlled.

Broadcasting organisations in Britain have full control over both production and transmission, with the exception of Channel 4. While Channel 4 will take programmes produced by independent companies, it remains full editorial control over what it will broadcast. Only the BBC, and the IBA through the commercial companies, and Channel 4, have the right to broadcast television programmes. Even if another agency is willing to pay for production and transmission, it cannot insist on the right to broadcast. Effectively, the State has allowed broadcasting to be placed in the trust of professional broadcasters who represent non one except themselves. This may be preferable to political control but it is surely not the only alternative. The consequence is that voluntary agencies or educational institutions who with to use broadcasting as a means of communications in a manner of their own choosing cannot do so in Britain. Broadcasting organisations may decide to do 'something' in an area of interest to a voluntary agency or educators, but when and how that something is done is entirely at the discretion of the broadcasters. Under such circumstances, broadcasters can only be paternalistic and condescending to other agencies, no matter how well-meaning or courteous they may be.

Thee is of course no justification for changing the present arrangements if most people are satisfied that they are working well. Few educators, though, are really happy with the present arrangements. I believe, broadcast frequencies are a national asset. This is recognised in the powers of the Home Secretary, who allocates the frequencies and regulates broadcasting. These frequencies no more belong to Granada Television or the BBC than does the River Thames or the MI. They are held in trust for all of us by the broadcasting agencies, and if the arrangements are no longer satisfactory, they should be changed.

What could be done to ensure a more equal partnership between broadcasting and education? Probably very little in the current political climate. The power of the broadcasting organisations is too strong and the will of the people and the interest of Parliament too weak. The simplest method would be for the government to set up a statutory body which would have powers to et educational and social action priorities for broadcasting, and to require from the broadcasting organisations certain minimal arrangements-such as adequate transmission facilities. In practice, such a body would operate through a set of committees very similar to the existing advisory bodies established by the broadcasters themselves. In any case, the membership of the current advisory councils needs to be extended or anew council established, to ensure representation of the interests of voluntary agencies which are inadequately represented at the moment. The advantages of a statutory body is that members would be appointed independently, and, more importantly, it would be in a position to insist on the use of certain transmission facilities for educational and social action purposes.

The decommitment to public service broadcasting

State regulation of educational broadcasting will be anathema to many in Britain, particularly in the broadcasting world. The realistic alternative, though is the end of educational broadcasting altogether. The whole concept of public service broadcasting is under serious attack in Britain, due mainly to increased competition from unregulated video-cassette use and new cable and satellite services. John Birt, programme director of one of Britain's biggest independent television companies, London Weekend Television, was reported by The Guardian in September, 1993, as saying.:

> The new area of competition is likely to mean that the scope for scheduling programmes of minority appeal during peak time will be limited. Indeed, soon there may be no case for it all...

He went on to argue that another 50 million a year should be spent on peak viewing programmes, while less popular slots such as current affairs, the arts, sport, religion and education should be 'pruned'. While these comments are contained in a discussion paper and are not policy, it highlights the problems likely to be caused through increased competition from cable, satellite and cassettes. Public service no longer appears to be fashionable. Populism, commercial profit and the maximisation of audience rating seem to be the main concerns. Working through some of the accounts of projects and research reports. I had the feeling that the only reason why some broadcast organisations do anything in the other agencies from gaining access to broadcasting frequencies. Maybe everyone in the long run would be happier if broadcasting organisations withdrew completely from specific educational activities. However, this would not only be a very real loss to education but also a clear indication of the decline in social responsibility in British broadcasting.

Broadcasting and education make an uneasy alliance. While often sharing common aims, broadcasters and teachers have different perspectives. Education is at the best of times a difficult and an ill-defined process, the values of broadcasting are not identical to those of education. Nevertheless, do we really want to see broadcasting become nothing more than a continuous variety show? If not, then vigorous efforts will be needed to protect educational broadcasting, and major changes will be necessary to ensure that it is used effectively in education.

Index

A survey of instruction budgets, 50

British Broadcasting Corporation, 1
Broadcasting, development of, 290
Broadcasting, freedom of, 282
Broadcasting, function of, 287
Broadcasting, future advantage of, 336
Broadcasting, importance of, 283

Corporation for public broadcasting, 63
Commission of Freedom of the Press, 110
Communications satellites, 57
Communication satellites, education in, 55, 64
Curriculum design, media in, 239

DDeveloping mathematical thinking, 13

Early bird satellite, 57
Educational stations, reservations for, 323
Educational broadcasting, future of, 328
Educational media, administration of, 237
Educational evaluation, 241
Educational broadcasting, new technology of, 1, 54

Federal Radio Commission (FRC), 127
Films, content of, 148
Four theories of the press, 102

Hutchins Commission on Freedom of the Press, 69
Hutchins, M. Robert, 110

Indian Space Organisation, 62
International Telecommunications Satellite Consortium, 57
International institute of communication, 34

Media improving, 246
Media materials, selection of, 50
Media responsibilities, misconceptions of, 124

Media, responsibilities of, 100, 134
Motion picture business, 172
Motion Picture Association of America, 158

Open university, 3, 6, 8

Perspectives in individualized learning, 244
Picture business, 144
Press councils, establishment of, 267
Press freedom, theoretical basis of, 65
Press, limitations of, 79
Press, social responsibilities of, 68
Press, social functions of, 65, 99

Radio Act of 1927, 126
Radio Corporation of America, 140
Responsible press, definition of, 110

Satellites, educational uses of, 58

The Washington, 253
Toward excellence in institution, 50

United Kingdom, 32, 34

World Publishing Co., 87